YEAR OF THE PIG

YEAR
OF THE
PIG

MARK J. HAINDS

The University of Alabama Press • Tuscaloosa

Cover image: The author being pursued by his
wily prey. Photo by J. J. Bachant-Brown.

All photographs courtesy of the author unless
otherwise noted.

Publication supported in part by Conservation
Southeast, Inc.

Typeface: Minion Pro
Designer: Michele Myatt Quinn

∞

The paper on which this book is printed meets
the minimum requirements of American
National Standard for Information Sciences—
Permanence of Paper for Printed Library
Materials, ANSI Z39.48-1984.

Library of Congress Cataloging-in-Publication Data

Hainds, Mark J.
    Year of the pig / Mark J. Hainds.
        p. cm.
    ISBN 978-0-8173-5670-5 (pbk. : alk. paper) —
ISBN 978-0-8173-8563-7 (electronic) 1. Feral
swine—United States. 2. Feral swine hunting—
United States. 3. Wild boar—United States. 4.
Wild boar hunting—United States. 5. Hainds,
Mark J. I. Title.
    SF397.83.U6H35 2011
    799.2′76332—dc22
                                2011002969

This book is dedicated to two forest ecosystems: the longleaf pine forests of the southeastern United States and the wiliwili forests of Hawaii. Longleaf remains on approximately 3 percent of its natural range and much of this land is fire-excluded and compromised by invasive species such as the feral pig. After four or five centuries of near-continuous decline, for the first time, longleaf acreage began to tick upward around the beginning of the new millennium. This turnaround coincided with the transfer of land from pulp and paper companies with a singular focus on short-term fiber production to landowners with multiple objectives and longer-term goals. The restoration of the fire-dependent longleaf pine forests presents an opportunity for the forestry profession to remain relevant in the southeastern United States. As a forester, it's hard for me to see that as a bad outcome.

The wiliwili forests of Hawaii face a different threat, an introduced parasitic wasp that defoliates the trees. Here we also find an encouraging note, as entomologists have found a bio-control agent in the form of another introduced insect that is beginning to attack the parasitic wasp, thus allowing the wiliwili to grow new leaves.

CONTENTS

FOREWORD

Steven Ditchkoff, associate professor of wildlife sciences at Auburn University's School of Forestry and Wildlife Sciences

In 1539, Hernando de Soto brought the first pigs to the North American continent. It was a common practice among early explorers to establish swine populations on islands and other favored sites. The pigs' hardy nature and ability to thrive in the wild ensured that there would be fresh meat (a valuable commodity among sailors in those days) when the explorers returned.

Over the next four hundred plus years, the combination of this practice and that of keeping pigs on open ranges (and the inevitable escapes from these herds) resulted in well-established populations of pigs across the southeastern United States. By 1982, approximately twenty states had populations of pigs, with Texas and Florida accounting for the majority. Since this time, the spread of pig populations has increased dramatically, and they are now found in forty-four states and some Canadian provinces. Why has the range of the feral pig increased so dramatically in the last quarter century relative to the previous four centuries?

The first answer is the popularity of hunting feral pigs, which continues to rise as the popular media (television and magazines) increase their coverage of pig hunting. And with a ready supply of domestic swine that can be released to establish new pig populations and recreational opportunities, many hunters have taken it upon themselves to assist with their spread.

The second source of many new feral pig populations is shooting preserves, whose operators have constructed "game-proof" fences to contain swine on the preserves. Well, the reality is that there is no such thing as a pig-proof fence. Yes, it might be pig proof for a while, but in the end its integrity will fail. Even the best fences, maintained by the most conscientious managers, will eventually allow pigs to pass. As pig hunting has increased in popularity, so have fenced hunting preserves that sell pig hunts.

The third cause of the rapid increase in pig numbers in the last twenty-five years is the domestic pork industry. Pork prices tend to be less than most other meats, and as a result, the profit margin for pork producers is very narrow. In the late 1990s, when the bottom fell out of the pork market, it was cheaper for pork producers to turn their stock loose than keep it because the cost of feeding was greater than the price they would get at market. As a result, many small pork producers couldn't afford to keep feeding their pigs and just opened their gates, further adding to an already increasing feral pig population.

The feral pig has been an incredibly successful invader, particularly resistant to control and eradication efforts. Pigs have an unusually high rate of reproduction for a mammal their size, and they become sexually mature and reproductively active at only 8 months of age. Considering the short gestation time of pigs (115 days, or 3 months, 3 weeks, and 3 days), a sow can produce her first litter before her first birthday. Feral pigs can have two litters per year and three litters in 14 months if conditions are good. Finally, the litter size in the wild is normally four to five piglets. The end result is that a female pig may produce eight to twelve offspring by her second birthday, when most other large mammals are just producing their first offspring. This incredible rate of productivity makes it nearly impossible to eradicate an existing population, and scientific studies have reported that pig populations reduced by up to 70 percent have returned to pre-reduction levels in only 2–3 years.

Feral pigs are also able to utilize a wider range of resources than most other species. Their diet consists primarily (approximately 80 percent) of vegetation, and they readily consume most nonwoody or fibrous plant parts. They are particularly fond of roots, fruits, and other soft and easily digestible plant materials. What makes them unique is their ability to also consume animal matter. They eat invertebrates (insects, earthworms, grubs, and so on), reptiles and amphibians, birds, and mammals—sometimes including livestock. Opportunistic carnivores, they will readily consume anything that crosses their path. In some parts of Texas, they are the second-greatest predator of livestock (the greatest is the coyote), usually consuming newborn animals. Most of these predations go unnoticed, because pigs consume the entire carcass.

Pigs have a unique method of obtaining food from below the surface of the soil called "rooting." Using their snout, they are able to turn over large volumes of soil as they search for roots, fungi, and invertebrates. This technique of foraging is particularly destructive to native vegetation and has several negative effects on the environment. It leads to increased soil erosion, which ultimately causes increased sedimentation in streams and other water sources. It increases the spread of invasive plant species, and it is speculated that it disrupts nutrient cycling as well. In addition to these impacts, the rooting behavior of feral hogs also causes problems for landowners, as the pigs tear up pastures, food plots, and planted crops, creating holes that can lead to broken axles on farm equipment and even result in injury to domestic animals and humans.

Finally, the greatest threat posed by wild pigs in North America is their potential to spread diseases to domestic swine. Pseudorabies, swine brucellosis, and hog cholera are three of the diseases that concern domestic pork producers. The pork industry has spent untold amounts of money to eradicate these and other diseases from our domestic stock. With infected swine roaming the countryside, there is cause for concern that these efforts could be undone in an instant. Feral swine are the same species as domestic hogs; free-ranging males are continually roaming around swine farms in search of potential mates. All it takes is contact through a fence for the transmission of disease.

This combination of traits makes the feral pig one of the greatest invasive vertebrate concerns for resource managers. Feral pigs are almost impossible to control or eradicate, are able to take advantage of a wide range of resources and habitats, and, to make things even more complicated, are extremely intelligent. They are impacting threatened and endangered species (plant and animal) and in Hawaii have even been documented breaking into homes to obtain food. All in all, feral swine directly or indirectly impact almost every level of ecosystem function, including soils, water resources, plants, invertebrates, vertebrates, and even humans.

Keep these thoughts in mind while reading this book. Without question, pigs are fun to hunt and good to eat, and I can understand the desire to have a huntable pig population close to home. But no good comes from introducing pigs to a new area: their negative impacts far outweigh their benefits. Remember that the primary goal of pig hunting is control and eradication. While it is sporting, pigs should be hunted and eliminated with extreme prejudice.

FOREWORD

Mark Bailey, director of Conservation Southeast

This is anything but your typical hunting book. Mark Hainds explores what I call "environmentally correct" hunting, about which I'm increasingly enthusiastic. Hunting of native game species is sustainable, of course, and may reduce environmental stresses from overpopulation, but given the choice between a ten-point buck and a 150-pound sow, you're doing Mother Nature and your farming neighbors a much bigger favor by putting a bullet into the hog. Plus, you'll have better sausage and tenderloin, guaranteed.

In extolling the virtues of wild pigs, one is pretty much limited to the rewards of pursuing and barbecuing them, as Mark artfully describes in these pages. Beyond that, he will be the first to argue that the critters' negatives outweigh any positives, and I know he would gladly join me in pulling the trigger on the last feral hog in the South. *Sus scrofa* is not a game species to be managed for sustained harvest—it's an invasive, exotic, ecological nightmare, a scourge on the landscape straight out of Pandora's box. Devastating to pristine natural areas and valuable croplands alike, feral hogs may seem as daunting to eradicate as fire ants, but something close to eradication could be achieved if we made it a priority. And we should. I have enjoyed hunting hogs with Mark, but we both know that hunting alone does not have a meaningful effect on established hog populations. The answer lies in concerted efforts combining public education, private landowner incentives, and integrated, persistent, and adaptive management programs at a landscape scale.

Our species is surprisingly good at driving certain others to extinction, but getting rid of feral hogs will be a tremendous challenge. In light of our relatively recently developed conservation ethic, the idea of deliberately eradicating a large mammal (even an introduced one) creates cognitive dissonance. But when it comes to wild hogs, hunt 'em if you got 'em. Leave no pig behind, and let's save conservation for the native wildlife, which needs it now more than ever.

ACKNOWLEDGMENTS

It would have been impossible to accomplish this project without the assistance of many people.

A special debt of gratitude is owed to my wife, Katia, for sticking with me through this challenging year. Unlike many others, she actually believed this book project was worthwhile. That belief was not enough to keep impatience at bay, however. Although she was at the end of her rope by the conclusion of 2007, she didn't divorce me.

An equal debt is owed to my son, Joseph, for loving and missing me. When Daddy was away on hunting trips, he would ask Mommy every night, "Papa? Papa?" When I returned, he would run to me and jump into my arms. His love and admiration are worth more to me than all the trophies I've ever collected or will collect.

Two names turn up repeatedly in this book: John Dickson and Michael Powell. These guys are the best of friends, and their support was critical to my success.

With some luck, the future will allow me to repay the outstanding efforts of my reviewers, Dr. Jim Dickson, Dr. Steven Ditchkoff, Mark Bailey, Shon Scott, and Beverly Childress. Steven and Mark made sure the biology in the manuscript was right; their corrections and suggestions made this book much better than it would have been. Beverly, my wife's friend, was only a passing acquaintance until she volunteered to read and review the manuscript. She caught numerous grammatical errors in the manuscript and offered many valuable suggestions. And what's really amazing is that her Spanish is as good as her English!

Hunts were purchased from Maui Hunting Safari, with Rodney and Dawn

Perreira, Rodney Perreira Sr., and Kekoa (Hawaii); MPI Outfitters, with Mickey Pophin and Ken Gould of the Rio Bravo (Texas); Jerry, Dan Thomas, Diego Miranda, and David Watson (Florida); Shiloh Ranch, with Matt and Cheryl Napper (Oklahoma); the Bryson Hesperia Resort, with Deedy and Karin Loftus and Tom Willoughby (California); and Wrangler Up Outfitters, with Mark and Justin Martin (Arkansas).

Friends who arranged hunts for me include John Dickson, at Bayou Cocodrie National Wildlife Refuge (Louisiana); Larry and Vickie Stallings, on their farm in Covington County (Alabama); Jimmy and Sierra Stiles, in the Talladega National Forest (Alabama); and Ben Miley, James Parker, and Stephen Hudson, at Fort Benning (Georgia).

Also, many thanks to my coworkers in Alabama, J. J. Bachant-Brown, Joel Martin, Dale Pancake, Teresa Cannon, David Padgett, and Davie Sightler at the Solon Dixon Forestry Education Center, and Dean Gjerstad and Rhett Johnson, the excellent codirectors of the Longleaf Alliance, Inc.

Many thanks to Beth Motherwell and all the staff at The University of Alabama Press. Beth kept me inspired and dedicated through the long and grueling process of publishing my first book. Her suggestions, encouragement, and guidance were vital to the completion of this project. After I thought the manuscript was finished, the copy editor, Robin DuBlanc, swept in with a whole new raft of suggestions that really pulled this book together.

YEAR OF THE **PIG**

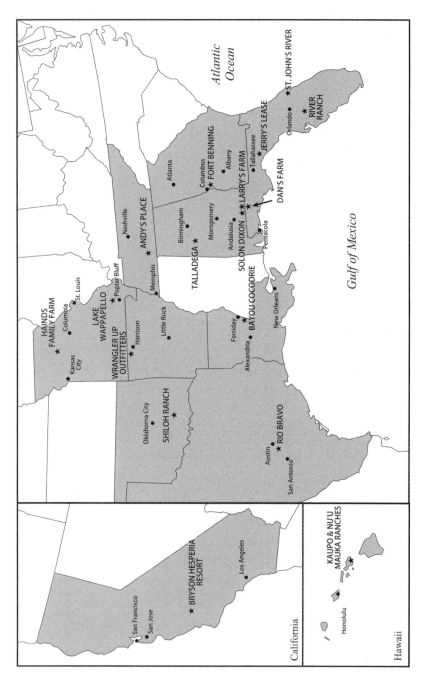

Locations of the seventeen hunts Mark Hainds took during his Year of the Pig.

PROLOGUE

To do this I must be altogether frank, or try to be, and if those who read this decide with disgust that it is written by some one who lacks their, the readers', fineness of feeling I can only plead that this may be true.
— ERNEST HEMINGWAY, *Death in the Afternoon*, 1932

This was not an easy undertaking. Most of those who are close to me looked upon my goal as quixotic at best. Several individuals simply didn't see the point, while others were outright hostile, regarding this as little more than "an excuse for Mark to go hunting every weekend." Some regarded me as selfish in the extreme.

A case in point: while I was still in the process of writing this book, our parish priest counseled me on the subject of spending more time with my family. I explained that I had set myself the goal of killing pigs in ten states over a one-year period, and this had required a tremendous devotion of time.

Father Den appeared quizzical. "Would that be a significant accomplishment?"

"I kind of figured it makes me a pig-hunting hero!" was my (somewhat ironic) answer.

Father, however, did not appear terribly impressed.

I grew up on a cattle, pig, and row-crop farm in Chariton County in north central Missouri. The nearest town of any size was Marceline, in neighboring Linn County. This property has been owned by the Hainds family since my great-great-great-grandfather settled the land in the early 1800s, and I was the sixth generation raised on the banks of the Mussel Fork. There are only two things in this world worth sacrificing for: children and land. And sacrificing for the latter is worthwhile only if children are there to inherit the land. Likewise, it makes sense to sacrifice for God or country only if the children of today, or the children of generations to come, benefit from the action. If God is merciful, my son, Joseph, will inherit the farm when I pass on. If God is kind, Joseph will grow to love and care for this land as much as I do.

Grandpa Joe Hainds once told me, "If you drink from the Mussel Fork, you'll always come back." So I slid down its muddy banks, scooped some water into my hands, and partook of its magical powers. Unfortunately, the Mussel had resident populations of beaver and muskrat. So I got giardiasis (aka beaver fever) and spent a week in the hospital.

But Grandpa was correct. I keep going back.

I usually drive or fly to Missouri for deer season in the fall. Sometimes I go by myself, and sometimes my wife and son come along.

And then, just before Christmas, we drive north for the holidays with presents, guns, and dogs in tow. In between family get-togethers, church services, and holiday feasts, we always do some rabbit, squirrel, and quail hunting, with a little time reserved to map out the next spring's tree planting.

By April, it's time again for the 920-mile (one-way) drive, with a truckload of tree seedlings and dogs. If there's a little extra time, I might do some turkey hunting, bass fishing, and searching for morel mushrooms. To us our farm is truly heaven on earth, and everything is done with the overarching purpose of leaving the land in better shape than when we first inherited it: more trees, bigger trees, older trees. We are also interested in improved aesthetics, fewer invasive species, more native ground cover, and a lot more wildlife.

Someday, when Joseph is old enough to understand the significance of the action, we just might share a drink from the Mussel Fork—but we'll boil the water first.

Subtracting the week for deer season, the week for spring tree planting, and two weeks for Christmas in Missouri, there are eleven remaining months when I reside in Lower Alabama (LA), in the Deep South. Here also I have favorite hunting grounds. For several years, a saltwater addiction required that I spend every other weekend in or on the Gulf of Mexico, with a rod and reel or a speargun in my hands. Then there was coon hunting. But I eventually had to start sleeping again, so I gave my hounds to a neighbor down the road.

After coon hunting, I discovered hog hunting, thus pulling a deep-seated, primordial trigger. It could be called a *Lord of the Flies* experience. Having hunted dozens of animal species, I can report that all of it is enjoyable. But hog hunting holds a special place in my psyche. This passion is shared by many. Vincent, a friend and pig-hunting acquaintance, told me, "I never feel so alive as when I am pig hunting."

Few people realize just how ubiquitous the wild hog (*Sus scrofa*) is. The first ever National Conference on Wild Pigs was held in Mobile, Alabama, in 2006. Based upon sightings reported at this conference, it can be determined that almost every state in the Union either has populations of feral swine or will have them in the near future. The continental United States and most of our islands, not to mention almost every other country in the world, have established populations of feral pigs, also known as wild boar, wild pigs, feral hogs, or feral swine. Many of these populations are expanding.

Excepting city dwellers in the North who never visit the Midwest or South, virtually everyone in America lives or vacations near or in wild hog habitat. You may not have seen them. You may not have recognized the signs, sounds, or smells that identify them, but they were there, lurking in the shadows.

Have you flown into Fort Lauderdale, Miami, Tampa, or Orlando lately? If you saw citrus groves, swamps, or virtually any wooded or shrubby habitat, you were close to pigs. Have you been to Atlanta, Los Angeles, San Francisco, Little Rock, or Memphis? Drive a little beyond the city limits and wild pigs won't be far away. How about New Orleans, Houston, or Dallas? A trained eye might find hog sign inside the city limits: along streams, in industrial zones, even in city parks!

With expanding pig populations there are increasing economic and ecological effects and, of course, more opportunities for hog hunters. Hog hunters are part of the solution—and at the same time part of the problem. Hunters are part of the solution when they help control feral pig populations, limiting the damage that pigs inflict upon agricultural fields and the environment. Hunters are part of the problem when they catch and relocate feral hogs to areas that were previously pig free. Most recent expansions or introductions of feral hog populations can be attributed to hog hunters looking for more opportunities to pursue their favored game species.

In most states there is no closed season on hogs and there is no limit on how many a hunter may kill. And in general, the hunter can shoot them with any legal firearm, bow, or crossbow. Some people pursue feral hogs with a spear. Or, for an up close and personal experience, try a knife! Personally, I like hog hunting because it's downright gritty.

And so we arrive at the reason behind this book. By January 2007, I had invested a decade in another book project: "A Field Guide to the Birds, Fish, and Crabs of Pensacola Bay and Surrounding Waters." I couldn't seem to stop adding new photos and descriptions, and I feared the book would never be completed.

In need of a finite project, I considered a book on hog hunting. I thought, "I could kill a pig in every state that has established populations of wild hogs. After ten states, I'll write it up and send it to a publisher." But without a deadline, this project could stretch out for years, too. However, around that same time it came to my attention that 2007 was the Year of the Pig in the Chinese calendar, and it all clicked. I had my goal, and I had my deadline.

Over the course of 2007, I hunted in eleven states, killing pigs with the sun high overhead, at dusk, and in the middle of the night. I hunted with big rifles, medium-sized calibers, and one of the smallest bullets ever made. Pigs were taken with a bow, a black-powder rifle, and a knife. There were hunts over bait, hunts from an airboat, and hunts with artificial light. I belly crawled into brush so thick that visibility was limited to ten feet or less and shots were taken as close as eight feet. I walked, ran, and stalked through woods, swamps, bayous, creeks, streams, rivers, mountains, volcanic rock, brush, fields, and pastures. Sometimes I hunted with friends or hunting guides and their dogs, but mostly I hunted by myself.

I witnessed differing approaches to ethics and the interaction between hunters, their prey, and the environment. There was forestry and wildlife management at its best and at its worst. Hunts took place in nearly pristine ecosystems and in tracts of land so degraded that invasive species were virtually the only survivors. On some properties the managers wanted every sow, boar, and piglet exterminated. On other landholdings, they imported pigs to increase the population.

My land ethic is not limited to our family farm in Missouri. As a research associate with Auburn University and as research coordinator for the Longleaf Alliance, I've devoted my professional life to restoring the longleaf ecosystem. Perhaps I'll do my small part in leaving the Southeast with a little more longleaf forest and one or two fewer pigs than when I first set foot in Lower Alabama.

1 LONGLEAF

From southern Virginia, down through the coastal plains of the Carolinas, Georgia, Florida, Alabama, Mississippi, Louisiana, and on into Texas, longleaf ruled.

—ROGER REID, *Longleaf,* 2006

Longleaf pine (*Pinus palustris*): The longest-lived, prettiest, toughest pine tree in the southeastern United States. It produces the best sawtimber, greatest percentage of poles, best pine straw, most attractive landscapes, and more lightered wood (aka fat lighter). When tree geneticists spend their careers breeding loblolly or slash pine for better form and more disease resistance, they are attempting to replicate that which longleaf pine does naturally. To give it an anthropomorphic bent, longleaf is what the other southern pines wish they could be when they grow up.

On a Friday evening I drove two hours and forty-five minutes northeast from my home in Andalusia to Auburn, Alabama. Earlier, some friends and former coworkers (James and Stephen) had invited me along for a hog hunt they had arranged at Fort Benning, Georgia, and after a good meal and a few beers, I crashed on their couch with a smile on my face in anticipation of ringing ears and squealing pigs on the morrow.

We got up early, picking up Ben at another house in Auburn before starting the drive east. All three of these guys are forestry graduates from Auburn University who had previously worked with me on longleaf studies in south Alabama. We cruised through Columbus, Georgia, arriving at Fort Benning about one hour after departing Auburn.

At the Base Recreation Center, I secured a visitor pass and a weeklong non-resident hunting license. Because Fort Benning requires hunters to sign into open units before entering these areas, James called Range Control, signing the four of us into three areas simultaneously. At each new location, we lined up perpendicular to the long axis of the unit and pushed forward, covering acre after acre and mile after mile.

After another Benning employee (Joe Ranson) joined us, our party consisted of five hunters, each with a different caliber rifle. Ben had a Marlin .35 lever-action rifle that would have looked at home in the hands of John Wayne. This traditional gun uses a heavy, large-caliber bullet that is considered ideal for shooting through thick brush. Stephen carried a long-barreled, bolt-action .270. This modern rifle still shoots a good-sized bullet, but it is smaller in diameter, faster, and more prone to deflection. It is a good deer/pig gun in open country, where shots may be taken at longer ranges.

Joe would be hunting with a Mini-14 (.223). Since the Mini-14 does not require the shooter to work a lever or bolt between shots, its main advantages are a more rapid rate of fire and lower recoil. James was shooting a semiautomatic .22 Magnum. This was the only firearm utilizing rimfire ammunition. Most hunters consider the .22 Magnum way too small for feral pigs. However, the .22 Magnum does have advantages: virtually no recoil, rapid rate of fire, and cheap ammunition. Lastly, my firearm was a trusty ol' Model 788, .243 Remington bolt-action rifle. This bullet was squarely in the middle of the pack, smaller than Ben's .35 or Steven's .270, and bigger than Joe's .223 and James's .22 Magnum.

The hunt started on the edge of a swamp. As we entered the woods, frost and hog tracks covered the ground. Normally, wetter is better when you're talking about hog habitat, but the temperature had dropped into the low twenties the night before and the pigs had avoided the icy-cold mud.

James was the first to see a pig. I was on the bottom of the line, up against a swamp, while James was positioned on the opposite end, near the top of a hill. Brush kept visibility to about fifty yards, and the adjacent hunter in the line would appear and reappear as our line tracked the contour. Reaching the end of the swamp, the four of us on the bottom grouped up, waiting for James to reappear before setting off in a new direction. James emerged from the brush, joined the group, and asked, "Did you see the boar?" None us had seen anything remotely resembling a pig.

James informed us, "There was a good boar up on the hill, and it headed downslope as soon it saw me. I didn't shoot because I hoped you all would get a chance to kill it." The boar had passed behind us, unseen.

Pigs: 1; hunters: 0.

One of the more interesting things about walking on a military base is the possibility of encountering unexploded ordnance. In fact, it is unusual to be out of sight of military detritus. Among the most prevalent relics are aluminum fins protruding from the soil or pine litter. Scores of .223-caliber blanks (M-16 ammo) are visible on any patch of exposed soil or sand. More ominously, rusty objects resembling grenades or RPG (rocket-propelled grenade) rounds occasionally protrude from the soil surface. It is likely they are dummies. Or else these munitions could be decades' old duds with the potential to take life or limb.

Ben and James had reminded me at the start of the hunt, "Don't kick shiny stuff!" before relating the story of a young boy who bought it a few years back while hunting on Fort Benning. No one noticed the explosion because he was hunting by himself. The poor kid may or may not have seen the round that killed him.

The hunt progressed, our group hopping from unit to unit as we worked our way around the base. After a few hours, we stopped to chow down on Meals Ready to Eat (MREs). With more than a decade between this hunt and my last active-duty service, I was reminded that the MREs aren't that bad. Joe had just gotten back from Iraq, so he was less enthusiastic about his MRE. To be sure, MREs have plenty of calories. Eating three full MREs a day, you'd better be humping some long distances. Our method of hog hunting fit the bill, so I consumed my MRE plus the other guys' unwanted portions.

Policing up our trash, we moved to a unit that was primarily bottomland hardwoods. Walking in, Ben told us about a big pig he had killed on this unit.

Ben worked on a feral hog project that Auburn University was conducting at Fort Benning. Through that study he and several colleagues had trapped, tagged, released, and tracked hundreds of pigs. They were attempting to determine the extent to which hog populations could be reduced by using all means necessary. Ben said, "I was walking in to check my hog trap. I came around this bend and saw a boar lying stretched out in the middle of the road. It looked like it was dead; then I realized it was just sleeping. When I shot it, the boar let out a short surprised squeal and ran into the woods. It didn't go far."

I asked, "Did you carry it out?"

Ben shook his head. "I didn't want the stinky bastard."

The five of us worked into a creek bottom covered with fresh sign. Based on tracks, wallows, rubs, and rooting, it seemed the resident hog population was more concentrated here than on any of the other tracts we had walked. Our hunting party followed a long loop out and back, occasionally walking through or around standing water. Somewhere on the loop, James disappeared. When the rest of us reached the vehicles again, we sat or lay down, resting our aching legs; at least *my* legs were aching. About ten minutes later, the sound of a shot came from the woods, followed by a pause, and then another shot.

Jumping up, I said, "It sounds like James is the first to draw blood." Taking a bearing on the shots, we went to look for him. Although the shots had sounded fairly close, James wasn't in the immediate vicinity. After a few minutes, we walked back and found him waiting at the trucks.

James shook his head in response to our unasked question. "I heard them in some blue palm and went in after them. They were staying in front of me and I got off a couple of shots, then my gun jammed. While I was trying to get it un-jammed, one stepped out in the open and looked at me for a few seconds. Then they all ran off. That was the first time this gun has jammed on me."

Pigs: 2; hunters: 0.

There was time to hit one more unit before dark. Ben suggested a very large food plot on an adjacent unit. The others dropped me off at the bottom of the plot with fifteen minutes of shooting light remaining.

The food plot was long and narrow, snaking through the woods. Deer tracks were everywhere, but there weren't any hog tracks. I was about two hundred yards in, hugging the tree line on the left side, when Joe emerged from the woods on the right. Joe and I moved forward on opposite sides of the food plot.

Ben hadn't been kidding—this food plot went on forever. As we reached the end, there was a good half mile of food plot behind us, with sawtooth oak planted the entire length of the field. Unfortunately, the mast crop (acorns) had been consumed a long time ago. Loblolly pine is the most overplanted pine tree in the United States, but at least it is a native tree species. Sawtooth oak, on the other hand, is an Asian species that's probably the most overplanted hardwood in the Southeast.

It was dark as Stephen and James picked us up at the end of the plot. Despite a heroic effort, the first day had been a bust.

The temperature dropped during the drive to our rented cabin on Fort Benning. There were a couple of dozen white-tailed deer in the wooded area near the cabins. Several were grazing within easy bow range.

Unpacking and settling in, we felt the cold. This was whisky-drinking weather, and I was proud to see a half gallon of George Dickel on the kitchen counter. I have a friend in Brewton, Alabama, named Shon. He has quit drinking but otherwise has pretty good judgment. Shon once told me, "Dickel makes Jim Beam want to slap his momma."

The heater warmed the cabin while the Dickel worked from the inside out. Tired out from a full day of walking over rough ground, we watched a television show on tropical diseases and called it a night.

Waking to temperatures in the teens, we had a frosty start, but we were hoping that the day's hunt would, with a little luck, yield more than a couple of futile shots in the palmetto.

James and Stephen were looking for a place to park on the first unit when Mark Byrd pulled up. Mark was the forester who had given me my first tour around Fort Benning ten years back when the Longleaf Alliance was working with a big Department of Defense (DOD) grant. Mark didn't have any interest in pigs. Turkey season opened in a few weeks, and he was listening for gobblers in the early morning hours.

Parking on a sandy ridge overlooking a deep drain, we noticed that the area had just been replanted in longleaf pine. James said they had kicked up pigs several times while planting this tract. As we got out of the truck, we saw fresh pig tracks crisscrossing the sandy road.

The five of us started down the slope. Reaching the stream at the bottom of the valley, Stephen and Joe took the far side. I stayed on the near side while Ben and James followed behind. The far side of the drain was an uncut, intact mixed-pine hardwood forest, trending toward mature hardwoods along the stream. To minimize erosion and deposition of sediment, a streamside management zone (SMZ) had been left. In this case, the SMZ was a strip of uncut hardwoods along the stream. To the right, above the SMZ, was a recently planted clear-cut.

Still waiting for Ben and James to get into position, Joe shouted from across the stream, "Pigs!"

A line of pigs was running between Joe and Stephen. Joe couldn't shoot because Stephen was in his line of fire. The pigs ran within a few feet of Stephen, and he swung his scoped rifle with the herd but never pulled the trigger. It's very difficult to make a good shot with a scope at close, fast-moving game.

The line of black and brown pigs passed Stephen, and I yelled, "Pigs coming!" to let Ben and James know the herd was headed their way. Shortly, Ben's .35 sounded: *Bang! Bang! Bang!* This was followed by loud squealing and a final *Bang!*

Converging on Ben and James, I asked, "How many did you get?"

Ben answered, "I've got one down in the ditch over there. They came down the stream, and I started shooting at the black boar in the brush to my front. I hit it good, but it was still dragging its hind legs and headed for the stream. So I shot the boar again, but it still rolled into the stream."

Following the blood trail to the ditch, we discovered a small- to medium-sized black boar with nice tusks dead in the stream. The spine shot had caused the boar to release some exceptionally pungent urine. Congratulating Ben on his shooting, we offered to help him drag the boar back to the truck. Ben declined. He had a high-wheeled cart designed especially for big-game retrieval, which in the South means pigs or deer. James stayed to help Ben with the pig while Stephen, Joe, and I walked out the surrounding draws.

Crossing a newly planted clearing, we found fresh pig sign. The pigs had uprooted recently planted longleaf seedlings. The seedlings, or "plugs," were lying on the ground, uneaten.

Farther down the drain, I found a nice lower jawbone from a hog that had met its end a year or two before. The three of us walked rapidly, covering about a mile before circling back to our starting point. Nearing the trucks, Joe picked up an old military compass, also recently uncovered by a prescribed fire. It was no longer functioning and Joe didn't want it, so I carried the compass and hog jaw out as souvenirs.

Back at the trucks, we found Ben and James with the boar. After snapping a few photos, it was off to the next spot.

Pigs: 2; hunters: 1.

The "skunk" was off our hunting party and there was new optimism. But over the course of the day, we walked several hours and covered many miles of ground. By late afternoon on this, the final day of the hunt, my enthusiasm was flagging again. With two hours of shooting light left, we held a powwow. Ben, James, and Stephen decided it was time for Shamanski Road. They had played all their other cards, and now it was time for their ace in the hole.

James signed us into a unit with a large firing range. A road passed through the range, into a big area of sand ridges covered with scrub oaks, longleaf pine, and sparkleberry, a classic "sandhill" longleaf community. Rounding a bend, we saw two large gut piles just off the road shoulder. Someone had recently killed large pigs here. Not a bad sign.

As we left the sand ridges behind, the "site index" improved. There was more groundcover. The longleaf pines were taller and there were fewer hardwoods. Annually, the Fort Benning forestry staff burns tens of thousands of acres. This frequent, low-intensity fire maintains beautiful, open, parklike stands of longleaf pine with a diverse herbaceous understory. Fort Benning has some of the healthiest woods I've seen on DOD landholdings.

As we moved down a long straight road, Ben said sharply from behind me, "There they are!" pointing to the right. I jumped up a high bank into a stand of longleaf with oaks and hickories scattered throughout. Stephen and James were on my left, and Ben was coming in behind me. The pigs were moving at a good clip from left to right, perhaps 150 yards out. The group consisted of two solid black pigs and a black pig with a white Hampshire stripe.

I leaned against a tree to help steady my aim as I picked the pigs up in the scope. They were moving fast and the woods were getting thicker. I took a hurried first shot. The pigs picked up speed as I fired a second, long, going-away shot just before they disappeared over a ridge. The first shot was questionable. The second shot hopeless.

The guys came up behind me, asking, "Did you hit one?"

Shaking my head, I answered, "I don't know."

It didn't take long to locate the pigs' tracks and follow their trails over the ridge. There was no blood, nor any sign of a hit pig.

Joe had been elsewhere during out afternoon hunt. When he rejoined us and heard the story of my missed shots, he gave some friendly advice. "Rather than squeezing the trigger, squeeze your whole hand."

While it was nice of him to offer the advice, I had always considered myself an above-average shot with a rifle. The pigs had been moving quickly, 150 yards out, in a wooded environment. Nevertheless, all three pigs should not have escaped. Still, it just didn't sit right, receiving shooting lessons from someone I'd just met.

Ben said, "Let's keep going. We'll find some more."

Pigs: 3; hunters: 1; Mark: 0.

The hunt continued, but a sinking feeling in my gut said, "You've blown your best and final opportunity."

With just over an hour of shooting light remaining, there was ground to cover. Having completed a circle through the unit, our party of four (Joe had called it a day) was working down a road in an open, fire-maintained longleaf stand when Stephen and James pointed at the same time and called out, "Pig!" They could have shot it themselves, but they wanted me to get my hog.

I didn't see it. Running forward and climbing the bank, I saw nothing. I had blown it again. Back at the truck, they told me it had looked like a large black boar.

Pigs: 4; hunters: 1; Mark: 0.

It was down to the wire and almost too much to bear, having blown two opportunities in less than an hour. Following Shamanski Road, we intersected with another trail we'd traveled earlier. Ben and James tried to keep my spirits up, assuring me, "The pigs are moving!" And they obviously were, but the inevitable doubts flooded in.

Only fifteen minutes of shooting light remained and I was beginning to resign myself to a fruitless hunt. But then, looking down the trail, all four of us recognized forms in the distance. There were two large pigs straight ahead! The pigs saw, heard, smelled, or sensed us, disappearing quickly into the woods. Ben pointed in their direction and said, "Go! Go!"

It was now or never. Blow this, and it would be a long, forlorn trip back to Lower Alabama (LA).

When last seen, the pigs were a good three hundred yards up the trail, just beyond my comfort range with the .243. I was pretty sure the pair had run right. Jogging forward, I saw a Hampshire-striped pig appear in the longleaf stand. It was headed down the hill, toward a much thicker hardwood bottom.

There was still a chance for a shot while the pig was in the longleaf, but the pig would disappear once it entered the hardwoods. I had missed two shots an hour before at lesser range in similar cover; the odds were not in my favor. Maintaining a steady jog on an intercept, if it came to it, I would take a low-percentage shot at the last second, just before the pig entered the bottom.

The pig stopped, giving me the option of kneeling and shooting long-distance at a stationary object. However, running had elevated my heart and respiratory rates, and the rifle would be less than steady. The odds were improving but still were not good. I kept moving, further narrowing the range. Another lucky break! The pig turned and headed back up the hill, so I veered slightly to the left.

The distance had closed to two hundred yards and my luck held as the pig stopped again. For some reason, the indecisive pig turned and headed back downhill! Veering right, I was still jogging as the distance closed.

It stopped again! Turning around, the pig headed back up the hill. This time, it had made up its mind. Only one hundred yards separated the pig and me. Rather than continuing on an intercept, I took a ninety-degree turn left and ran a few yards to the open trail. Reaching the middle of the trail, I dropped to one knee and shouldered the .243. A second or two later, the pig broke from the woods on the right. I immediately picked it up in my scope about seventy to eighty yards out and squeezed off a shot as it reached the middle of the path. At the shot, its front legs folded and the pig flipped over with a loud squeal. My heart was racing as I worked the bolt and jogged forward. To my back and right Ben shouted out a loud "Woohoo!" in response to the shot and squeal. Ben had been following on my right wing, just in case the pig turned back on us.

I ran up to the pig and observed that it was already dead.

The four of us had seen two pigs just moments before. While this pig made my trip a success, there was another black pig out there somewhere. Looking to my left, I saw a black object about eighty to a hundred yards out. Unfortunately, black stumps are a dime a dozen in fire-maintained longleaf forests. However, stumps tend to remain stationary, and this object was moving quickly through the woods paralleling the trail. The woods were thicker on the left side of the road but still relatively open. Drawing down on the pig, I recognized the remainder of the pair we had first spotted three hundred yards out.

The pig entered an open area at a fast pace and I squeezed off a shot as it disappeared over a ridge. Running forward, I found a large draw stretching to my right and left. The pig wasn't on the other side of the draw, nor to the right. Walking forward at the ready, I saw another immobile black object in some charred holly stems. Putting the scope on the object, I recognized the large black pig standing beside a tree. Moving the crosshairs just behind the right front quarter, I pulled the trigger. There was the *thwack* of a solid hit. The pig flopped over. Working the bolt, I advanced, but it wasn't getting back up. Now it was my turn: "Woohoo!!!"

The second pig was a big black sow. The first shot had hit it a little too far back. It wasn't enough to knock it down, but the sow had only run about a hundred yards before stopping at the base of a big longleaf where I found it and finished it off.

Hanging my fluorescent orange hat on a shrub to mark the spot, I jogged, or perhaps I just floated, back up the hill to find James, Stephen, and Ben gathered around the black-and-white pig. It was another sow. High-fiving and shaking hands, the guys congratulated me on finally getting my first Georgia pigs. We later weighed them out at 128 and 154 pounds.

I realized that, by some lucky break, we'd gotten on the same pigs I'd shot at less than one mile away.

It was dark by the time we got the black sow back to the trail for some photos. From the depths of pessimism, I had levitated to a post-kill euphoria. Two days of solid, hard hunting, and I didn't have my Georgia hogs until the final ten minutes of hunting light.

Hunters: 3; Mark: 2. Whatever points the pigs had accumulated, they were zeroed out at dusk on the last afternoon of our hunt.

2   TITI

Any person who would seriously consider it is almost by definition beyond the sway of reasoned argument.

        —Jon Krakauer, *Into Thin Air*, 1997

Titi (*Cyrilla racemiflora*): A shrubby tree found in wet sites. Titi swamps are synonymous with tough going. In thick stands the gnarled branches weave together to block out the sun. Occasional holes in the canopy are filled with giant banana spiders, whose webs may span twenty feet or more. The air is filled with humidity and the drone of mosquitoes. The ground below is sand or black-organic mud populated with water moccasins and alligators.

    The original story broke in May 2007. The article on MSNBC read like "Hogzilla II," but I smelled a rat. The photo was the first hint at deception. As most any fisherman or hunter knows, it's easy to make vanquished game appear larger than life: just play with perspective. By standing a few feet behind an animal, it's easy to create an illusion that the animal or fish is much larger than it really is. For example, if a three-pound bass is held close in front or to the side, the fish will look like a two- or three-pound bass. If the same fish is held at arm's length, it magically appears twice as big.

    In MSNBC's photo, the kid who shot the pig looks like he is standing ten yards behind the boar. This makes the pig look gigantic, but the perspective was overkill, and the pig resembled a hippopotamus. The article claimed the "wild hog" weighed 1,051 pounds, an astounding weight for a feral pig. The point is the pig weighed over half a ton. There was no need to make it look bigger than it was. If the kid had simply stood behind the pig at about arm's length, it would have appeared more realistic. The photo displayed a willingness to distort reality in a big way.

The second worrisome factor was the sheer size of the pig. With few exceptions, feral hogs tend to be relatively lean animals. To survive in the wild, they cover large distances and eat almost anything: frogs, salamanders, grubs, mushrooms, roots, leaves, baby rabbits, bird eggs, even the occasional fawn. Wild hogs are omnivores, and occasionally out-and-out predators.

You've heard of the Arkansas "razorbacks"? There are two possible explanations for this name. For some time, I believed they were called razorbacks because many feral hogs are so thin, their backbones stand out like razors. There is another explanation in the book *The Complete Guide to Hunting Wild Boar in California* by Gary Kramer. He attributes the name razorback to "[t]he band of long hair extending down the back and forming a ridge." Mr. Kramer also asserts that this band of long hair on the back is a sign of "European ancestry."

Feral hogs may reach impressive sizes. Alabama's best-known pig killer is an Alabama Game and Fish employee named Chris Jaworski. Chris told me in 2005 that two hunters brought in boars at the Lowndes County Wildlife Management Area here in Alabama that maxed out their four-hundred-pound scales. Chris and I frequently give presentations at landowner workshops across the state. When we met up at a Monroe County Field Day in the fall of 2010, Chris told me that of the eighteen hundred feral hogs he had personally shot, only four boars had exceeded four hundred pounds. There are some big hogs out there, and maybe one in ten thousand tops five hundred pounds. Anything beyond that comes in at one in a million. There are no statistics to back that up; that's just my experience and best guess.

So how did this pig reach an excess of one thousand pounds? The only answer is: virtually unlimited feed.

Besides the distorted photo and the pig's gigantic size, the story was pretty fishy. This pig was reportedly shot numerous times over a three-hour period. It takes a special set of circumstances for someone to get this many shots over this length of time.

Of course, the truth eventually came out, as reported by the AP story: "'Monster' Pig Was Huge—Just Not Wild." It wasn't a wild hog. In fact, it had a name; this porker went by Fred. Poor Fred was raised to 1,051 pounds and sold to a high-fence shooting preserve. Then stalked and killed by a boy. And they call this hunting?? No! It's not hunting! Fred was shot nine times over three hours because he was in a high-fenced pen! Fred couldn't get away. Don't call this hunting. This is shooting, and there is a big difference.

Let me tell you about hog hunting.

While I was an apprentice hog slayer under the tutelage of the Master Pig Killer, John Dickson, I picked up the fine art of "point-blank hog hunting." Point-blank hog hunting requires a slightly demented mind, a firearm, wild pigs, and an interminably thick patch of brush.

In the heat of the day, pigs lie up in the thickest stuff they can find. Here in the Deep South, our pigs are partial to privet thickets adjacent to streams and creeks. John told me, "Locate one of these privet thickets. Pick a hog trail in. Then bury yourself in the thicket by crawling on your hands and knees. Visibility will be extremely limited, typically less than ten feet. If you can stay downwind, you can crawl right up on the pigs and maybe get off a shot at point-blank range." Never one to pass on life-threatening adventures that involve big fish or game, I took right to it.

Let's compare and contrast how Fred was shot with one of my hunts that took place shortly after I read Fred's obituary.

My .243 rifle was in the truck as I hopped in and drove to the Solon Dixon Forestry Education Center, where feral hogs had been tearing up our peanut fields. Certainly I wanted to help mitigate the economic destruction the hogs were causing, but I had another motivation: I'd seen the biggest boar in Covington County on the edge of what we called the Sheep Field about two weeks back.

It was a pleasant ride through the longleaf pine woods to the edge of a clear-cut above an abandoned beaver pond. Just the week before, I'd heard a pig in the ditch running through the old pond. Although the pig was only ten yards away, it was invisible in the thick brush. The road ended a couple of hundred yards above the beaver pond. Parking the truck and walking twenty yards down the hill, I heard a pig squeal from somewhere near the beaver pond. My heart was pounding as I threaded a trail through the broomsedge and blackberries, trying to get to the pigs before dark.

At the bottom of the hill, I entered the dry channel of the ditch. Another pig squealed. They were upstream, straight ahead of me. The streambed normally held a few feet of water, but LA was in the middle of a severe drought and the channel was dry.

Luck was with me on two counts. First, the moss-covered streambed allowed for silent walking. Second, the year before, this same beaver pond was down to a few holes of concentrated water and fish, and I had found six water moccasins in a puddle not more than fifteen feet across. The cottonmouths were still around, but at least they weren't directly in the dry stream channel. The banks of the stream were lined with titi.

Pigs snuffed and grunted from the brush ahead. Step by step, I closed the distance. A black pig emerged, crossing the channel from right to left, about twenty yards upstream. It was gone before I could find it in my scope. Visibility was good up to twenty yards ahead, but I could see only ten feet into the titi on either side of the channel. As I was standing still with the rifle at port arms, a pig stepped back into the channel, this time crossing from left to right. The crosshairs immediately settled on the pig and fire leapt from the barrel as the pig disappeared into the brush.

Pigs scattered in all directions, with one moving to the left about ten yards out, but brush obscured everything. Another pig split right. This pig was also within ten yards, and it was also invisible in the thick brush. Bending down and peering into the foliage, I saw only glimpses of movement in the solid thicket of stems, vines, and leaves. Other pigs moved straightaway, following the channel upstream.

Another round was already cycled into the bolt-action, scoped rifle. The first shot had felt good and I hoped I would get a second chance if another pig crossed the stream to my front. Although pigs milled all around, no additional opportunities presented themselves. The pigs departed as darkness descended, requiring a trek back to the truck for a flashlight. It was 8:25 p.m.

Cottonmouths and rattlesnakes slithered through my thoughts as I walked back down the hill, returning to the spot where the targeted pig had last crossed the ditch. It was easy to identify the place—a "fan" of blood, lungs, and stomach contents marked the spot.

I was sure the injured pig had taken one of several trails to the left. Working each trail out and back, I found neither blood nor sign of a shot pig. Having examined the immediate area, I expanded the search pattern in concentric half circles on the left. After an hour of searching, my spirits were flagging; there are few things more depressing than losing wounded or dead game.

Returning to the blood fan, I backtracked to the empty shell casing and studied the angle from the spot where the trigger had been pulled to where the pig had caught the bullet. It was 9:45 p.m.

Maybe the pig had wheeled and run straightaway at the shot? Walking up the stream and rounding a slight bend, I found blood on some cane. Fire ants were collecting on the blood, necessitating a quick follow-up before they disposed entirely of the bits of gore. After running straightaway, the pig had circled back to the right, straight into a solid titi and greenbrier thicket.

Was the pig wounded and pissed off? Dead? Or had it run to the next county? I would soon find out. It was "point-blank pig time" as I got down on my hands and knees to follow the blood trail into the wall of brush. Visibility was limited to three or four feet and a long, scoped rifle was the wrong gun for the job. I dislike pistols, so a short-barreled twelve-gauge shotgun would have been ideal. But this was not the ideal situation. Hopefully, the rifle would be pointing in the right direction when I found the pig, or it found me.

Crawling through the titi, my progress was measured at a few feet per minute, or a few minutes for each foot when greenbrier entangled me. The blood trail was very good and my confidence increased, but eventually the thicket became impenetrable. Backing out and circling around, I reentered the thicket from downstream. A few minutes later, I was about ten yards in, simultaneously watching for the pig, looking for cottonmouths, and dripping sweat in the eighty-degree heat and 100 percent humidity.

Suddenly, I recognized the form of a pig in front of me. The pig wasn't lying down, but something wasn't right about its orientation. The pig was dead, but the brush was so thick that the carcass was lodged upright in a bunch of titi stems. Success! It took a while to extricate the carcass from the brush, dragging it out backward. It was 10:30 p.m. by the time the pig was loaded into my truck. I drove back to the main complex on the Dixon Center, to a concrete pad with skinning gambrels, scales, and everything one needs to dismember a pig, turkey, or deer.

That was pig hunting.

Do you see the difference? No fences. The need for a silent stalk. The potential for the pig to exact some payback. This black pig didn't have a name. He wasn't a pet.

Fred, on the other hand, wasn't killed by a hunter. He was killed by a little kid just learning to shoot straight. That sure isn't hunting. That's shooting in a pen.

The day after my pig hunt in the snake-infested beaver pond, we cooked a batch of ribs from a pig harvested a mere twenty-four hours before. The menu was an epicurean's dream: ribs rubbed in fresh minced garlic and *completito* (a Peruvian seasoning), whole Vidalia onions wrapped in tinfoil, and fresh corn on the cob, grilled with the shucks on. The meal was delicious and my conscience was clear.

3 OVER BAIT

[H]aven't you ever wondered why human eyes face forward as do those of every other land predator or bird of prey?
    —Peter Hathaway Capstick, *Death in the Long Grass,* 1977

Laurel oak (*Quercus laurafolia*): In botany, there are lumpers and splitters. Lumpers are pragmatists. They look at two separate plants that are identical in nine out of ten characteristics, and they issue their pronouncement: "Both trees are laurel oak. We shall name them *Quercus laurafolia.*" Splitters look at the same two trees, focus on a slight variation in the leaf, and issue their verdict: "This one is laurel oak. We shall call it *Quercus hemisphaerica.* That one is diamond leaf oak. Henceforth, it shall bear the name *Quercus laurafolia.*" Whether it is one or two species, laurel oak is recognized as a weedy, fast-growing, evergreen oak that rapidly invades upland sites in the absence of frequent fire. Should his bluetick hounds strike a cold raccoon trail, eventually work it out, and bark treed, the houndsman will inevitably find his dogs at the base of the laurel oak—the only tree with all its leaves still in place, thus forcing the coon hunter to imitate a coon squawl, flicker his lights, and employ all manner of techniques in an effort to trick the coon into peeking from its hiding place. Laurel oak makes good firewood but mediocre lumber, and it comprises a large proportion of the logs on hard pulpwood loads moving up and down the roads of the southeastern United States.

There are many ways to locate a hog hunt. It always helps to know people who have access to large tracts of land with established populations of feral pigs. That's how I lined up the successful hog hunt at Fort Benning.

For the Web-wise hunter, the Internet is another great place to locate hunts. In the past, one site I had used (with mixed results) was eBay. Previous bids had produced only one pig hunt, in New Mexico. I decided to give this auction site another try.

Locating a reasonably priced hog hunt near Austin, Texas, I submitted a bid and won the auction. The auction options allowed the winner to add other hunters at the winning bid, so I called my friend John Dickson from Louisiana. John agreed to go along and bring his friend from Texas, Vincent Gay. Also, my good friend Mike Powell agreed to meet us with his son Tyler, to make a group of five. The Texas hunt was placed on the docket for early October, before the Texas deer season (rifle). Once gun season opens for whitetails, most ranches and hunting preserves focus almost exclusively on deer hunting.

A second search on eBay turned up a combination deer/hog hunt in Laurel Hill, Florida, only forty miles away! Searching on eBay can turn up items from Hong Kong to Anchorage, Alaska. Searches for "Hog Hunts" always turn up domestic offerings, but finding a hunt forty miles away was a real stroke of luck. Between my place of work, the fifty-three-hundred-acre Dixon Center, and the family farm in north central Missouri, I had plenty of deer-hunting access. The hog half of the eBay hunt in Florida was what caught my eye. The hunt sold for a reasonable price, but I did not submit a bid. I was guessing the landowner might be open to a lower negotiated price on a straight hog hunt in the summer. The seller's name was Dan, and he lived just south of the Alabama state line in the Florida Panhandle.

Dan was easy to deal with, offering to pre-bait the area for $25. Any number of hogs could be shot, at $50 a head. For a paid hunt, this was the best deal I'd found so far. I quickly agreed to the conditions and Dan started preparing the area for my hunt.

A couple of weeks later, Dan sent me a photo via e-mail. A hunter from Ohio had vacationed in Panama City, Florida, and made a side trip to hunt hogs at Dan's. The hog hunter walked his climbing stand up a tree over the baited spot, and twenty minutes later a herd of twenty-five to thirty-five pigs of all colors and sizes came to the bait. Dan said, "According to the hunter, three huge black ones brought up the rear. He intended to wait and shoot one of those, but he was afraid the others would smell him, so he shot the pig in the attached photo." The photo showed a pretty red pig that Dan estimated at 100 to 120 pounds. This was just what I was looking for.

Arrangements were made for a hunt on July 6, 2007. I would show up around 5:00 p.m., set up my climber, and be in place a little earlier than the Ohio hunter, who had set up around 6:00.

With a little luck, this hunt would allow me to harvest my first pig with the newest addition to the Hainds' arsenal, a 7 mm Remington Magnum (7 Mag). Having sighted the rifle the week before, my shoulder was fully recovered. Frankly, the gun hurt. I didn't want to shoot the "7" any more than necessary, but a well-placed bullet should stop the biggest boar in its tracks.

On Friday afternoon, I finished work and drove southeast through Florala, Alabama, to meet with Dan. I had brought a bucket of corn and a few older bananas to add to the bait pile on his farm. Following Dan's directions, I pulled into a well-tended yard with attractive flowerbeds lining the driveway and surrounding the house. Dan invited me in to his living room. He offered me a seat and we discussed the local hog population. I asked, "Are you seeing more pigs in recent years?"

Dan confirmed, "Yes, there do appear to be more pigs lately, and I think you stand a good chance of killing one. But make sure to stay on the stand until it is dark."

Dan didn't have to tell me the last part. "I know what you are talking about. It seems like a few minutes before and after dusk is a critical time period for seeing hogs."

Dan gave directions to the stand. "You'll want to park just inside the gate. Walk across the newly built-up road and you will see the hog trap at the top of the hill. That's where I have been feeding them. You'll see the trails where they've been coming to the feed."

Dan wished me luck and I drove to the site. I mounted my climbing stand on a laurel oak about fifty yards from the spot where Dan had been feeding the pigs. Next, I scattered the corn and bananas on ground that was torn to pieces from hog rooting. Whatever corn Dan had put out had been completely eaten—it was a good thing I had brought extra.

After I had been on the stand for several minutes, a doe emerged from the woods on the other side of the hog trap. It grazed for a while before disappearing back into the woods. After the doe, a gray squirrel came out to eat some corn. A couple of hours into the hunt I heard a grunt from the woods to my right. Putting my book down, I picked up the 7 Mag.

It was impossible to see beyond the edge of the forest. The landscape was typical of much of the Florida Panhandle. It had been cut decades before, removing much of the longleaf pine that would have covered this site. After the harvest, fire was excluded and the land regenerated to a mixed pine/hardwood forest. In place of a stable, longleaf pine forest, this stand was now dominated by fast-growing weedy species such as loblolly pine and laurel oak.

After several minutes of quiet, I returned to the book.

As the light faded, I put the book away and focused on the woods around me. This was the peak time period and hopefully the pig I had heard earlier, if it was indeed a pig, was about to make its appearance. Through the gloom, two black shapes appeared over the corn. The crosshairs settled on the closest shape. It was a raccoon. The barely audible sound of cracking corn reached my ears as the coons ate the bait.

Thirty minutes later, it was too dark to shoot. Loading my gear in the truck, I met Dan on the way to his house and paid him $25 for putting out the corn. Dan encouraged me to try again the next day.

Saturday afternoon I drove straight to the spot where Dan had been feeding the pigs. Carrying my climber up the hill, I was disappointed to see the corn still on the ground. If the pigs had located the corn the night before, there was a good chance they would return at an earlier hour. Since the pigs had not visited this site in the last twenty-four hours, there was only a slim chance of seeing pigs this afternoon.

Climbing a tree on the opposite side of the trap, I was settled in a few hours before dark. It wasn't long before company arrived. Two does and a yearling came in from behind. This time they approached to within bow range. I watched them graze for a while before returning to my book.

Mourning doves landed in the corn. Then a newcomer came out, a rabbit that appeared to be eating the corn. The best I could remember, this was the first time I had seen a rabbit eating shelled corn. Just before dark, the coons reappeared. Thirty minutes after dark, I walked the climber down the tree and drove to Dan's house to give him another report.

We settled on a plan: Dan would keep feeding the pigs. If the pigs returned at least two days in a row, he would give me a call and another shot.

My first attempt at Florida pig hunting wasn't quite the "sure thing" that Dan and I had thought it would be.

4   PRIVET

Like a hunter long familiar with his or her woods, who comes somehow to know where the quarry might be taking refuge, and who wanders a seemingly convoluted path that nonetheless eventually takes him or her to the exact place where hunter and quarry will intersect with such synchronicity that in retrospect the confluence will seem foreordained—the hunter sometimes even dreaming the night before of the manner and circumstances of the kill, so that the next day, or the next, it is not the dream that seems like life, but life that seems like the dream.

—RICK BASS, "Activism's Paradox Mountain," 2007

Privet (*Ligustrum sinescens*): An introduced shrub/tree from Asia that grows rapidly and produces prodigious amounts of seed. Birds eat and spread the seed across the southeastern United States. Stop mowing a pecan orchard and privet will appear as if by magic. Stop mowing a yard or weeding a flower garden, and it will become a privet thicket. Stand still long enough, and it will sprout between your toes. Privet thickets are especially common and dense in fire-excluded areas with moist soils near streams and field edges.

As research coordinator for the Longleaf Alliance, I work out of the fifty-three-hundred-acre Solon Dixon Forestry Education Center, between Brewton and Andalusia, Alabama. As the crow flies, the Dixon Center is about ten miles from the Florida line. By automobile it's an hour and a half to Pensacola, and two hours to Mobile, Montgomery, and Dothan, Alabama. The Dixon

Center is owned by Auburn University, and every graduate with a BS in forestry passes through the center, generally between their sophomore and junior years. The Dixon Center abuts the eighty-three-thousand-acre Conecuh National Forest, timber company holdings, and neighboring farms.

The Dixon Center has many vegetative cover types, varying from fire-maintained, upland longleaf stands to fire-excluded bottomland hardwoods. The center has stands of timber varying in age from one year to more than one hundred. It has pure pine stands, mixed pine/hardwood stands, hardwood stands, agricultural fields, food plots, and some pasture ground.

Shortly after my employment began at the Dixon Center, a plane crashed on our property. One reporter started her story, "Reporting from the middle of nowhere, this is . . . " If shopping malls, people, multiple-lane highways, and traffic congestion identify a given location as "somewhere," then the Dixon Center is indeed "the middle of nowhere." But if longleaf pine, rivers, streams, blackwater creeks, pitcher-plant bogs, and an incredible diversity of plants and animals outrank Atlanta, then the Dixon Center may be viewed as the very center of the universe.

My employment started in June 1995, and for the first ten years feral hogs were infrequent visitors. From 1995 until 2005, only three groups, or "sounders," moved onto our property and set up shop. The first group, of five pigs, was eliminated in a two-minute period that may have been my ultimate shooting performance with a rifle.

It was several years before another group of three pigs moved onto the Dixon Center. It wasn't long before I ambushed them in a clear-cut with my .243, laying the group down with no survivors.

The third group showed up in the Conecuh River bottom and a good friend, coworker, and hog killer extraordinaire by the name of John Dickson killed five out of six, allowing only one lucky survivor to escape.

In 2006, the equation changed. Several sounders invaded simultaneously. The first people to notice the pigs were a married couple, Jimmy and Sierra Stiles, good friends of mine. They were out doing herp surveys: trapping snakes, turtles, frogs, salamanders, and other assorted reptiles and amphibians for an Auburn University study. They were working a ridge directly between the two locations where the previous invaders had met their demise. They were going in to check their traps when a herd of pigs walked up on them. Once Jimmy passed on this information, I initiated an intense pursuit, but it was a few weeks before the hogs and I crossed paths.

One weekday afternoon, I was traipsing back and forth, measuring longleaf seedlings in a flatwoods clear-cut, when a squeal arose from a nearby privet thicket. Work was suspended a little earlier than normal that day.

I drove to my house to pick up some buckshot and a twelve-gauge pump shotgun, returning to the clear-cut by 4:00 p.m. No noticeable breeze could carry my scent in the heavy, humid air, so it would be a direct assault.

Following a pig trail to the ditch, I was forced to my hands and knees by a wall of privet and greenbrier. Just to keep the shotgun out of the sand and pointed forward was an effort. The crawl was hot and slow. Grunts and squeals identified the quarry as a sow with piglets. Visibility was limited to five yards or less. With brush this thick, crawling was the only way to make forward progress.

My mouth dried as the distance narrowed to ten yards or so, judging by sound. Continual grunting and snuffling kept me oriented on the pigs as I inched forward with the twelve-gauge pointing toward the sound. A black pig appeared to my front. I centered on black and fired as the pig disappeared. The pigs went silent before quickly exiting the area.

A closer inspection revealed my mistake. The black pig had crossed behind a black stump, which absorbed the buckshot: so much for my attempt at "point-blank hog hunting."

Despite my nonstop scouting, Jimmy was the next to see and shoot at the pigs. He chased them with a determination that closely mirrored my own pig addiction, pursuing the pigs each day before and after checking his herp traps in the surrounding timber, hunting every single day for two weeks.

On one of his morning hunts, Jimmy followed the streams and swamps surrounding the clear-cut that held my longleaf pine study. Jimmy was expecting a close-range shot, so he carried a twelve-gauge with slugs. Unfortunately, the shotgun was a smoothbore, which severely limits accuracy. Most people who pursue pigs or deer with shotguns and slugs have graduated to more accurate slug guns with rifled barrels.

Jimmy told me, "I crawled in and out of the privet, emerging from the dense thickets into the clear-cut, when I looked up to see two large black pigs. The pigs were walking quickly from right to left. I shouldered the twelve and took a freestanding shot at the trailing pig, the larger of the two." Jimmy had sized up the pigs; the pig he targeted "sported exposed tusks," meaning it was a true trophy boar. After the shot, both pigs wheeled and ran for cover. Jimmy said, "It looked like two elephants lumbering across the clear-cut."

Jimmy pumped in another round and fired again, but to no avail. He found no blood or sign that he had connected with either shot.

As later verified, these *were* very sizable pigs. The lead pig may have been the large black sow that I was to cross paths with in the coming months. The trailing pig was the largest boar ever seen on the Dixon Center. Over the next couple of years, I would come to know its habits, recognize its tracks, and respect its exceptional wariness. I carried a rifle or shotgun to the field nearly a hundred different times while pursuing this boar. Other pigs were harvested as opportunities presented, but the primary target was the black boar that dwarfed the rest.

My first digital game camera was installed on a tributary of the stream that flowed around the clear-cut and into the bordering swamps. Tracks and photos told the story: A handful of pigs, including a large boar, were following the open sandy streambeds. It wasn't long before the camera captured the first images of the boar. It was clearly a very large pig, but none of the photos gave a clear view of the head or tusks.

Over Alabama's long deer season, numerous hunts in and around the tributaries of the swamp failed to produce a single pig. After deer season ended, my climbing stand was relocated to a gum tree directly over a streambed in the middle of the privet thickets where the hog sign was thickest.

The following spring found me remeasuring the longleaf seedlings in the clear-cut surrounded by swamps. Once again, squeals arose from the privet thicket, the site of my earlier attempt at point-blank hog hunting. This time, rather than burrowing straight in with the twelve-gauge, I circled well out and downwind of the last place I'd heard the pigs. I entered the tributary that bordered a nearby area called the Round Field, its sandy streambed allowing me virtually silent passage. As I advanced toward the pigs, a privet thicket enveloped the stream-bed forcing me out onto meandering pig trails where fresh tracks and sign blanketed the forest floor. It took only a few minutes to intersect the main stream channel that separated the Round Field from the clear-cut.

The temperature was in the nineties. Pausing to gather my breath, listen, and assess the situation, I noticed that my clothes were already soaked with sweat. There was a light breeze out of the west and the pigs were upwind. The wait was short. After I'd stood a minute or two at the stream intersection, a squeal sounded from the west, precisely where the pigs had been the year before.

The streambed led west but the brush forced me out onto the pig trails again. It sounded like they were about 150 yards downstream. Trying to move as silently as possible, I was forced to crawl on my hand and knees. Greenbrier laced the privet thicket. Its thorny vines grabbed my clothing and skin, forcing frequent stops to clip the vines with a Leatherman (a plierslike tool with similarities to a Swiss army knife). After several minutes of crawling, I had so many holes in my extremities that a halfway decent tracker could have blood trailed me!

Progress was incredibly slow in this superthicket. Every few yards there was evidence of recent hog beds. The pigs recognized cover that would normally exclude hunters. Perhaps that's why they kept returning to this safe haven.

The distance narrowed to about fifty yards. History was repeating itself. Near-continuous grunting and squealing kept me oriented, with visibility limited to five yards in most directions—sometimes a little more, sometimes a little less. In some spots, maneuverability was so limited that it was impossible to swing the gun barrel to either side. I tried to locate and follow paths that allowed me to keep the barrel pointed toward the pigs.

I was tight in, estimating the distance at less than twenty yards, when the way forward was blocked by a large area covered with dry sycamore leaves—a minefield where a hand or knee on any of these leaves would blow up the hunt. To clear a path, I resorted to gently picking the leaves up one at a time and setting them to the side.

Had the pigs been visible, they should have been in range of the double-ought buckshot. It's hard to explain just how exciting this type of hunting is. But when the hunter has closed to within a few yards of his prey and the animal is making near-continuous noises, the heart wants to jump out of the chest.

A few yards of leaves still blocked the way when the pigs went silent. The sycamore leaves had been my downfall. After a minute or two, it was clear the jig was up. This ol' sow was a wily one, and if she raised her shoats to be as cautious as she, it would prove extremely difficult to keep the Dixon Center "hog free."

It took a few minutes to push through the privet thicket and emerge from the drain. The clear-cut had been wide open two years back. Now it was solid shrub and herbaceous growth. The dense, nearly impenetrable privet was replaced by dense, nearly impenetrable grass eight to ten feet tall. It was even thicker than the privet thicket. Visibility was limited to little more than an arm's length in any direction.

Hog sign was just as prevalent in the clear-cut as it had been in the privet. After picking up a pig trail, I pushed west, with my shotgun pointing straight up to minimize entanglements. A few dozen yards in, something stirred in the grass three or four feet off my right leg. When I looked down, my vision was obscured by a wall of grass, but small patches of black appeared through holes as the animal moved forward, parallel to the pig trail.

The action that followed lasted perhaps two or three seconds, but the scenario would be replayed in my mind hundreds of times in the year to come. Those few seconds became some of the longest of my hunting career. Seeing the small patch of black, for some reason the first thing that came to mind was "raccoon." The shotgun was still pointing straight up but I started to lower it while watching the grass to my right and front. The animal was still moving through the grass when it dawned on me that this critter was too big for a coon.

About eight feet to my front, an enormous hog's head with exposed tusk emerged into the trail. No longer in doubt as to what the animal was, my brain screamed, "Down! Down! Down!" willing the barrel lower, but the shotgun seemed to move in super-slow motion.

Recognition was mutual and simultaneous. Before the barrel was down, the hog launched itself across the trail, shooting toward the ten-foot-high wall of grass on my left. It was now or never as I swung the twelve down and around, pulling the trigger before the shotgun touched my shoulder, firing buckshot into the closing grass as the boar disappeared.

I started forward but my wobbly legs gave way. Kneeling in the trail, a few controlled, slow breaths allowed me to regain my composure and load another shell before moving into the grass with a fully loaded shotgun. Examining the spot where the boar had entered the grass, I saw no blood, no hair, no bone. Opportunity had knocked; I just didn't get to the door in time.

It took about half an hour to thoroughly search the surrounding area and confirm that the shot had been a clean miss. I trudged back to the truck; soaked in sweat, covered with weed seed, spiders, and detritus.

Despair haunted my memories, but this pig wasn't dead or gone yet. As long as the chase persisted, there was a reasonable chance we would cross paths again.

Hogs kept working the streams and swamps around the clear-cut. Later that spring, I moved my digital game camera a little farther downstream, closer to the clear-cut and privet thicket that so enamored these pigs. The camera started picking up more images right away. In early March 2007, the camera took a photo of four pigs in the same frame. This and other photos showed my quarry as a very large boar, another large pig that I assumed was a sow, and two smaller pigs that appeared to be the offspring of the big sow. This group was solid black, excepting one of the smaller pigs, which had a few brown hairs running the length of its back.

Months after my missed shot at the big boar, and a few weeks after my trail cam captured the boar's image with the sow and shoats, I was sitting in a tree stand overlooking the privet ditch and some adjacent trails. It was late in the afternoon when I heard the pigs coming. They milled around in the privet for several minutes before emerging into the stream below. It was dark beneath the hardwood canopy and I was just able to locate a large black pig in my scope, but the crosshairs were invisible in the dim light. All I could do was center the pig and pull the trigger. All four pigs immediately disappeared at the shot. Over an hour of searching didn't turn up a single drop of blood.

There was no sign that the pig was hit, but the sow disappeared while the other three pigs returned to the area within a few weeks. More than likely, I gut shot the sow and the bullet did not exit. Or it could have been another clean miss. The odds are pretty good that the pig's bones are somewhere in the surrounding woods. Whatever the case, there had been four, and now there were three.

Several more hunts from the same stand failed to produce a kill. Then, on another late afternoon in March, I started down the hill to the ditch in the afternoon dusk. It had been dry for a while and the leaves and twigs along the trail crunched underfoot. Starting about eighty to a hundred yards above the ditch, I took two steps and then stopped, counting to fifteen and listening for pigs. The trail camera flashed while I was still fifty yards from the ditch. It took willpower to resist the impulse to cover the remaining distance quickly.

Progress continued, two steps at a time. The ditch to my front ran straight north half a mile to U.S. Highway 29, and the sound of a large truck rumbled down the ditch. Under the covering noise, I covered the remaining twenty yards to the ditch at a steady but cautious pace. When I reached the ditch, moist sand allowed for nearly silent progress.

I still hadn't heard any noise from the pigs, assuming it had been they that tripped the camera. As I faced downstream, I noted a solid wall of privet to my right. To my left, depending on the brush, vines, and trees, visibility ranged from a few feet to twenty yards. Rooting and trails crisscrossed the whole area. Scanning left, right, and forward, I inched down the ditch, reaching the bend without seeing or hearing a thing. Maybe there were no pigs in the area? My pulse slowed.

I had just reached a bend in the ditch when the camera flashed again, about twenty yards away. Before the flash faded, I was back on red alert and my mouth dried as I rounded the bend. At first nothing was visible besides the surrounding brush and the empty streambed. Then two pigs stepped into the main channel from the right bank. I immediately shouldered the rifle, the crosshairs settled on the nearest pig, and I pulled the trigger. The pig rolled forward into the stream and the other one disappeared before the muzzle flash faded.

Which pig had I just shot? It looked pretty big at first glimpse. Was it the boar?

Working the bolt, I watched the pig kick once or twice in a final spasm, and then lie still. It was one of the two smaller pigs, the one with brown hairs on its back. It wasn't huge, but I was nearly exhausted by the time I dragged it out of the ditch, up the hill, and back through the food plot to my truck. If you are given the choice of a 140-pound deer or a 100-pound pig, drag the deer. Pigs are very compact and something about their shape makes them much harder to drag than a deer of the same weight. Back at the main complex of the Dixon Center, the sow weighed in at 114 pounds, about 20 pounds more than my estimates from the most recent photos.

The small sow had been eating well and had nearly two inches of fat over the whole body. The only damaged meat was the left front shoulder, a meager sacrifice in exchange for not having to trail a wounded pig. To date, every pig I have shot in the front shoulder dropped in its tracks. Since my pigs never seem to leave blood trails, the front shoulder is my preferred target.

The pursuit had started with a group of four. Then there were three. Now there were two.

The meat from this pig was fantastic, but my freezer was filling up from many successful deer and hog hunts. I persuaded two married coworkers, Larry and Vickie, to take some roasts and loin. Even though Larry is a cattle and row-crop farmer, he's grown accustomed to the dry, tasteless pork sold in supermarkets. He didn't like the taste of feral hog, although I believe that sow produced some of the best-tasting, most tender pork I've ever eaten.

A couple of weeks later, I had just gotten home from a speaking engagement in Georgia when Vickie called and asked, "Do you want a pig?"

Oh, no! Which pig had been killed? "Is it a sow or a boar?"

She radioed Larry, who relayed back that it was a boar. My freezer wasn't lacking for pork, but Larry may have killed my boar, or perhaps the littermate to my recent kill. I had to know.

Vickie told me to meet Larry at the Pecan Orchard. I arrived to find Larry waiting with a forestry student. I asked, "Where's the pig?"

Larry said, "I'll take you to it."

Was this going to be my boar?

But when we reached the pig, I saw that it was not. There were no visible tusks. This pig was too large to be the littermate of my recent kill, but too small and young to be the boar. Older boars are more heavily weighted to the front end and they have long tusks. This was the first I'd seen of this pig.

Larry had been on the edge of the old pecan orchard when he had seen the pig crossing the food plot. He had made a nice two-hundred-yard shot with his .270 as the pig headed for the timber at the bottom of the hill.

Addressing Larry, I said, "Look, I am going to clean this pig but you can have all you want."

Larry wasn't too excited. "As far as I'm concerned, it can lay there and rot. I don't want any."

Larry drove home while I took the pig to the cleaning shed. When I winched the boar up, it tipped the scales at 140 pounds live weight.

A couple of weeks earlier, the director of the Dixon Center, Joel Martin, had told me that some of the Auburn University forestry students had expressed an interest in cooking a whole hog. Just as I finished gutting the boar, some of them pulled up. This was my chance to offload the pig. "Any of you all want a pig?"

They excitedly answered, "We'll take it off your hands!" For the second time in one evening, relief flooded over me.

A couple of days later, they cooked the whole hog, and several of them told me it tasted pretty good. Joel said he detested the boar smell and there was no way he could eat one. Joel had killed hundreds or maybe even thousands of pigs at his previous place of employment in southeast Georgia. He said they had killed pigs all year long, trying to reduce the pig population so that they could have more deer and fewer, larger hogs on the property.

Few experienced hog hunters or pig farmers can stomach boar meat. One exception is a U.S. Fish and Wildlife Service biologist I work with from Fairhope, Alabama. Over the years, Randy Roach has shot or trapped dozens of pigs on his hunting lease in south Alabama. Randy told me he likes to soak his meat in a cooler with ice and water for at least twenty-four hours prior to cooking. In his opinion, all feral hogs are decent table fare.

The Dixon Center leases its agricultural fields to a local farmer named Bill. In 2007 he planted peanuts south of Highway 29 and west of the Rome Road in what we call the Sheep Field. East of the Rome Road, in Danny's Field, Bill planted corn. By midsummer, hog sign was all around the planted fields.

After work, I spent most afternoons scouting ditches and checking my digital game camera off Reed Break Road. I was driving out Reed Break Road one afternoon while Bill was going in to spray his fields. As we pulled up beside each other, Bill asked, "You hunting pigs?"

Actually, I was scouting for pigs, but that's a technicality. "Yeah. I had a camera up and got photos of four different pigs earlier this summer. I've killed the sow and one of two shoats. The other shoat should be in the one-hundred-pound range. And there is one heck of a big boar that I've been hunting for over a year."

"I saw that boar."

He had my attention. "No kidding!"

Bill told me, "I pulled into this field a week back and looked down there"—he pointed above the head of a ditch—"and I thought, 'Boy, that is a big weed out there.' The next thing I knew, it was running for the ditch and I could tell it was a huge hog."

I assured Bill, "I am hot on his trail." That was true, but the more people who saw this pig, the higher the odds that someone else would get the final trigger pull.

In the following weeks, the boar moved frequently. The trail cam picked up several more photos of him on the ditch bordering the Round Field. Then the boar's tracks started appearing in and around the Sheep Field. Over the previous winter, the pigs had spent considerable time in this field digging up volunteer peanuts after the residual corn was exhausted. When the Sheep Field was planted back to peanuts in the spring of 2007, it didn't take long for the boar to start raiding the field at night, working his way down furrows on the back, or south and west, sides of the field. This part of the field was the least visible from U.S. 29. It was also close to thick, wet, brush-filled drains where the boar probably bedded in the daytime.

Noticing the rooting in the Sheep Field, Larry clued me in to the boar's new location. A few days later, the assistant director of the Dixon Center, Dale Pancake, came in late in the morning and told me he had just seen either a rhinoceros or a huge pig in the Sheep Field. It had casually walked down a row and into the woods less than a hundred yards away.

Now it was turning serious. If the pig was hitting the peanut field in daylight hours, it would only be a matter of time before Larry or Bill knocked him down.

Furthermore, Joel told Dale, "Let me know the next time you see that boar. I've got a 7 mm 08 that'll take care of him."

Threats to my boar were coming from every side. Having already invested over a year in chasing this pig, I would not be pleased in the least if some interloper pulled up on U.S. 29 on his way to or from work and plugged the boar.

I left work the afternoon after Dale reported seeing the boar and parked on the edge of the Sheep Field with the intention of scouting for sign. My rifle was at home, but the sun was high overhead and I didn't foresee any chance of crossing paths with a pig in the middle of a sunny, hot afternoon. I noted considerable rooting on the southeast edge of the field, but most of it was a few days old. Walking over a small ridge, I was stunned to recognize the boar walking a row of peanuts about two hundred yards to my front, right where Dale had seen him the day before.

Dropping to my hands and knees, I crawled back over the small rise before breaking into a full run for the truck. Ignoring speed limits, I raced home to get my rifle and was back at the Sheep Field in fifteen minutes. The boar was gone, so I sat on the field edge until dark, vainly hoping the pig would come back for one more mouthful of peanuts.

My rifle accompanied me everywhere from that point forward, regardless of the time of day. The boar continued raiding the peanut field, but there was no sign from the privet ditch for another two weeks. By the second week in July, the smaller black pig was back in the privet ditch and the sow had two piglets, which appeared to weigh about five pounds each.

First there were four. Then three. Then two. Now we were back to four. This was a microcosm of the difficulty involved in controlling feral hog populations, even with dedicated and persistent effort.

When my camera captured images of the sow and piglets three days in a row, it was time to get back to the ditch. Arriving well before sunup, I took a comfortable seat at the base of a large water oak that had broken about fifteen feet up. The privet beneath the oak was so thick that it propped the top of the oak tree several feet above the sandy soil along the nearby stream.

My collar was turned up, and my hands were tucked in my pockets to minimize exposed skin. The mosquitoes had been so bad on the previous trip, I had suffered dozens of bites, even with repellent applied to my face and clothing. My position at the base of the water oak covered two trails on the left and one to my front. The trails all converged at the ditch.

Two hours into the hunt, the *ruhhh ruhhh . . . ruhhh ruhhh* of piglets dispelled the fog of sleep and brought me to full alert. Piglets often use low grunts to keep track of each other or to locate each other if they get separated.

I sat up, raised my gun, and looked to my left and front. Nothing. An alarm snort sounded behind me: *Frwoooh! Frwoooh!* The sow was visible over my shoulder, about five yards to my rear, looking straight at me. I rolled to my left, but the pigs disappeared into the privet before I could get the gun up. So goes hunting.

Surprisingly, the game camera picked up the sow in the same area two days later. Four days after the close call in the ditch, I was returning from another fruitless hog hunt in Florida and decided to give the Dixon Center privet pigs another attempt.

Morning found me in the same privet ditch, but at the base of a different tree. There wasn't time to fall asleep before the *ruhhh, ruhhh . . . ruhhh, ruhhh* of piglets reached my ears. By the sound of it, they were just where I wanted them to be. The pigs were about forty yards away in the thicket on the left. Inching silently down the ditch, I closed the distance to twenty yards, but the way forward was blocked by the top of that broken oak tree entwined in the privet. I took a knee where a small hole in the privet provided a shooting lane.

The pigs rooted to the left for about five minutes. It was torture holding my position, but there was no safe way to approach them. Eventually, the sow let out a long, low grunt—a pause—and another low grunt: *urrrrrr . . . urrrrr.* The piglets went silent and the jig was up. The sow had winded me.

To be on the safe side, I waited another five minutes before pushing through the privet branches. Of course they were long gone. My kill record was abysmal in this ditch.

On Tuesday, July 10, all four of the pigs' tracks showed up again. Perhaps the sow had come back into estrus? Each successive day, there were fresh tracks from the boar, the sow, and her two new piglets. Anticipation mounted as I psyched up for the hunt.

I would be carrying a brand-new rifle. It had a black synthetic stock and it was chambered for the 7 mm Remington Magnum cartridge. This was a considerably larger cartridge than the .243 that I had hunted with over the last twenty-five years or so.

Before daylight on July 14, I put on a T-shirt, a pair of gray camouflage bib overalls, and my old army forest camo BDU (battle dress uniform) top. Two or three layers of clothing on my upper torso would limit mosquitoes to the exposed skin of my hands, neck, forehead, and ears.

Arriving at the Dixon Center in the early morning hours, I parked a half mile from the ditch and hiked in. Although water had run in the ditch during the night, there was only one puddle in the immediate vicinity. The pure sand in the streambed formed a flat delta that seemed to suck up everything the stream had to offer.

Since the two prior shooting positions hadn't panned out, I selected a new location. The day before, Friday the 13th, I had cleared dead branches and cut away greenbrier and privet, opening clear shooting lanes extending about thirty yards in four spokes from the center hub.

A towel separated me from the sand as I lay down and practiced rising to a shooting position to my front and rear. Satisfied that I could rise up and acquire my target quickly and quietly, I sprayed 40 percent DEET into my hand and rubbed the repellent onto exposed skin to slow the mosquito onslaught. Lying back on the towel with the 7 Mag across my chest, I dozed fitfully as time passed. The concentrated DEET kept the mosquitoes at bay and I drifted in out and of sleep as time passed and the skies began to lighten.

The soft grunts of piglets penetrated my subconscious, causing me to wake and open my eyes. Had I been dreaming? Or was the grunting real? I was still lying on my back, looking through the tree branches above me. The sun wasn't fully up, but the sky had mostly cleared of clouds. There was just enough light that the crosshairs should be visible, even deep in this privet thicket.

Soft grunts drifted from the privet to my left. Now fully awake, I rolled over, reversed directions, and took a knee. Looking down the shooting lane that ran southeast from my position, I could hear the pigs on my right. They would not see me. Neither would they hear me. But would the sow smell me?

The pigs drifted closer. It sounded like they were thirty to forty yards to the front and right. About five minutes passed as they worked in the brush.

I watched the trail intently. An eye! A head! A very big head! The left front leg entered the shooting lane as the rifle came up. The shooting lane was only ten feet wide and the pig wasn't stopping. Its head was already in the brush on the other side and only a fraction of a second remained when I squeezed the trigger, rocking backward from the recoil. When my vision returned, my ears were ringing and the pig was gone.

The piglets were still grunting to the right. Had that been the sow? It looked too big, but the targeted pig had been visible only for a couple of seconds. The piglets headed straightaway through the brush on the right, never crossing the trail.

The pig had been in the crosshairs but the shot was hurried. Perhaps the bullet had struck too far back? Surely, the bullet had exited and there would be a solid blood trail?

The question remained: Was it the boar or the sow? The piglets were too small to make it on their own so they shouldn't have left the area. They had not followed the big pig that crossed the trail. This seemed to indicate that the piglets were still with the sow, and they had moved off as a group.

Was the pig lying just off the trail? There was no blood trail in the area where the pig had crossed the trail to give an indication. Numerous pig trails led off in every direction. Even without blood, bone, hair, or any sign of an impact, I couldn't believe I'd missed a pig that big and that close.

With a compass on a lanyard around my neck and a bearing from the starting point, I crawled into the privet. I repeatedly followed trails to my left, searching the sand and brush for spots of blood. Fresh tracks covered the ground, making it impossible to determine which were today's versus the previous days'. Sometimes the meandering trails emerged into the dry streambed or the fire line that circled the Round Field. Sometimes the trails led back to my original starting point.

In *The Complete Book of Wild Boar Hunting,* Todd Triplett writes, "[F]ollowing up on a wounded boar can be dangerous, particularly in thick cover." Along the same vein, Bob Gooch, author of *Hunting Boar, Hogs and Javelina,* says, "Following a wounded boar or a hog into a thicket is just as risky as heading in after a bear."

Despite their advice, the third time I came back to my starting point, I left the 7 Mag leaning against a tree. It was just too heavy and too long to carry on the pig trails. A wise hunter would have already purchased a sidearm, but I hadn't gotten around to it and would just have to take my chances.

After an hour of working to my left, it was time to search trails straightaway and to the right. Perhaps this pig had pulled the same trick as the last one at the beaver pond, darting to the left but circling back to the right.

My luck was no better regardless of the direction. Two hours into the search, my clothes were wringing wet and exhaustion was clouding my judgment. If I happened to crawl around a clump of privet to face an injured angry boar, my ability to react quickly would be compromised.

I drove home and took a short nap before returning to the Dixon Center. This time, Maggie, my eleven-year-old Brittany spaniel, accompanied me. She'd never found big game for me, but maybe she would bark, growl, or give some indication if she located the pig.

Entering the ditch, Maggie ran out of sight while I continued working the brush near my stand. Fifteen minutes into the renewed search, I saw a large black object on the ground. As I walked toward it, the picture clarified. This wasn't a stump or a log. This was a very big hog. A few more steps and I knew it wasn't the sow—this was my boar.

Standing over the dead boar, it was clear that this was the biggest hog I had ever killed. The boar was black from the snout to its hooves and to its tail. The hair was sparse and the bullet hole was almost dead center, length and height of the torso. The boar was lying against a four-inch-diameter hardwood. The leaf litter had been cleared away by the boar's final thrashes or spasms, exposing the bare mineral soil. There was a little blood in the mouth but no discernible blood trail. The bullet had not exited.

This was not just another kill. This was the most magnificent animal of my hunting career. The pursuit had lasted for almost two years. I had shown photos of its tracks to my buddies on a New Mexico elk-hunting trip. The boar's habits and patterns had become familiar to me. As time passed, the boar had invaded my dreams, and it had earned my respect. Now the hunt was over, but there was no smile on my face. I felt just a sense of relief and, at the same time, a feeling of loss.

In my youth, I had heard or read that Native Americans offered a prayer of thanks for the gift of each animal they killed, while they also asked forgiveness from the spirit of the animal whose life they had taken. As a young teenager I had taken this on as standard practice with my large game. Kneeling beside the boar with my hand on the coarse hide, I said a prayer of thanksgiving and asked for forgiveness.

My eyes were blurry with fatigue. My clothes were soaked with sweat. I smelled awful. Finding the carcass had only been part of the equation. Now it was time to extract it from the brush. Luckily, there was a labor pool readily available. Three Auburn University forestry students helped drag the boar out of the woods. Back at the Dixon Center, the boar weighed in at an incredible 317 pounds.

I typically make it back to Missouri for deer season and Christmas. A few years back, I visited a second cousin and his new wife on New Year's Eve. "Little George" had killed an incredible ten-point whitetail in November, during Missouri's short rifle season. The antlers on this once-in-a-lifetime kill grossed 198 points before shrinkage. Of note, George was my second relative to kill a world-class buck within twenty miles of our family farm.

As we had a few drinks in his living room, the conversation turned to his spectacular deer season. George told us, "Until recently, every night when I laid down in bed all I could think of was sex. Now, when I lay down at night, I think, 'I killed a really big deer.'"

I knew just what George was talking about. For weeks to come, each night when I lay down, I thought, "Man, I killed a really big pig."

5 OAK/HICKORY

It is comforting to know that there is something out there that is at least arguably dangerous. A life without rattlesnakes, lived safely under the umbrella of the rescue squad, would seem a little diminished. Let them pass. Snakes have seniority. Besides, it would be a lesser world without them.

—John C. Hall, *Headwaters*, 2009

Oak/Hickory (*Quercus/Carya*): The oak/hickory type is the most common upland forest of the midwestern United States. Where pines do not comprise a significant percentage of the canopy, the oak/hickory type is also the dominant forest of much of the eastern and southeastern United States. This is the forest type in which Billy Charles Hainds showed his young son how to tell the difference between red oaks and white oaks. This is the forest type in which a farm boy, who would grow up to be a forester, first gained an appreciation for the beauty and value of our natural forests.

By August of 2007, it was time to pick up the tempo if there was any hope of killing pigs in ten states in one year. Logging onto eBay, I found a hog hunt near Counce, Tennessee. Counce was less than six hours away, and if the hunt was successful, it would add an additional state to my list.

There was one big negative: it appeared that the seller had not received registered feedback on a single sale. This could be the first time the seller had offered something for sale on eBay. As a frequent eBay customer, I rarely bid on items from sellers that who sold fewer than twenty items on eBay, preferring established sellers who have offered up hundreds or thousands of items and have at least a 98.5 percent positive rating.

Because Tennessee would be a good score, further investigation was warranted. A few e-mails increased my comfort level. Andy (the name has been changed), the seller, owned property bordering the Shiloh Battlefield National Park, just north of the state line with Alabama. He also said the pigs were concentrated on sixty acres of bottom ground. Andy added, "I am confident you'll see pigs on this site and all the hogs I've seen have been more than 125 pounds."

We discussed dates, and Andy said the coming weekend was fine for him. He wanted hunters to come sooner rather than later, because the hogs were tearing the forest up and he wanted to book as many hog hunts as possible before deer season started.

The description sounded good—but as often as not, glowing descriptions are followed by skunked-out hunts; just recall my recent Florida hunts. Few people realize just how much sign a handful of pigs can leave. Unless a hunter is familiar with feral hogs and interpreting hog sign, it's hard to tell the difference between the activity and sign from five pigs or five hundred pigs. A handful of hogs can leave lots of tracks, rubs, and rooting, and it's easy to overestimate the number of pigs in a given area.

Another factor to consider is that hogs respond very quickly to hunting pressure. A large group of hogs may work a given area every day, but shoot one hog out of the group, and the survivors frequently relocate, ending all activity in a given locale for days or weeks to come. That's probably what happened with my first Florida hunt, where another hunter shot one pig out of a group of twenty-five to thirty-five pigs. My Florida hunts were booked while the survivors were still giving the property a wide berth.

Based upon Andy's description and my previous experiences, there was no call for pessimism. But it didn't hurt to discount optimistic stories and/or descriptions, and then be pleasantly surprised when and if they turned out to be spot on.

Logging onto eBay at 5:30 on Thursday morning with a cup of coffee in hand, I discovered that the Tennessee hog hunt was mine! Andy had already e-mailed me: "Congratulations on winning the hunt! Should I count on you coming up this weekend?" Either Andy had stayed up later than I had, or he had gotten up earlier. Sooner was better than later, so the hunt was booked for the following Saturday morning.

Later that day, I gave four talks in Troy on various aspects of longleaf artificial regeneration to a group of foresters, tree planters, nurserymen, herbicide applicators, and private landowners. One of the questions posed was "I've heard that wild hogs like to eat the top out of these longleaf seedlings. What can you tell us about that?"

Addressing the group, I said, "Actually, I am hoping to go hog hunting in Tennessee this weekend. And a few weeks back, I just killed my biggest boar to date—weighing in at 317 pounds." (I seldom missed an opportunity to mention my recent pig-hunting triumph.) "That hog had been working our peanut field over, but I didn't see any evidence that he was eating longleaf seedlings."

The story continued: "From what I have seen of hog damage on one site in Geneva County, on the Dixon Center, on Fort Benning, Georgia, and in west Alabama, hogs root up longleaf but they generally don't eat the seedlings. On one field in Geneva County and another field in west Alabama, I inspected longleaf plantings that were complete failures, because the hogs had essentially turned the fields over. The pigs 'plowed' those fields.

"Two more cases: earlier this year at Fort Benning, and two years back with a study on the Dixon Center, hogs rooted through new longleaf plantings. My photos show extensive rooting, but the container-grown longleaf seedlings were lying on the ground uneaten.

"So the answer to your question is: You may suffer mortality or planting failures if the hogs are free to root up the whole field or clear-cut, but feral hogs don't appear to eat longleaf when they have better food sources available.

"There is an exception to this rule. Many of you know the former director of the Dixon Center, Rhett Johnson. Rhett worked on an island in South Carolina that had extremely high hog numbers. Under that situation, where food was very limited, Rhett reports that he saw hogs start on the lateral roots of longleaf and work right down the root, pulling it up and eating the cambium all the way back to the bole. So at some point with very high pig numbers, you could see actual feeding on the tree seedlings or even on mature trees!"

As the meeting was wrapping up, one attendee let me know that he was having problems with hogs in his cornfields. Handing him my business card, I told him to give me a call if he needed a professional pig hunter to reduce his population.

The next day, Friday, I took off work at 3:30 p.m., ran home, showered, packed, and was on the road by 4:45. Crossing into Tennessee, I stopped at the Welcome Center on I-65 and picked up a map, choosing 64 West, which would take me just above Counce, where my hotel room was waiting.

As I drove west on 64, the headlights illuminated a recognizable form in the middle of the road—a big timber rattler, and as I feared, it was too late to save the animal. Someone had run over the snake, smashing its guts onto the asphalt, but it wasn't yet dead. The rattler was trying to crawl to the road shoulder, but even if it had cleared the road, it was doomed to a slow, excruciating death. Its innards would tangle in the brush and the fire ants would attack from all angles, eating it alive.

This was a big snake and it was, justifiably, in a very bad mood. I popped my trunk and removed a camera tripod—the only suitable weapon at hand. After applying the coup de grâce, I dropped the snake in a forty-eight-quart cooler full of ice. The next day, I measured the rattler at fifty-one inches.

Arriving later in Counce, I left Andy a message, checked into the hotel, and was in bed around 1:00 a.m.

Andy picked me up very early the next morning. We shook hands and loaded my bow, rifles, and cooler into his truck before heading to the field. He told me his truck had six hundred thousand miles on the body, and it was on its third motor, adding, "I've got a two-hour one-way commute to Memphis."

I hoped it wasn't that far to his property. "How far to the site we'll be hunting?"

He relieved my worries. "It's about twenty minutes away."

Passing a Civil War battlefield, I observed 150-year-old cannons standing in formation on mowed fields. I wasn't that familiar with the history of battles in Tennessee. I knew more about the conflict in Missouri, where my family suffered indignities and mortal danger straight out of the script from *The Outlaw Josey Wales*. One of my ancestors had apparently fought with Sterling Price, the namesake of Rooster Cogburn's cat in *True Grit*. Partly because of this history, these are two of my all-time favorite movies.

Sericea lespedeza lined the road shoulders. It's impossible to go anywhere in the South without seeing invasive species such as this one. Tragically, people are still planting these nonnative species, often because some ignorant biologist found it in his out-of-date "quail food" book. When landowners, foresters, or biologists ask me about planting Asian lespedezas, I tell them, "Budget $1 to plant it and $10 to control or kill it down the road."

Andy parked next to a small tractor and farm implements. My bow, quiver, backpack, and camcorder were going to the field with me. It had been a long time since my last bow kill, and with a little luck, we'd get the hunt on video.

Andy strapped on a large silver revolver and led the way, whispering, "There'll probably be some pigs under the stand, so be ready." He led the way through a disked food plot and into the woods. The overstory was primarily oaks and hickories. The midstory was moderately thick, and visibility ranged from ten to fifty yards with the leaves on.

The trail wrapped around the ridge, following the contour. Perhaps fifty yards into the timber, Andy pulled up and pointed straight ahead. A black hog, somewhere in the range of 100 to 150 pounds, stood beneath a ladder stand on a slope overlooking a slough/oxbow to the right. Later, Andy told me this was an old channel of Snake Creek, with the main channel just around the bend. Beside the black hog, a larger white hog, 150 to 200 pounds, was rooting around the forest floor. Andy hadn't pulled my leg about the number of pigs on his property.

We knelt in the trail and assessed the situation. The pigs were less than fifty yards out, an easy rifle shot, but well outside my effective range with the bow. So far, the hogs were not alarmed.

Andy pointed down the slope. I'd also heard rustling from that direction. The source was a big spotted boar in the slough below. The boar started up the hill toward the stand to our front. This hunt was progressing rapidly.

Both the black pig and the white pig had sensed us. The pair stood still with their heads up, while the boar continued up the slope, oblivious to our presence. I had an arrow already nocked. I went to full draw just before the spotted boar entered the trail to my front, presenting a clear broadside shot at fifteen yards. Andy was still trying to get the camcorder out of its carrying case.

This was no time to dally. Video would have been nice, but it wasn't worth passing up this opportunity. With the boar stopped broadside, I aimed just behind the front shoulder and squeezed the release. *Twang—thunk.* The arrow hit a little farther forward and higher than intended, quivering in the top of the front shoulder. It was hard to judge, but the penetration looked pretty good. The boar snorted and ran a short circle back to the spot where it had caught the arrow. It faced us with its head down, looking about as pissed off as a pig could look. The pig's expression said, "Okay, which one of you bastards stuck this thing in my shoulder?"

Andy gave up filming, dropping the camera, and drew his revolver while I frantically tried to nock an arrow. The arrow slid into position as I turned to face the pig again. Though injured and surly, the boar found discretion the better part of valor, disappearing into the brush before my peep sights settled on him.

Advancing down the trail while watching all sides, I rounded the hill and came face-to-face with another large pig in a surly mood. It snorted, facing my direction about twenty yards out. The pig pawed at the earth like an Andalusian fighting bull. But instead of using its front legs, it used its hind legs to scrape at the earth.

There was no protruding arrow. This was not the spotted boar that I'd just stuck. After attempting to stare us down for a moment or two, the white pig and the black pig, the pair we'd seen initially on entering the timber, exited to the right. Just as they were leaving, a larger, light-colored hog joined them before disappearing into the brush. Was that my boar? If so, it was walking without any obvious infirmity, which was a bad sign.

Back at the ladder stand, Andy asked, "Did you see him?"

Not sure, I replied, "I think so. Three pigs followed the hill around to the right."

Andy said, "I think we better let him have plenty of time to bleed out."

In total agreement, I answered, "I hear you!"

As I climbed the ladder stand, I noticed numerous vines clinging to the bole of the white oak, paralleling the ladder. Andy crawled up on a downed oak tree about four feet above the ground and said, "I should be high enough to be safely out of their reach." Andy's extreme concern struck me as curious. Also, the pigs' behavior was unlike anything I had witnessed before from feral hogs.

Reaching the top of the ladder stand, I found the view obstructed in almost every direction by poison ivy. It took about five minutes of clipping with a Leatherman to clear a field of fire to the left, front, and right. Andy held the camcorder, sitting five yards to the left and rear.

The wait was short. Perhaps five minutes after I'd settled in, rustling leaves signaled a hog to our front and left. Andy pointed the camcorder across the slough to our front. Shortly, a large white boar emerged from the herbaceous growth, following the slough from left to right, about a hundred yards away. At the closest point, it passed sixty yards to my front.

Minutes later, leaves rustled on the opposite side of the slough. Andy pointed and mouthed, "Boar." No pigs were visible from my elevated seat, but the top of a twenty-five-foot tree was moving back and forth. The boar was rubbing the base of a tree about eighty yards away. There was more rustling behind Andy. Pigs were moving all around us.

The next pig to appear was a black-and-white boar in the two-hundred-pound range. The pig walked down the hill to the edge of the slough, where it stopped and rooted about forty yards away. Smiling and nodding at Andy, I knew this pig was plenty big enough for me. If the range closed by another ten yards, it was time to stick a second hog.

For a good five minutes, the boar hung up about forty yards out, pausing occasionally to listen and scent the wind. At least once, Andy shifted his position on the log, causing the boar to lock up, listening and smelling. Eventually, the boar caught our scent, snorted, and ran off with its tail straight up. In a way, this encouraged me. By running at the scent of humans, this pig demonstrated a degree of wildness and caution that the other pigs had not exhibited.

To keep the mosquitoes at bay, Andy had brought some spray repellent and a Thermacell, a device that emits a gas that repels mosquitoes. Andy had said I could use one or both but, not initially noticing any mosquitoes, I had declined the offer. Once I had settled on the stand, however, a healthy population of mosquitoes made its presence known, biting my hands, forehead, and cheeks.

After an hour of fairly consistent hog activity but no good opportunities for shots, it was time to see what had become of the wounded spotted boar. Turning to Andy, I said, "Should we look for the hog?"

Andy was ready. "Yeah, let's trail him up."

Andy found blood ten yards past the spot where the boar caught my arrow. The blood trail led us a hundred yards around the hill before we lost it. We were still under the impression that the third pig that had disappeared around the hill was the wounded boar. Andy said, "Why don't you continue following that trail and I'll work up the hill."

Hog sign covered the trail following the contour, but there was no blood, bone, or other evidence of a stuck boar. Downslope, a slough was covered with wallows, tracks, and trails, but no pigs were in sight.

It took about ten minutes to circle back to the starting point. Andy was standing on the near edge of the slough. He whispered, "He pulled a trick on us and cut across here. I followed the blood right down to the water." Andy pointed to a wide blood trail with good splashes in the grass and forbs, saying, "See if you can find a crossing point."

There was some firm ground to the right, with downed logs over the worst mud. Crossing the slough, we quickly picked up the blood trail on the other side. This side of the slough had a thick herbaceous layer, but visibility was good above the grass, which stood about four feet high. We could see about fifty yards in most directions. Following the blood another twenty yards, we simultaneously recognized the form of a pig lying on its right side. Andy said, "He's still alive. Be careful."

I cautiously approached to the left of the boar with an arrow nocked. The boar remained lying in place, with the broken-off stub of the arrow protruding from its shoulder. It was breathing rapidly and frothy blood was bubbling up around the broken arrow. It was a high lung shot and it appeared that this pig was down for good. Addressing Andy over my right shoulder, I said, "I should have brought my knife. It's in my backpack beneath the stand."

Andy asked, "Do you want to use my pistol to finish him off?"

"Sure." I took the silver revolver. "What am I shooting here?"

"It's a 45. It's pretty loud."

As I approached the pig, it sprang to its feet. Still in command of its faculties, this pig was done running and ready to start chewing on something. I was lowering the boom when Andy yelled, "Shoot!"

Just as the sights settled on its shoulder, I pulled the trigger. The boar stumbled backwards, took a few steps, and went down in its final death throes. This time the boar was down for good, and it expired quickly.

After a few photos and a quick field-dressing job, it was time to get the tractor to extricate the boar. Andy led me through the woods to a trail that circled back toward the pickup and the tractor. As we approached a drain, Andy pointed to a low wallow surrounded by brush and said, "There's a pig in there!"

A large black-and-white pig was just visible through the brush. We eased forward until the distance closed to fifteen yards. This was a big hog with wide shoulders, quite possibly equaling or exceeding the weight of my recent super boar from the Dixon Center. I went to full draw with the boar facing me, intending to put the arrow into the chest, between the shoulder and the neck. My finger was tightening on the release when Andy tapped me on the shoulder. "You won't be able to get through the shoulder on that one."

Andy either didn't recognize the shot, or he was mistaken as to my intention. Andy pointed up the hill for a different angle. Frustrated, I tried to ease past the boar, but it was a hopeless approach. The boar looked up and froze. Brush blocked any shots from my new position. The boar snorted, wheeled, and disappeared down the ditch. It was not to be.

Andy and I split up at the truck and tractor: Andy started the tractor and drove off in search of a way through the timber, while I went to retrieve my backpack and cameras from the stand. As I reentered the woods, a decent-sized black boar snorted. Although it didn't run too far, I never had a clear shot and it eventually disappeared.

Andy was almost to the boar with his tractor. Above the sound of the tractor, there was rustling from downslope. Andy pointed to the slough below and mouthed, "Sow." Later he told me, "That sow came straight to the sound of the tractor."

I was standing upslope, scanning the creek bottom below, when a black pig with a Hampshire stripe emerged from four- to five-feet-tall weeds. The sow was on the other side of the slough, the same side as Andy and the downed boar. Step by careful step, I stalked downhill to the slough's edge, where the mucky soil allowed for nearly silent progress. In a few minutes, the distance closed to twenty yards, but the pig was still in the grass. Holding my position on the edge of the slough, I saw Andy to my left, snapping photos with his digital.

The pig stepped into the open and looked straight at me. Was the gig up again? The sow put its head down and went back to rooting. Going to full draw, the sow turned broadside, facing left. Aiming just behind the front shoulder, I triggered the release.

The arrow disappeared into the front shoulder as the pig squealed and started running straight at Andy. Andy wheeled and ran for the tractor as I broke out laughing. Just as Andy reached safety, the pig piled up. The sow made it only twenty yards before collapsing, kicking a few times, then lying still.

Crossing the slough, we both converged on the downed pig. Andy had called it correctly; it was a lactating sow. The arrow had passed clean through and was lying on the ground about five yards past the spot where it struck the pig.

Riding the tractor on the way out, Andy called out, "There's a black boar down here."

It's interesting what sounds will scare a pig. People talking and/or walking through the woods puts most pigs on high alert. Yet, a pig will allow a truck to approach closer than a person on foot. Tractors are a whole different matter. Andy had told me before the hunt, "The sound of a tractor actually draws these pigs in." A former assistant manager of a large plantation in southeast Georgia had told me the same thing: "When we decided to start thinning out our pigs, we took to carrying guns on the tractors. We were able to kill dozens before they associated tractors with danger."

If, as suspected, these pigs spent most of their lives on the neighboring Shiloh National Battlefield, the pigs had probably grown accustomed to following mowers and bush-hogs on the battlefields. Mowing tall grass causes collateral damage to small species. Bird nests are knocked down, dumping eggs and chicks. Rabbit warrens and nests are exposed. Snakes are chopped up. Most disturbing, fawns frequently lie in place until the last second, when they jump up just in time to have their legs amputated. Pigs, being the intelligent omnivorous animals they are, learn to associate a running tractor with ready, available food.

Under the terms of the hunt, the winning bid was for one pig. Each additional pig would cost $100. The two pigs on the bush-hog would fill my coolers and empty my wallet. I told Andy, "I can't afford another one!"

On the ride back to Counce, Andy explained how pigs had been introduced to the area. "A few years back, the price on pigs went to nothing. It got to where it cost more to butcher a hog than the farmer could get for the meat. A local farmer turned all his pigs loose during the bad market."

Not long after I started working at the Dixon Center, the price on feeder hogs dropped below $0.20 a pound. That would have been about ten years back, and could have coincided with the establishment of this population of feral hogs.

Andy told me he worked as a real estate agent, so we discussed the local housing and land market. He relayed, "I just sold a quarter-million-dollar home for $80,000. It was a nice clean house. But the neighborhood is full of meth heads. They break into their neighbors' houses and steal from peoples' yards."

Alabama has the same drug problems as Tennessee—or Illinois, for that matter. My brother was a physician's assistant at an infectious disease clinic in Chicago, where he worked with plenty of meth-addicted HIV patients. I wondered, "Just how long will it take this drug craze to play out?"

Pulling up to Andy's house, he backed up to a big oak tree. Using a low-hanging branch, we weighed the pigs. The boar weighed 208 pounds sans intestines, while the sow pegged out at 128 pounds field dressed.

Tennessee was a great addition to my list of hog-hunted states, and to date, it had yielded the easiest kills. It's exciting to have so many good opportunities, but those pigs were not far removed from the farm. Both of my Tennessee pigs had large, floppy ears, whereas most feral hogs exhibit smaller, more upright ears. Neither the spotted boar nor the Hampshire-striped sow exhibited much wariness. I suspected that these pigs spent much of their time in the national park, where they were protected from hunters and were not forced to adapt or evolve to hunting pressure.

These kills just weren't that challenging. As my Year of the Pig progressed, I hoped future hunts would lead to encounters with much cannier animals.

Caveat Emptor

On July 22, 2008, I received a call I could have done without. Tennessee Game and Fish was investigating the guide who had sold me the hog hunt near Counce. The organization suspected he was buying pigs and releasing them on his property. Describing my hunt to the game warden, I admitted that the pigs were not very wild, but I had attributed this to Andy's land being adjacent to the Shiloh National Battlefield Park, where hunting was prohibited.

I am too trusting, as my wife repeatedly points out. When Andy told me, "The local farmers turned their pigs loose when the price got too low," I believed him because that had reportedly happened in other areas. When the sow came toward the noise of the tractor, it was curious, but not implausible, because I'd heard reports from other farmers and land managers of wild pigs coming to the sound of machinery.

I have left this chapter almost exactly as it was written, to reflect how I perceived the hunt at the time. But after this phone call, I replaced the seller's real name with a pseudonym. If those pigs were released, then this was the second time I had been suckered on an eBay hog hunt.

The first misadventure occurred in New Mexico, where John Dickson, Mike Powell, and another friend, David Jones, all participated in the same hunt with me. That hunt started with a search for feral hogs around dairies in eastern New Mexico. The evening's hunt failed to turn up any pigs, so John, Mike, David, and I got about three to four hours of sleep before our hunting guide, Shannon (not his real name), called us at the hotel. "I've got some hot pig tracks. Hurry on over!"

Arriving at Shannon's, we led his pig dogs to a three-acre grove of salt cedar around a settlement pond, below a feedlot. The dogs disappeared into the salt cedar. After thirty or forty minutes, they bayed a pig. Shannon charged through the salt cedar with his semiautomatic pistol drawn, putting forth his best effort to add drama to the situation. The dogs had bayed on an old, black razorback sow that I promptly dispatched with a rifle.

Meanwhile, Mike, David, and John had covered the back of the grove, in case the pig attempted to escape across an open cultivated field. While I was killing the sow inside the grove, John Dickson worked out the real story behind the hunt in the salt cedar, although it was nearly a year before he told me what he had found. John had located tracks from a truck and trailer and had also seen the spot where someone had stopped and unloaded the pig earlier in the morning.

These situations are not unique to hunts sold on eBay, but having been burned twice, I will be much more wary in the future.

In retrospect, I realize that during both of these hunts, the guides had behaved as if hunting feral hogs was roughly equivalent to following a wounded cape buffalo into tall grass that was populated by a pride of man-eating lions. In other words, they were just acting out their part in an overly dramatic play.

6 IRONWOOD

They were the product of their time and beliefs, and I of mine, and after I reached what the Bible defines as the age of reason, we didn't converge on too many issues.
— MICHAEL SWINDLE, *Slouching towards Birmingham,* 2005

Ironwood (*Ostrya virginiana* and *Carpinus caroliniana*): True to their name, both trees produce a very strong, durable wood. To avoid confusion, some foresters and most dendrologists refer to *O. virginiana* as "eastern hophornbeam" and *C. caroliniana* as "American hornbeam." Both species are attractive, hardy, shade-tolerant trees found in bottomlands and south-facing slopes of southern, eastern, and midwestern forests. Because neither tree is suitable for the production of stud-quality, warped, knotty, two-by-four lumber (much of which comes from loblolly pine), most foresters would consider both trees to be "weed" species.

One of my main duties as research coordinator for the Longleaf Alliance is to train foresters, landowners, herbicide applicators, land managers, and tree planters in appropriate, effective, and economical methods for the establishment and management of longleaf pine. One of the best ways to transfer this knowledge is through artificial regeneration workshops.

In 2007, the Longleaf Alliance held five longleaf workshops across Alabama, with the final workshop scheduled at Marion Junction in west central Alabama on August 22. Sensing a pig-hunting opportunity, I called my good friends in west Alabama, the herpetologists Jimmy and Sierra Stiles. They were contracted by the Forest Service to do herpetological surveys on the Oakmulgee District of the Talladega National Forest in Chilton, Perry, Hale, and Bibb counties. Jimmy had been regaling me with descriptions of high hog populations and tremendous sign on national forest property near Marion Junction. Marion Junction is near the Oakmulgee District.

Jimmy invited me to come up to Centreville for an afternoon hunt the day before the workshop. He had an extra mattress for me to crash on and there would be time for another quick hunt in the morning before the workshop.

Before heading north, I started the day at a forestry herbicide workshop in Andalusia. The audience for many of my forestry-oriented presentations tends to be pretty homogenous, with the vast majority of attendees being older, southern, white, well-educated males. But when the audience is wildlifers and/or ecologists, then one finds a much more diverse crowd.

After my presentation, I drove home to pack some clothes, plenty of water, the 7 Mag and the .17 Hornady Magnum Rimfire (HMR). Kissing Katia and Joseph good-bye, I left for Centreville. Driving I-65 north, I noticed that my vehicle's thermometer read 106 degrees. It was brutally hot and exceptionally dry. Alabama was in the grip of a long streak of 100-plus-degree days. Even the old-timers couldn't remember a hotter streak than the current one. The public radio station out of Selma reported local temperatures of 102 or 103, so the car's gauge may have been a bit high. Regardless, this was less than ideal hunting weather. Temperatures 50 or 60 degrees cooler would have been just right.

I arrived in Centreville at about 5:00 p.m., finding Jimmy under his carport, typing an abstract for an upcoming Gopher Tortoise Council meeting. It didn't take long to change from speaking clothes to hunting clothes and carry my gear into their house. Sierra was in the kitchen. She told me, "I hope you all get some pigs."

There was no disagreement on my end. "Look, if Jimmy doesn't get one on this trip, I am going to start calling him Hard-Luck Jimmy."

Jimmy had been trying to kill a pig for about ten years now. Given that Jimmy routinely killed several deer annually and he was very familiar and comfortable with the outdoors and hunting, he had to be the single unluckiest hog hunter in the history of modern-day hunter-gatherers carrying high-powered rifles to the woods.

When Jimmy walked into the room with his .30-06, Sierra and I giggled and informed him of his new nom de guerre, Hard-Luck Jimmy. He took it in stride. "Yeah, it's about time for me to get one."

We loaded up Jimmy's SUV, which had five doors and two working door handles. Jimmy immediately rolled down the windows, so the air-conditioning was probably not functioning either. Their other vehicle was a Subaru. As for its condition, Jimmy said, "Don't even ask. It will just get me mad."

Herpetologists really need to form a union and demand better pay. What would you call such a union? Snake Handlers of America (SHA)? I kind of like the Federation of Associated Reptiles, especially Turtle Studiers, or FARTS. And that's not half as bad as another acronym that comes to mind.

A few years back, the Forest Service had a large ongoing project at the Dixon Center called the Fire Surrogate Study. At any given point, half a dozen graduate students and undergraduate hourly workers sampled birds, arthropods, herps, and all the other biota associated with the longleaf ecosystem. To save money, the students rented a house a few miles away near the Shady Hill Baptist Church. It didn't take long for the students to designate their home away from home as the Shady Hill Institute of Terrestrial Studies.

While I was working on a master's degree at Auburn, my field research was at the Jones Ecological Research Center in Baker County, Georgia. The students there printed T-shirts saying, "I Work for the JERC." When you get down to it, scientists, biologists, and ecologists have a sense of humor that tends toward the downright corny and profane.

Leaving Centreville, the road passed through Brent, and Jimmy and I arrived at the Talladega National Forest at about 5:30 p.m. According to Jimmy's thermometer, the temperature had dropped all the way down to 99 degrees.

Jimmy laid it out during the thirty-minute ride. The Wildlife Management Area (WMA), part of the Oakmulgee District, was closed for hunting until dove season. When dove season opened in September, hunters could use shotguns and shot as large as #2. No one in their right mind hunts doves with #2 shot, so this was clearly a concession to the pig hunters. Jimmy said, "I'm going to put a full choke in my twelve-gauge and see if I can punch a hole through a pig."

A few months back, Hard-Luck Jimmy had hunted turkeys on the Oakmulgee during the spring season. He carried his twelve-gauge into the woods with #4 shot, which is a pretty good load for turkeys but too small for a large feral hog. Sure enough, a big boar walked up and Jimmy shot it in the head. He knocked it down but the boar got up again, so he put another load of #4 shot into the pig. The pig went down again, but then got up and ran through a hole under a fence and into a nearby swamp. The pigs had rooted under the fence, pushing the fence up and pointing it toward the swamp. Jimmy told me, "I was sure I could get in, but not necessarily out, especially in a hurry." Jimmy had carried only three rounds, and he was worried that he might shoot the pig again, not kill it, and be stuck with an empty gun, facing an injured, pissed-off boar.

There are a couple of lessons to be learned from Jimmy's story. Number one: Always, always, take more ammunition than you think you might need, especially when there are pigs in the area. If there's a chance of getting into pigs, consider carrying a minimum of ten rounds for a large-caliber rifle. If carrying a rimfire rifle, expect more shots in a shorter period of time because of the minimal recoil. A hunter should probably carry a few dozen rounds of rimfire ammunition.

Number two: No guts, no glory. In Jimmy's situation, with just one round remaining, a wounded boar, and the pig squealing down in the swamp—yes, a rational person could pass on this opportunity. But I am not a rational person. When people tell me they are scared of snakes or pigs or wildlife in general, the first thing that comes to my mind is "Maybe you should just stay on the front porch."

As sure as day is day and night is night, I would have gone in after that pig, using the last round at very close range to maximize penetration of the shot. If that didn't kill him, the situation probably would have devolved into a knife fight.

Anyway, the WMA was closed. Jimmy told me, "We'll be hunting a drain just across the road [from the WMA] that's torn to pieces." Jimmy had been doing a fair bit of scouting, and he had found fresh tracks in this drain for three consecutive days. He didn't know what time they were coming in, but with all the sign, he figured we had a pretty good chance of seeing some pigs.

Jimmy drove past the hunting spot to give me the lay of the land. The road was midslope, following a ridge that ran east and west. The WMA was south of the road and mostly uphill. To the north, the hill dropped off to a small creek that paralleled the road. There was a short, steep drop-off that was fairly dry. Farther downslope were wet, mucky soils in the depressions and stream bottoms.

Circling back, Jimmy parked and led me into the woods. Stepping off the road, I could easily see that the ground was rooted up in all directions. As we moved downslope into the drains, the forest floor turned to mudflats from repeated hog rooting. Tracks were absolutely everywhere, most left by sows with piglets.

One hundred yards in, Jimmy left me to my own designs. He would be hunting about a quarter of a mile to the east. There was an hour and a half of shooting light remaining. A few hundred yards into the woods, there was a small rise with a downed oak tree that looked like a reasonable location. Sitting against the oak tree would allow a decent view of the surrounding forest, and the bole would break my profile. I swept away the dry leaves, exposing the spongy humus layer beneath. With the noisy leaves out of the way, I practiced rising silently to a kneeling position. Scanning the area to the front, I saw that an understory of sweet shrub obstructed the view, so I employed the Leatherman tool to remove the offending stems, just low enough to provide clear shooting in most directions.

I was now settled in, my clothes already damp with sweat. The temperature was still in the 90s. Positioned beneath an ironwood tree, I observed that the overstory was comprised of large-diameter white oaks, loblolly, ash, and sycamore. The midstory held sweet shrub, American holly, and the attractive and unique big-leaf magnolia. Pileated woodpeckers occasionally drowned out the constant drone of mosquitoes circling my head and neck. I should have brought the repellent.

My arms were itching. Belatedly, I realized my mistake. A few years back, I had seen some ironwood trees in seed and thought, "That would make an interesting addition to my nursery stock." After I grabbed a few handfuls of seed, it only took a few seconds before my hands were itching like mad. Ironwood seed capsules are covered with short, sharp bristles that penetrate exposed skin like fiberglass insulation. Apparently, leaf litter from an ironwood produces the same result.

The remainder of the hunt was spent swatting mosquitoes, scratching my arms, and sweating. It was a hot, itchy, all-around miserable hunt.

Barred owls chimed in as dusk approached, but there was no sound from our friends, the feral hogs of the Talladega National Forest. With shooting light behind me, I put on a headlamp. My compass kept me pointed south in the thick underbrush. Emerging from the forest onto the gravel road, I turned east. Jimmy flashed his light from the side of his vehicle. He asked, "Did you see anything?"

All I had seen were birds. "Pileateds and barred owls were the only thing active in my neck of the woods. How about you?"

Hard-Luck Jimmy's voice took on a resigned tone: "I screwed up. I got in the creek, and I was hurrying down the channel trying to reach a place where I had seen a bunch of sign. I wasn't quiet enough and the next thing I knew a pig was running up the bank into the brush. I found the spot where it was standing right on the edge of the stream. It must have seen me and spooked up into the woods. That was about it."

Back at their house in Centreville, Sierra cooked a delicious plate of Conecuh brand pork sausage with new potatoes and yellow bell peppers. After a couple of beers, it was time to get some sleep.

At 4:00 a.m., Jimmy was grinding coffee beans in the kitchen. A quick shower and a cup of Kona woke me up. Jimmy drove us back to the same spot we had hunted the day before, except this time, my seat wouldn't be under an ironwood tree.

The morning hunt was pleasant, but neither of us saw or heard any pigs. After a couple of fruitless hours, I said good-bye to Jimmy and drove south to my next longleaf pine workshop.

7 DEATH IN THE WILIWILI

Aaahh, one more invasive species introduced to the islands
Invades the wiliwili tree and devastates the population across the
Hawaiian Islands
Aaahh, what's next?

—Pekelo Cosma, "Nā Wili Wili Eha," 2006

Wiliwili (*Erythrina sandwicensis*): It would be difficult, if not impossible, to come up with a more appropriate name than "wiliwili" for a tree species that appears to have been appropriated from the pages of Dr. Seuss.

Although my wife, Katia, had been incredibly patient with the mounting expenditures and time on the road my project was exacting, her forbearance was not inexhaustible. It was time for a family trip to a location everyone would enjoy. If there could be some good hog hunting along the way, so much the better.

While there are plenty of islands close to the United States worthy of a visit, hog-hunting opportunities are somewhat limited in Aruba, Nassau, and Bermuda. Hawaii, on the other hand, has some serious pigs. Polynesians brought pigs to the Hawaiian Islands on their rafts nearly a millennium ago, possibly all the way from Tahiti.

Like Texas, Hawaii has some additional large invasive mammals. After pigs, the feral goat has been on the Hawaiian Islands the second longest. According to some sources, goats were first introduced by Captain Cook and the population was later augmented by Captain George Vancouver. Subsequent introductions of large invasive species included cattle, axis deer, and black-tailed deer, to name just a few. Hawaii has no native mammals other than bats. Virtually every mammal on the island has been introduced by humans, some with disastrous repercussions.

Some of the biggest ranches and best hunting opportunities are found on the "Big Island," but there are hunting opportunities on many of the islands. It was time to research hog hunting in Hawaii using both traditional and nontraditional methods. In my two years of tracking hunts on eBay, not a single hunt in Hawaii had come to my attention. YouTube had dozens of hunting clips from Hawaii, but no ground was gained by e-mailing several people who had posted clips of hog hunting, goat hunting, and even cow hunting in Hawaii.

There was still a question as to which island was best suited for our trip. In talking with several friends and acquaintances, I noticed that Maui consistently received better reviews than either Oahu or the Big Island. Those two latter islands have many of the most visited tourist sites, like Pearl Harbor, Waikiki, and active volcanoes. But Maui is less urban, with many interesting natural features including rain forests, cloud forests, volcanic-sand beaches of many colors, and Haleakala—a giant, dormant volcano.

The Hawaii Department of Natural Resources (DNR) was very helpful when I called. A friendly and knowledgeable woman listed which islands had rifle, archery, and dog hunts for various species, and what the seasons were. With a little more time, a self-guided hunt would have been a reasonable option, but time was a limiting factor. A one-week Hawaiian vacation was affordable, but it wouldn't be a real family vacation if Katia and Joseph were on their own while I spent several days chasing pigs in the rain forest. Scouting and/or hunting needed to be confined to one or two days if my marriage was to remain intact.

The Hawaii DNR provided a list of licensed hunting guides who offered pig and goat hunts on Maui. I contacted several of the guides on the list, but only one replied to a few questions, and then he stopped responding. Finding a hunt was proving to be more difficult than expected.

I found that the most prominent hunting Web site associated with Maui was Maui Hunting Safari. When I opened its Web page, there was a smiling Rodney

Perreira holding a "trophy goat." Maui Hunting Safari offered hog hunts "Hawaiian Style," describing this method of hunting as using dogs to bring the hog to bay. Once the pig is bayed, it is killed with a knife stab to the heart. YouTube had several clips of this type of hunting, and it looked pretty exciting.

In addition, since feral goat hunting was totally new to me, this would be an excellent opportunity to experience both a new hunting style for pigs and a new target species. This combination of hunts would be the single most expensive hunting trip of my career (in fact, it would cost more than all my previous 2007 hunts put together!), but Maui Hunting Safari advertised a 95 percent success rate on Polynesian pigs and a 99 percent success rate on goats. It was time to give the operation a call.

Dawn, Rodney's wife, answered the phone. Her calm, reasonable voice reassured me. After discussing various options of the hunt, I no longer had any doubt. This was the hunt for me. Biting the bullet and mailing in a $300 deposit, I locked in a one-day Polynesian Pig hunt, "Hawaiian Style," to be combined with a "Trophy Goat Hunt" for one billy goat over twenty inches. The following day was scheduled for a "Management Goat Hunt" for three "meat" goats.

Luckily, it didn't take long to locate a great deal for flights, a condominium, and a rental car. I booked a package with the Maui Vista option, an early morning flight out of Pensacola, and a full-sized rental car at the airport in Kahului.

This was the first trip to Hawaii for all three of us, not counting a two-hour layover in the Honolulu airport I shared with my mom, dad, and little brother, Curtis, on our way to Australia a decade before. I will draw a veil over the trip itself. Suffice it to say that after a long, arduous journey that began at 3:30 a.m. in Andalusia, and that included one incident of Joseph hurling onto his new Hawaiian shirt and several transfers of luggage, we arrived in Maui by 6:00 p.m. Pacific time.

It was a pleasant drive to the Maui Vista in Kihei (pronounced *Key-Hay*), and we eventually got situated in condominium #3,210. Exhausted from the long travel day, we bought some groceries at a local supermarket, ate, and went to bed.

I was up first on the morning of August 29, 2007, rising at 7:00 a.m. A pot of Kona helped get me going. Katia was still worn out from the day before, but

Joseph was full of energy and excited about his new surroundings. It was sunny, warm, breezy, and humid. Salt hung in the air. The tropical vegetation and sea breeze transported me back in time to the beaches of Santos, São Vicente, and Guarajá, Brazil.

I returned to the present, and called Maui Hunting Safari to notify them of our arrival and contact information at the Maui Vista.

This vacation would be a series of "firsts." My first goat hunt. My first pig hunt with dogs. Joseph's and Katia's first trip to Hawaii. And with luck equivalent to winning the lottery, perhaps my first billfish? I made a few more phone calls, booked a fishing trip, and was instructed to report to slip #12 at the Lahaina Harbor between 5:00 and 5:15 Thursday morning.

With the main objectives settled, it was time to set up activities for Katia and Joseph. The concierge, a nice lady named Caroline, arranged for a bus to pick them up for a ride to the top of Haleakala, a dormant volcano that, at 10,023 feet, is the highest point on Maui. Caroline also suggested the Oceanarium, just north of Kihei. Our tickets to the aquarium were good for anytime during our trip. A first-time Hawaiian trip wouldn't be complete without a luau, so Caroline booked us for the Wailea Marriott luau on Monday evening. She also suggested a glass-bottomed boat tour for Katia and Joseph while I was pursuing billfish. The following day was reserved for another trip, the "Road to Hana"; Curtis, my brother, had made the drive and highly recommended it. With a full roster ahead of us, the whole family was excited about being in paradise.

A couple of days later, it was time for my oceanic fishing trip. The sun wasn't up yet, but the surfers were already in the water. On the way out to sea, the boat captain talked about living and working in the Caribbean. "It's the same everywhere. Natives see you [Caucasian/American], and they tolerate you because you're a tourist and you are their livelihood. But when they keep seeing you, and they start recognizing you at the grocery store, they hate you. Because once you're living there, you're stealing their jobs, you're driving up their rent, you're stealing their daughters—they just f—ing hate you."

Those few short sentences had quite an impact on me, because for years, when the difficulties of life had threatened to pull me down, my thoughts had turned to Jimmy Buffet and the Caribbean. Many are the times I've told someone, "I am one step away from the island life," believing a job on the islands as a dive instructor would provide blissful surroundings and all the fishing and fun I could handle.

Now this boat captain had just blown my fantasies to hell. But to be honest, he wasn't the first to sow doubt; he was just the confirmation. As I slowly began to understand, that same tension between native islanders and Caucasian tourists existed here in Hawaii. The guidebook *So You Want to Live in Hawaii* explained that *haole* once meant "foreigner," but now it means "white person." In the parking lot near our condo, a pickup truck had a sticker in the back window: "Respect the Locals." This was a relatively tactful way of saying, "We live here all the time. You're just visiting. Remember that."

The fishing trip was a bust: an eight-hour ride without a single strike. Talking to the boat captain, I learned that long-liners encircled the islands several times over with thousands of miles of fishing line. A few fish filtered through to the waters we were trolling. This handful of survivors sustained the fishery, but it was a joke. The odds of actually catching a fish are so low that, in my opinion, it's not worth the investment in time or money. I talked to several people who went fishing in Hawaii, and they all reported the same result: hours on the water and not a single fish. Until someone gets the long-liners under control, allowing fish stocks to rebuild, blue-water fishing in Hawaii is an exercise in futility for many paying customers.

Then the day came for my hunt. Rodney picked me up at the Maui Vista at 4:20 a.m. We shook hands and then picked up Kekoa, a native Hawaiian teenager who would be assisting in the hunt. From there, it was a long drive to the opposite side of the island. Along the way, Rodney Sr. pulled in behind us. I was glad Rodney Jr. was behind the wheel as he drove the twisting roads with cliffs above and cliffs below. Occasional peninsulas jutted into the Pacific Ocean on our right. Many of these peninsulas had trucks parked on them, although it was still well before dawn. Rodney explained, "There's a big fishing tournament going on. They are fishing for the *ulua*." These hard-fighting members of the jack family are considered Hawaii's top game fish by many island fishermen.

The steep cliffs and giant waves were in stark contrast to the Gulf of Mexico, where I was used to fishing. I told Rodney, "It looks like pretty challenging fishing."

It was more than challenging. Kekoa had hopped in with Rodney Sr. so Rodney Jr. gave me some background. "Before Kekoa started helping us out, we had another Hawaiian teenager who helped us on the hunts. He and his twin brother were fishing out here for ulua one night when a big wave came in and swept them off the rocks and out to sea. The young man we used on our hunts made it back to shore, but his twin brother was never seen again. It broke him up pretty bad and he ended up getting into meth. He hasn't straightened out yet."

The skies lightened as Rodney drove the winding roads. Some birds that looked like grouse ran across the road in front of us. Although it was my first time seeing these birds, I thought I recognized them from photos of introduced game birds in Hawaii. "Are those francolin?"

Rodney answered in the affirmative: "We have gray and black francolin."

The sun wasn't quite up at 6:00 a.m. when Rodney stopped at the gate to the Kaupo Ranch. Above us rose Haleakala. Perhaps a couple of hundred yards in, Rodney stopped, saying, "There's a pig!" He was looking out the driver's side window.

The lower slopes were covered in grass. It took me a few seconds to locate the pig, but there it was, a black speck moving midslope on an adjacent ridge. "Okay, I see him."

Rodney Sr. pulled up behind us with Kekoa. Everyone exited the two trucks and Rodney Jr. said, "Let's put this one in the bag. Then we'll go for another one." Rodney and Kekoa strapped water bladders onto their backs for the dogs' benefit. They would need water after the chase.

I threw on my full backpack. It held a compass, a digital camera, a headlamp, two water bottles, plastic gloves, bags, matches, and a knife. My camcorder and 35 mm camera bags added bulk, but it would be worth the extra effort for good video and photos.

My guides let the dogs out of the truck box one at a time, leashing each dog before it could run off. We hurried down the hill, and the dogs were loosed just below the ridge where the black pig was last seen. Seconds later, a pig was squealing to our right, not more than fifty yards away in a small patch of trees.

Approaching the melee, I turned on the video camera, recording the unholy racket—hogs squealing and grunting, dogs barking. Drawing closer, I saw one dog, which looked like it was part blue heeler, come flying out of the brush sideways, thrown into the air by a large, pissed-off spotted boar. The boar turned around and charged back into the brush, hitting a red dog, which went flying out of the brush on the other side. While the boar was wreaking havoc, another pig was squealing from deeper in the brush. The invisible squealing pig was the focus of the dogs' attention.

Suddenly, all the action moved away from us as the pig that was squealing broke free from the dogs and made a short run into the grass. The dogs followed the previously bayed pig about twenty yards, then grabbed it again and the squealing resumed.

The boar kept grunting, but it decided to make its exit now that the dogs had moved a short distance away. For some reason, none of the dogs followed the boar, preferring the squealing pig that we had yet to view. The boar nonchalantly trotted off through the grass while Rodney Jr. and I watched helplessly. If the camcorder in my hands had been a bow, a good Polynesian boar would have already been "in the bag."

Kekoa caught the squealing pig, holding a medium-sized sow by the hind legs. Rodney Jr. said, "Let's turn that one loose and see if we can get back on the boar."

Apparently, the large black pig seen from the road below was long gone. Having watched the spotted boar disappear into the grass, Rodney seemed to think we had a good shot at locating and catching him, a much more impressive pig than the sow we'd just released.

The dogs ran out of sight, heading in the direction of the spotted boar. Rodney thought he heard the dogs barking in the distance. But thirty minutes of walking didn't bring us any closer. Rodney Jr. and Rodney Sr. called back and forth on handheld radios, attempting to triangulate on the barking. The dogs were finally located, leashed, and loaded into the truck. With the dogs in hand, we gave up on both the black and the spotted boar and drove farther up the mountain/volcano.

Arriving at another gate, Rodney said, "We'll probably get on some pigs here. We catch a pig every time we put out in this area." Unlocking the gate and driving through, Rodney stopped, parked the truck, and turned four dogs loose. The fifth mutt stayed in the box; it was an old dog that was only good for a run or two. Rodney told me they brought this one along more for the pleasure of the dog than the benefit of the hunt.

It wasn't much over two minutes before we heard a pig squealing in the timber. Double-timing it to the edge of some thick brush, I turned on the camcorder and passed it to Kekoa. "Just point it in my direction. I'm going in."

Rodney Jr. had already passed me the knife and burrowed into the brush himself. Rodney grabbed the pig by the hind legs. He said, "Stick him here!" motioning toward the pig's right side.

The struggling pig moved before I could get into position. Now the left side of the pig was exposed. Stepping forward, I plunged the knife into the pig's side, just behind the front quarter, pushing the knife down a few inches. Hot blood splashed over my hand. Rodney appraised the stab. "That's good!"

The blood stopped and the pig finished bleeding out internally as its squeals rapidly lost volume. The pig kicked a few more times and then the body relaxed. Less than ten seconds after being stuck, the pig was dead.

Grabbing the red pig by a hind leg, I dragged it out of the brush while Rodney held the dogs. With the sow lying on the road, Rodney said, "Congratulations!" shaking my hand.

It was a lean red sow. I told Rodney, "That's one feral-looking hog. You said a lot of them in this area were red?"

"Yeah," said Rodney, "quite a few." He pointed back to the woods and said, "Look over there. See the mangoes?" Large, ripe, orange mangoes hung in the palms. "That's why the pigs are hanging out here."

Rodney started to pose the hog, but the photo shoot was interrupted by the squealing of another hog. Rodney said, "Let's go!" and charged down the road. As we closed the distance, the pitch of the squealing shifted from very high to slightly lower. Maybe a hundred yards past our first kill, and just across the fence, the dogs held a small, thin, white pig with black spots, weighing twenty pounds at the most. Rodney jumped the fence and pulled the dogs off the piglet. The skinny pig ran down the hill on wobbly legs. Three pigs caught. One killed. Two released. These were the first pigs intentionally set free during my hunting trips.

Although I didn't need the meat from the two hogs we caught and released, it would have been ecologically correct to kill them. Perhaps more than any other invasive species, pigs have altered and diminished Hawaii's native flora and fauna, and they continue to have a large impact today. But hunting leases and fees contribute a substantial and positive addition to the economics of the Kaupo Ranch. And high populations of hogs present more options for paying hunters like me. In a way, feral hogs are being managed just like the cattle that cover the pastures on the slopes of Haleakala. Whatever impact the hogs have on the Kaupo Ranch, however, it is nothing compared to making the whole place into subdivisions.

Rodney came back across the fence and we started down the road. Just ahead, a small, chewed-up red pig lay on the ground, gasping for air. Rodney said, "I'll put it out of its misery." He stabbed the piglet with the knife and we kept going. The dogs had caught this piglet and then abandoned it when it ceased fighting. Having done this small piglet in, they moved to the next closest piglet, the small spotted pig we had just released. Now I understood why the pitch of the squealing had changed while we were running toward the dogs.

The dogs ran way ahead and up the side of Haleakala, disappearing into thick timber, heading straight up the slope. Rodney turned to me. "Welcome to hell!" We started the climb. Up, up, up we went. Rodney stopped every few hundred yards to determine the dogs' direction with the electronic tracking collars and locator unit. Those collars would have been handy back when I was hunting coons three or four nights a week. I asked Rodney, "Has the price come down any on that equipment?"

Rodney answered, "No, if anything, the price has gone up." Maui Hunting Safari was sitting on some serious fixed costs, running an operation like this. For pig hunting, there were feed and vet bills for five dogs. They were running five tracking collars at $300 a unit, and the main tracking unit was another $1,000. Rodney Sr. told me the lease on one of the two ranches "was $40,000, but it went up."

The chase continued uphill for another thirty minutes or so, weaving in and out of trees, over lava rock, over and through old rock fences and new barbed wire fences. Rodney's tracking equipment showed that we were closing in. I asked him, "Do you think they are on a pig?"

"They won't be alone." The words were barely out of his mouth when the dogs came down the hill—alone.

Hunting is unpredictable. It was worth a chuckle. But I'd made many similar pronouncements while coon hunting that proved false often enough.

Rodney and Kekoa caught and leashed the dogs before dumping each of them into a water tank to cool them down. Rodney said, "Let's take a seat in the shade and let them rest. Tired dogs can't catch pigs." Rodney explained that they had lost two dogs the year before to heat stroke, when a pig ran too far, too fast, and they couldn't catch the dogs in time.

Fifteen minutes later, our group started downhill. Stopping at a small opening in the timber above a drain, Rodney said, "We generally get a pig in this draw." Rodney and Kekoa turned the dogs loose. We followed the dogs; perhaps five minutes passed before someone noticed the barely audible barks and squeals in the distance. The chase was fast but difficult, over lava rock and through the brush. As we pushed through heavily wooded areas, green thorny vines repeatedly entangled us, slowing progress. The pig kept breaking free, extending the chase.

A few minutes into our pursuit, I turned on the camcorder. The distance was closing somewhat, but my breath was coming in gasps. Ten minutes after the chase began, the dogs were raising Cain and a pig was squealing loudly as we broke free of the brush into a clearing. Rodney charged fifty yards ahead, grabbing a spotted pig by the hind legs. Kekoa took the camcorder as I pulled the knife out of Rodney's sheath, stepped up, and plunged the knife into the pig, behind the front leg. I pushed down, slicing another couple of inches; the blood splashed over my right hand, and the pig quickly died.

Two good sticks. Two good sows.

This one was a pretty spotted sow, and just like the other one, she was a razorback all the way.

Rodney and Kekoa propped the pig on a rock. The dogs were hot and exhausted, lying in nearby shade. This time, our photo shoot was uninterrupted. Rodney and Kekoa showed their professional experience, arranging and posing the pig for the best possible photo. Rodney Jr. probably takes several hundred photos a year of successful kills.

Rodney estimated the second sow at about 120 pounds, adding, "If this were winter, she would be 30 pounds heavier, and you'd be looking at a good 150-pound sow."

These sows looked different than mainland pigs. I asked Rodney, "What are the traits of a Polynesian pig?"

Rodney pointed. "Polynesian pigs have small ears." This was true. Most if not all my pigs from the other states had bigger ears than these two.

Rodney identified a second trait. "They have sharp ridged backs." Both the red and the spotted sow had prominent ridged backs. I had taken sows in Texas and Tennessee that could have been described as "razorbacks," but I didn't remember any of the mainland pigs possessing ridges quite as pronounced as these two Maui sows.

Rodney finished, "The sows have tusks like a boar, and the top sharpeners." I agreed, but were these sows' tusks larger or better developed than some of the older sows from Texas or Georgia? I wasn't sure on that trait.

To my eye, the most distinctive characteristic of these hogs was their small ears.

I queried Rodney further. "Is there any Russian in these pigs? Do you see striping in the piglets?"

Rodney answered, "No, I don't believe there is any Russian in Hawaiian pigs, and I haven't seen any piglets with Russian striping."

A few years back, on a Texas hunt at the Mad Island Wildlife Refuge, I shot two old sows, and our hunting party caught four of their piglets. All four had striping characteristic of piglets with Russian or European blood. As the piglets age, the stripes fade and the pigs can turn almost any color, including black, brown, red, or spotted. Those Texas sows also had extraordinarily long snouts, much more so than these two Maui sows.

As we worked downslope toward the road, it was clear that the main tracking dog, Cue Ball, was done. He was tired and held close all the way down. The remaining three dogs disappeared into the forest. The tracking equipment kept us headed in the right direction, but eventually the dogs ranged too far away and Rodney could not pin them down.

A *kukuey* nut tree provided shade as we took a seat. Earlier in the morning,

Rodney Sr. had explained, "The native Hawaiians would split these nuts, put them on a skewer, and light them for torches."

A couple of days before this hunt, Katia, Joseph, and I had driven the Road to Hana. We had rented a Geo-Trek device that had given us some additional information on trees along the route, including the English name for the ku-kuey tree: candlelight tree. I said, "I heard or read that the Polynesians brought these with them when they came to Hawaii?"

Rodney Sr. replied in the affirmative. "Look, I may not be a genius, but the best I can tell, volcanoes don't spit up much but gas and lava. *Everything* on these islands came from somewhere else."

In geological terms, the islands are comparatively young, and new immigrants or additions are bound to take hold at every opportunity. It didn't make me feel any better about the devastation wrought by mongooses and the like, but maybe some of the "naturalized" species like the pig and goat had earned their spots in Hawaii by virtue of being here several hundred years. An ecologist would argue, "No way!" The native Hawaiians would probably argue in favor of the presence of goats and pigs as "natural."

Three of the dogs came back, but the fourth was nowhere to be seen. After a long wait, Rodney Sr. pulled up in his new Nissan truck. Rodney Jr. went back up the mountainside to look for the missing dog, returning fifteen minutes later with the collie-looking dog, saying, "It came in lame. But at least we've got them all now."

Rodney Sr. and Kekoa hung the red sow in a tree they called *vive,* and Rodney Jr. made short work of the cleaning job. Rodney saved the ribs at my request, but they were so thin they were barely worth retaining.

With the dogs in their boxes, we returned to the lower slopes, where a mixture of tall grass glades and wooded forests dominate. Parking in the shade, Rodney Jr. unpacked lunch.

There was a small herd of goats not more than fifty yards away. I unpacked my camera. Using boulders and trees for cover, I approached to within twenty yards of the feral goats. I clicked away at a medium-sized billy, some nannies, and a kid or two. This was easy bow range.

Back at the truck, lunch was sandwiches and chips eaten while sitting on lava boulders beneath some trees. We washed the food down with a couple of cans of Aloha Maid juices and a bottle of water.

It was time to kill some goats.

Over lunch, Rodney Jr. had regaled me with tales of three hundred goats at a single water tank. These tanks were scattered across the Kaupo Ranch, and they consisted of old tractor tires fed by black PVC piping. As we now approached the famous water tank, it was disconcerting to find it surrounded by hundreds of Angus and Hereford cattle. The sounds of lowing cattle and howling wind were intermixed with the bleating of a goat. A kid goat was weaving its way through the cattle in search of water. As I was able to get within a few meters of the kid, it would have been another easy kill with my compound bow or .17 HMR.

The wind was blowing hard, kicking up dust and sand from the trampled area around the water tank. Over a twenty-minute period, as we sat beneath trees some twenty yards away, we watched as a few nannies, kids, and one black billy approached the tank. Unfortunately, the cattle herd had not dispersed but remained standing in a half circle behind the water tank. I let Rodney know, "I'm going to be pretty uncomfortable shooting a goat with all those cattle behind it."

Rodney was of the same mind. "Let's go see what else we can find."

Not hunting the tank was a disappointment. According to Rodney, two weekends before, when a Japanese client had sat at this same tank, "a huge red goat with near-thirty-inch horns came in. I told him to take it, but he declined, saying, 'I don't like the color of that one.'"

Amazing! Who cares what color the goat is? That hunter passed on a goat that may have been among the top five goats ever harvested because he wanted a black goat. If a purple goat came in with thirty-inch horns, I would knock it down without a second thought.

Rodney, Kekoa, and I walked over a ridge to see goats grazing and walking in every direction. It was hard for me to judge the horns, but Rodney's eye was well trained to the task and he picked out potential trophies as we worked our way to another water tank, passing a few dozen goats along the way.

The three of us took seats beneath some trees above another water tank. The wind howled across the opening. There weren't any cattle at this one, but there were goats. It was about fifty yards to the water tank: a "give me" with a rifle, but a near impossibility with a bow, considering the distance and wind.

Goats worked the hill from our rear left to our front left. The goats behind us were too far away to identify as trophies, but those to our front left were only two to three hundred yards away and Rodney was able to assess some of them as having decent horns.

A scattering of nannies approached our water tank, but it was pretty slow. After thirty minutes, Rodney grew impatient. "There are several billies over there, and I just saw one that looks pretty good, bedding down beneath the tree with the orange flowers."

Rodney Jr. led the way. I was second. Kekoa brought up the rear. As we left the clearing, the goats were about a hundred yards out. Tension mounted as we picked our way through the trees, brush, and lava rock. The distance closed to fifty yards. Rodney whispered, "They're on the other side of that big rock." The rock was about the size of my living room, and the goats were upwind in the heavily browsed brush. At a distance of thirty yards, the strong smell of goat assaulted my nostrils. It was easy to see why they call wild goats "stinkies" in Australia.

Rodney eased ahead. It wasn't a question of shooting just any goat. The object was to take a "trophy" goat, and Rodney could better locate and identify the right goat if he were in the lead, although I was less than comfortable in the follow-on position.

At twenty yards, some of the goats sensed our presence and stood up, but they didn't run away. The three of us stood motionless and before long, the goats started grazing through the brush and trees.

There were several attractive billies in all different colors: black and silver, red, red and black, and pure black. Rodney studied the horns and finally pointed at a large black goat mostly obstructed by tree branches. "That one looks pretty good."

The goats moved downhill. Rodney led the way left on an intercept. As we emerged from the trees, there were about twenty goats from sixty to a hundred yards out. My trigger finger was getting pretty itchy.

Rodney glassed the herd with his binoculars, again finding the black goat with the good horns. But they moved back into the brush, still angling to the left and downhill.

Rodney led through the brush to an opening on our left, arriving ahead of the herd. If the herd continued on course, the larger opening would afford more time for locating and shooting a good goat. Rodney said, "They'll be coming into the opening and crossing in front of us." In a moment or two, his prediction came true as nannies, kids, and billies emerged into an open draw beneath us.

A red billy with good horns stepped out of the brush, drawing my attention. Rodney said, "There he is." Hadn't he been talking about a black billy? But I was focused on the red billy. Glancing around, I saw that nothing else looked as big. The billy moved up the draw, approaching more cover. Rodney said, "That's a good spread."

Rodney had brought shooting sticks and the .308 rested in the crook of the sticks as I watched the goat through the rifle scope. The billy was quartering away. With a slight adjustment to move the crosshairs a little farther back, the bullet should angle up into the vitals, exiting through the front shoulder on the opposite side. Lighter, higher-velocity rounds may deflect or change trajectory once they enter the body. Heavier, slower rounds maintain their direction better. From what I knew of the .308, this should be a decent angle.

Seeking to confirm the target, I questioned, "The one in the draw? I can take him."

Rodney said, "Go ahead."

I pulled the trigger. The rifle barely kicked and the report disappeared into the wind. The goat ran but the shot felt good. The red billy crossed a small ridge and collapsed. I told Rodney, "He's down!"

The three of us walked eighty yards up the hill. Rodney looked down at the goat. "Ohhhh, its red."

My heart sank. "I shot the wrong goat. You were talking about the black one we saw earlier."

Rodney confirmed, "Yeah, it was a much better goat." Was my "trophy" goat hunt blown?

Rodney continued, "No, this isn't a bad goat, but it's not what we're looking for. We'll just count this one as one of your meat goats."

Sighing in relief, I swore to not make the same mistake again.

Rodney went to work, skinning and boning out the goat. Now that Rodney had let me off the hook, it was a little funny. Kekoa held out pillowcases for the meat, and Rodney asked, "Do you want the head?"

I did. "Sure, if it's no problem."

Rodney assured me, "No problem at all."

As Rodney cleaned the goat, I pondered which, if any, animals would dispose of the remainder of this carcass? I hadn't seen any buzzards on Maui. If the remains of this goat were left in an Alabama field or a Missouri forest, black and turkey buzzards, coyotes, and opossums would all take their portions. I asked Rodney, "Will something eat what we leave of this goat?"

Rodney answered, "Mongooses will be all over this tonight." The mongoose is another unwanted foreign addition to the fauna of Hawaii.

Finishing with the goat, Rodney said, "Let's keep on going up the hill." Goats had been filtering by at twenty to fifty yards the whole time he was cleaning the billy.

Working uphill, Rodney turned to me and said, "I don't think many of the goats heard the shot in this wind."

Our group of three closed in on another herd of goats. This group was mostly black billies. The herd crossed grassy openings two or three times, allowing clear shots, but these billies weren't big enough for Rodney.

The billies went out the far side of the trees and started up a slope. Goats were still filtering out of the brush, so there may have been a trophy in there somewhere. The three of us hurriedly made our way to the edge of the trees. A group of eight or ten billies stood on a ridge above us. Without the sheltering trees, the wind was blowing at gale force. Rodney glassed the herd with binoculars as I looked through the scope of the .308, which rested on the shooting sticks.

Rodney announced, "There's a good one!" Was it the same black one that escaped us minutes ago? Rodney pointed it out. "It's the fourth one from the front, with the big horns, behind the other goats."

I acquired the fourth billy in my scope. My view of the goat was obstructed by other billies and the wind was rocking me badly. "Okay, I think I see him."

The goat dropped its head. Rodney said, "He just dipped his head!"

No mistakes this time. "Okay, I saw it." The herd shifted positions, opening up a clear shot, but the wind was blowing my sight picture all over the place. I stayed focused, willing the crosshairs to hold still, my body rocking back and forth on the sticks. The wind calmed for just a moment, and the crosshairs settled behind the billy's right front shoulder. *Boom!*

The herd ran forward but one head suddenly dropped over the ridge. Rodney said, "He's down!" Rodney, Kekoa, and I jogged up the hill. The black billy was lying five yards from where it was shot.

Rodney pulled out a tape measure and measured the right horn: "Twenty-four and a half inches!" He pulled the tape on the left horn: "Twenty-four and a half!" This was a trophy goat. The terms of my hunt allowed me to kill at least one billy over twenty inches, and this one beat that handily. It was a pretty black goat with a good beard, and I had no complaints.

Admiring the goat, Rodney Jr. patted my arm. "I like you. I think we can do better."

The offer floored me. "Are you sure?"

Thank goodness, he was. "Yeah, let's ease on down this peninsula and see what we can find."

This black billy was awesome, but I wasn't about to turn down an opportunity to kill something bigger. I left my backpack, cameras, and the goat. Kekoa stayed behind to watch everything as Rodney and I headed downhill towards a flat, grassy peninsula that jutted into the ocean.

Small specks moved in the distance. It was a herd of goats, about half a mile away on the peninsula, and there were plenty of goats between us and the distant herd. On the way down, Rodney told me, "Just a couple of weeks back, I was glassing the peninsula with a hunter, and I saw a goat that may have gone thirty inches down there. I told the hunter, 'There's your trophy,' and he said, 'There's no way I'm going all the way down there!' So we stayed up here and shot a smaller goat."

Shaking my head in disbelief and pointing to the barely visible top of Haleakala, I said, "If you told me we needed to go to the top of that volcano to shoot a trophy, I'd say, 'Let's go.'"

We worked downslope, glassing the brush and trees. There were goats everywhere. Rodney said, "There are some billies bedded down beneath those trees." He pointed about one hundred yards ahead.

Using some large boulders for cover, we approached to about sixty yards and took a seat, still scanning the surrounding area. There were at least two decent billies lying on the near side of some trees. It was up to Rodney to select a trophy, and it wasn't long before he did. "I see a billy in the brush behind the two that are bedded down. All I can see right now are the horns and they look really good."

Scoping the area, I didn't take long to find the billy. It was another black goat, but it looked quite a bit larger than the second billy I had shot moments before. Rodney asked, "Do you see him now? He's black and his horns curl back a little."

I did. "Yes, I see him."

Rodney advised me, "Let's wait on him. He'll walk into the open."

We held our positions. The rifle rested on a boulder, and despite the extreme wind, my low profile allowed a steady sight picture. The billy worked to the right, feeding on the lower branches of trees, occasionally standing on its hind legs to reach higher branches. The billy turned slowly, facing straightaway before circling back to the left. Rodney reassured me again. "Hang on, he's going to clear that tree."

Steadying my breathing, I tracked the goat. The odds were good that the billy would eventually emerge, but my cardinal rule is: Once a desired target is positively identified (unlike my first billy of the day), the hunter must take it at the first viable opportunity. When you pass on a good shot, hoping for an excellent shot, there is a good probability that the animal will spook or disappear, and those are the missed opportunities that haunt you for the rest of your life.

The billy stopped broadside with its head down and a front shoulder exposed through a fork in the tree. It was good enough. I let Rodney know, "I've got him!"

Rodney had seen enough of my shooting and stabbing to trust me. "Take him!"

The crosshairs were settled on the left front shoulder as I squeezed the trigger. At the report, the billy flipped forward with its hind legs flying as it kicked in a circle. Rodney was pleased. "Good shot!" Rodney handed me a fourth bullet as we walked down the hill. One more good shot and the day would end with four goats for four shots.

The billy was beautiful. Rodney grabbed a horn and dragged it to a flat, open, shady area beneath another tree. The body was much larger than the two previous billies. This black billy had a longer and larger beard. No doubt about it, this one was going on the wall.

Rodney patted his pockets. "Did I bring the tape?" He found it. "Let's see what we've got." He pulled the right horn: "Twenty-six inches!" He pulled the left horn: "Twenty-six inches!" He taped the spread: "Twenty-five and a half!" Rodney explained, "We needed twenty-three inches on each side to make the book, and he beats it by three inches on each side!"

"I'm in the book!" After thirty years of hunting and tens of thousands of animals, I finally had a kill that made a record book. Although, to be truthful, I really hadn't given much consideration to ever having an animal in "the book." Having killed an animal that qualified, I could see the attraction record-book hunting has to some hunters, especially wealthy, globe-trotting trophy hunters. It's enjoyable to take photos and put heads on the wall, but that's not why I hunt. From my perspective, it's still thrilling to make a good shot on a white-tailed doe, and who knows how many of those I've taken over the years.

Some other hunters are focused on numbers. They boast about how many bucks they take in a year, regardless of quality: shooting large numbers of one-and-a-half- or two-and-a-half-year-old spikes, four-pointers, and six-pointers with "basket" racks. Had they let these bucks walk, in a year or two they would have been much nicer eight- or ten-pointers. Trophy pig hunters focus on tusks. Once a person is fixated on trophies, however, it detracts from many other aspects of the hunt. Instead of the pursuit, the experience, the table fare, or the story, they focus on the end product and bragging rights.

Later, Rodney described an extreme case in point. "I have a client from California that flies out fairly regularly to shoot trophy goats. On a recent trip, he told me he was going to kill the world-record *Watusi* [a breed of cow from Africa]. So I asked him, 'How do you know you are going to get the world record?' He told me, 'They have already measured the horns. They've got it penned up in a paddock on the West Coast.'" Rodney had just described "trophy hunting" at the silly and extreme end—the point where it is no longer a sport, but a joke.

He carefully caped the last billy. Besides being a hunting guide, Rodney is a supervisor for a metals fabrication plant and a taxidermist! He said he would be glad to mount the goat and help me submit the paperwork to Safari Club International for my record-book entry.

With all three billies boned out, both Rodney Jr. and Rodney Sr. suggested harvesting a nanny goat for the best table fare. With our gear loaded and the meat and heads on ice, we drove a short distance to the nearby Nu'u Mauka Ranch. It took less than five minutes to locate a herd of nannies. With several targets in easy range, I chose the biggest black nanny and dropped it in short order.

They hung the nanny in a wiliwili tree, and Rodney Jr. made short work of the goat, peeling the loins and then the meat off the hindquarters. The .308 had blown out both front shoulders so he didn't mess with them.

The wiliwili trees had an interesting green, warty bark. Wiliwili is a native tree species, growing on parts of the Hawaiian Islands that are intermediate in rainfall between the rain forest and the desertlike conditions on the mountainsides above Lahaina. Most of these wiliwili trees were completely defoliated. Rodney Jr. explained, "An introduced parasitic wasp is killing the trees. They're all dying."

Although defoliated, several were in bloom. Rodney Sr. pointed. "They have different-colored flowers. See, there is one with orange flowers, there is yellow, and there is white."

With the successful hunt concluded, Rodney Jr. drove us back through a large forest of wiliwili trees, stretching over scores if not hundreds of acres. "This ranch has some of the largest tracts of wiliwili trees on the island. My daughter is saving the seeds of the wiliwili trees. If they can figure out how to stop the wasps, she wants to replant them." Picturing Rodney's daughter in the wiliwili forest, collecting seeds from the dying trees, put me in a very melancholy mood.

The day after the hunt, Katia, Joseph, and I walked beneath a giant banyan tree beside the old Lahaina Customs and Courthouse. A Hawaiian was singing and playing his guitar while an older, spectacled haole accompanied on his guitar. Joseph climbed into the banyan tree while several women danced the hula and the music drifted through the banyan branches. The music was good enough that, despite crimped finances, I forked over $20 for his CD. Later that day, I listened to the music in our rented car while Joseph slept in his car seat and Katia shopped for souvenirs. The singer's name was Pekelo, and the CD cover described his music as "Traditional Hanaiin Slack-Key Guitar." Pekelo was a native from the town of Hana. Perhaps this style of music is unique to that small community, thus "Hanaiian" style. The sixth song on the CD was "Nā Wili Wili Eha." I learned the plight of the wiliwili tree from my hunt guides, and now I was hearing the sad story in song.

Tuesday, September 4, 2007: time to pack and go home.

Having purchased a large cooler in Lahaina, I planned on putting my biggest goat head in the cooler, along with all the meat. There were forty bags of goat and pork in the freezer. Each bag contained just enough meat for one meal for a family of three.

Joseph loves pork. But would he eat goat? Could I eat goat? Of the three of us, Katia, who was born and raised in Peru, was the only one of us who had eaten *cabrito* or *chivo,* and she said it was pretty good.

My plans went awry rather quickly. Regardless of any angle I tried, I couldn't fit the goat head into the cooler, and I found that only thirty-five of the forty bags of frozen meat would fit. The skulls from the two sows and the red billy had been boiled and scraped and would fit, but the black billy head with the twenty-four-and-a-half spread was intact. It looked like all four heads were going to have to go into my luggage, including the head of the bloody, stinky billy goat. The nanny's head had stayed in the field, while the record-book goat head stayed with Rodney for later mounting and shipping.

The housekeepers at the Maui Vista got five bags of goat meat.

At the airport, all passengers, including me, had to clear the USDA checkpoint. Three middle-aged men were staffing the inspection area. Two watched the X-ray machine, scanning checked luggage, while a third stood out front, questioning passengers. A sign said "Carry-on bags do not have to be X-rayed, but all agricultural items must be declared or face forfeiture of said items."

The two guys watching the X-ray machine were talking and joking, not paying much attention to the screen. The third guy walked up to us. I announced, "I've got some skulls in my luggage."

His expression turned quizzical. "What have you got?"

"I've been hunting, and I've got pig and goat skulls in my checked luggage. I also have a large cooler of meat."

"Oh, I see." He had another question for me: "Is the meat frozen?"

"Yes." The meat was frozen, but that dang billy's head was just a little cool by now.

While I placed the bags on the conveyor, the two guys carried on their conversation and the third guy said, "Hey! He's been hunting here on Maui and he killed some goats and pigs!"

Seeking to draw their attention, I smiled broadly and stated loudly, "It was an awesome hunt!"

My bags made it through with pig skulls, one partially cleaned goat's head, and one intact head with the beard still on. Wheeee!!!

Now, would the bags make it all the way to Pensacola? Or would a sniffer dog go nuts while inspecting our luggage? How would the police respond to this macabre collection?

It was another exhausting series of flights, but the three of us and our grisly luggage made it back to Pensacola, Florida, arriving at 2:30 p.m. on September 5.

Several months later, I tracked down a phone number for the Hawaiian singer Pekelo Cosma, leaving a message and my phone number on a Friday afternoon. An hour later, Pekelo called me back at the Dixon Center, just before I left to go home for the weekend. We talked about the recent Georgia–Hawaii football game. Since Missouri got eliminated from the Bowl Championship Series, I told Pekelo, "I was hoping Hawaii would beat Georgia, and then they would at least have a claim on the national championship."

After a bit more small talk, Pekelo asked, "So what can I do for you?"

I answered, "Last summer, my family took a vacation in Maui. And while we were there, I saw the wiliwili forest on the Kaupo Ranch, and I learned about the wasp that was killing it. A few days later, I saw you playing beneath the banyan tree by the old courthouse in Lahaina and I bought your CD, which I really enjoy. In particular, I was affected by the song 'Nā Wili Wili Eha.'

"I work as research coordinator for the Longleaf Alliance and we promote the restoration of the longleaf pine forest. It once covered 92 million acres of the southeastern United States, and now we are down to 3 million acres. So I am sensitive to the decline of our native forests.

"And I am writing a book. I want to dedicate this book to the longleaf pine forest of the southeastern United States, and also to the wiliwili forest of Hawaii. I wanted to bring attention to organizations working for our native forests, like the Longleaf Alliance, and if there is a similar organization for the wiliwili forest, I would like to mention them also."

Pekelo answered, "Ahhh, the native people of Hawaii have been crying out for centuries, and no one heard. But now the wiliwili tree is endangered, and people pay attention."

I was taken aback, but understood what he was saying. "I have read some of the history of Hawaii, so I know of what you speak."

Pekelo told me a little about himself. "My mother was Hawaiian and my father was a Filipino, but when he came to Hana, he learned everything he could about the native culture and environment. He passed this on to me: where and how to fish, how to plant by the moon, how to live in harmony with nature." While Pekelo was talking, roosters crowed in the background. The sound took me back to my childhood on the farm in Missouri and, more recently, many trips to South America.

Pekelo continued, "I recently played an event. As I was going in, I saw some young girls in T-shirts. They were raising money for the wiliwili tree, and they said to me in Hawaiian, 'Uncle, uncle, uncle!' So I said to them, 'Niece, niece, niece!'" Both of us laughed over the phone. "I was so proud that they had taken the time to learn the language and that they were concerned about the wiliwili tree. It has been so important in our culture and history. The symbolism is very important. We tell our children, 'This is an important tree,' and all of a sudden, something comes along and devours it. This is not only about the tree, it's something we can tap into and communicate to the young ones, about the tree and the people."

Pekelo was not aware of any organizations similar to the Longleaf Alliance focusing on the wiliwili. He told me that scientists at the University of Hawaii were conducting research on possible biological controls, but there was not much optimism for the wiliwili forests of Hawaii.

Pekelo left me with this: "Maybe my song will help a little bit. I am not a researcher, I just do what I can, and my way of helping out is to put it into song. My children are going to see the world through my eyes, and I want them to remember and know the wiliwili tree. And I thank you for what you are doing."

8 BEAVER POND

Because of our largely urbanized existence, I suspect that some readers
may find this book "gory." If this is so, then it is because the truth is gory.
—PETER HATHAWAY CAPSTICK, *Death in the Silent Places,* 1981

Black gum (*Nyssa spp.*): There are several hardwoods species in this genus, all of which are adapted to hydric soils. Much like bald cypress and the average American, black gums develop tremendous butt swell as they age. A black gum or swamp tupelo with a four-foot-diameter butt may taper to a mere twenty inches at eye level. Also, like the bald or pond cypress, gums tolerate inundation for months at a time. Cypress/gum swamps are relatively inhospitable in the summer months, unless you are a mosquito, spider, water moccasin, or alligator. But load your shotgun with steel shot in the winter months, and these swamps are magical places to pursue the darting, plunging, climbing, shrieking, most beautiful of all waterfowl—the wood duck.

My professional life is oriented around science. My personal life, at least in recent years, has been oriented around pig hunting. The two, the professional and the personal, blend rather well.

When my attention becomes fixated on a given subject, be it spearfishing, coon hunting, how to plant a longleaf seedling correctly, or how to kill a pig, then I tend to expend a disproportionate amount of time and energy on this fixation. The greater the challenge, the greater the fixation. The more often I hear "It can't be done," the more likely I am to attempt it.

When I purchased a .17 HMR, I was told by several gun enthusiasts, "You cannot kill [cleanly and ethically] a wild boar with this gun."

Some of the best public hunting opportunities in the South are found on our numerous Wildlife Management Areas. These are typically managed, and sometimes owned, by the state in which they are located. Alternatively, they are privately owned and leased from forestry companies or federal ownerships such as the Army Corps of Engineers. WMAs offer fishing, hiking, bird-watching, camping, and other activities, but hunting is probably the single largest draw for most WMAs.

WMAs often have restrictive regulations concerning how, when, and where various game animals may be legally pursued. For instance, one of the earliest hunting seasons to open in many states is squirrel season. During squirrel season, several WMAs limit hunters to rimfire rifles .22 caliber or smaller, which includes three common rounds, the .22 long rifle (LR), the .22 Magnum, and the .17 HMR.

Having fired tens of thousands of .22 LR rounds through several rifles, I know this is an excellent bullet for squirrels, rabbits, and other small game species, but it isn't powerful enough to consistently put down large feral hogs in the woods. But John Dickson, a good friend of mine in Louisiana, shoots pigs with the .22 Mag on the National Wildlife Refuge where he works.

After some additional research, I found that some WMAs do not allow the .22 Mag during squirrel season, but all the WMAs and refuges that I investigated allowed the .17 HMR. Comparing the .17 HMR's ballistics with the .22 LR and the .22 Mag, many of the gun nuts I know prefer the .17 HMR. Having weighed the evidence, I went with a .17 HMR.

Next, this rifle needed an appropriate bullet. The Hornady twenty-grain XTP patterned well, and after quite a bit of testing and shooting, this became my bullet of choice.

Driving back from a talk in Monroeville, Alabama, on the afternoon of September 14, 2007, I arrived home a little after 4:00 p.m. After changing into hunting clothes, I drove my truck back to the Solon Dixon Center. Hog activity had dropped off considerably since I had killed the big boar on July 14. My trail cam hadn't taken a single photo of a pig in the last two months, but there had been some fresh pig rooting in our peanut field. I wondered if my camera had captured any new pig photos.

It was clear that the pigs had been very busy just off U.S. 29. There were dozens of spots where pigs had rooted up the peanuts. The activity was heaviest on the western edge of the field, near a thick stand of mixed pine and hardwood.

After circling the field, I followed a field road along a recent clear-cut, through an open, parklike stand of longleaf and slash pine, parking at the end of the road. Several acres of thick brush and timber stood between me and the peanut field, providing good cover. The adjacent peanut field provided food and there was water in a drain running through the woods. Basically, this was hog heaven.

Carrying the .17 HMR, I walked to the trail cam. There was fresh sign in the area and five new photos on the card. Farther down the drain, an old beaver pond had produced one pig earlier in the year. I even had a path cut through the brush for a silent approach to this hot spot. On the other side of the old beaver dam, there was more fresh sign: rooting, rubs, tracks, and new trails through the grass.

I worked through a relatively open area, with a cypress gum swamp to my rear, water to my right, and a privet thicket to my left. I looked up to see a large black hog in the 200-pound range. The pig saw me and broke left, immediately disappearing into the privet. A second black pig in the 120- to 150-pound range followed the bigger pig into the privet before I could acquire either one in my scope. The pair had been only twenty to twenty-five yards away. I admonished myself. A slower, quieter approach would probably have resulted in a good shooting opportunity.

From the privet, a pig let out a low rumbling growl that probably meant "Pay attention!" The pig followed that with a loud snort that meant "Danger!" I thought to myself, "There goes my first opportunity to kill a pig in two months of hunting on the Dixon Center! And yet, there was still a slim chance I could kill a pig. Often, when the alarm snort is sounded, the rest of the sounder will freeze for one to three seconds before running to thick cover.

Amazingly, the backs of four hogs were visible to my right front. All four had their heads down, rooting in the organic, mucky soil. They either hadn't heard the snort or weren't paying any attention. Either way, natural selection was kicking into high gear.

The four pigs were obscured by waist-high grasses and sedges. I took two steps forward and leaned against a small black gum tree. If I had been carrying a large-caliber rifle, my position and angle would have been good enough for a high-percentage shot, but with the .17 HMR, it was a different story. There was zero room for error in this swamp. A twig or even a single blade of grass could deflect the bullet, leading to a miss or a wounded target. A wounded pig would almost certainly lead to another excruciatingly difficult pursuit through the surrounding privet thickets, as with my three previous experiences this year.

Two pigs turned toward me, rooting through the grass. This was good fortune. A head-on shot, square between the eyes, is the preferred bullet placement for killing pigs in traps. Unfortunately, grass continued to obscure my shot even though these two pigs had closed to within ten yards.

Holding still, I slowed my breathing, steadying the rifle, and waited for a clear shot. It was difficult to remain calm and steady. These pigs could spook at any moment, and it was a matter of seconds before they would wind me.

A red hog rooted behind the two closest pigs, stopping broadside, facing to my left. It raised its head above the grass, looking in my direction from less than fifteen yards away. The crosshairs immediately settled above and behind the left eye, just below the pig's ear. *Crack!* At the sound of the shot, the three other pigs finally got the message the big black hog had transmitted moments before.

The red pig dropped in its tracks. I worked the bolt as a black pig ran almost straight at me, passing six feet to my left before disappearing into the privet. All three survivors were gone before I could reload and find another pig in the scope.

The downed pig was a young red boar with long, curly hair. In some places the hair was nearly black from rolling in the mucky, organic soils of the gum drain. Its tail was long. There were no tusks, so this was a young hog. On the negative side, it was disconcerting to see the hog's large testicles and smell the distinct odor of a musky boar. With larger boars, this muskiness is adversely correlated with edibility.

After a long drag across the beaver dam and up the hill to my truck, I loaded the pig a couple of minutes before 6:00 p.m. Clouds gathered and the sky darkened as I left the woods. Ten minutes later, the skies opened and lightning crashed all around.

That's when I realized that these pigs had probably been exclusively nocturnal for months. No one had seen a pig in daylight hours since the big boar in the peanut fields a couple of months back. But pigs, like many other large game animals, respond to approaching weather. This herd had sensed the gathering thunderstorms and ventured out in daylight hours, to its peril.

Had I expected to encounter pigs, I probably would have carried a bigger rifle and missed this opportunity to kill a pig with the .17 HMR. Everything had fallen into place for a perfect shot and kill. The .17 HMR is nobody's first choice for a hog gun, but with a steady rest, the right bullet, and precise placement, this small round can do the job.

9 HILL COUNTRY

Maybe I don't have to be good but I can try to be
At least a little better than I've been so far
But when I drink . . .

—AVETT BROTHERS, "When I Drink," 2006

The Hill Country: Dry, shrub- and tree-covered hill ground of central Texas. Most of the Hill County is classified as oak/hickory or pinyon/juniper. In times past, it was known for its oil and cattle; more recently, for hunting and subdivisions. From a forester's viewpoint, there aren't many trees in the Hill Country that will make a grade log. From a hunter's viewpoint, this is a good place to pursue deer, turkey, and pigs.

Texas was another eBay hunt, purchased as a one-day, dawn-till-dark or dusk-till-dawn, hog hunt through Mickey Pophin and MPI Outfitters. Apparently, MPI had different locations to send its pig hunters. After a few phone calls and e-mails, the hunt was scheduled for the last weekend in September on the Rio Bravo.

I invited my best friend, Mike Powell, who was temporarily working in Atlanta, and his son, Michael Tyler, who lives near Kansas City. I also called up John Dickson, who had taught me many of the finer points of hog killing. Since John lived in Louisiana, this hunt would be a lot closer for him than it would be for Mike or me. There were extra spots available at the winning bid, so I told John he could invite his Texas friends, some of whom I'd hunted with before.

He called Vincent Gay, who a few years back had killed one of the biggest boars I'd ever seen on the Mad Island Wildlife Refuge along the Texas Gulf coast. There weren't any scales at Mad Island, but the long, black boar easily topped three hundred pounds.

John, Vincent, Mike, and I had all killed Texas pigs on previous hunts. If the pigs were there, we'd know what to do.

Mickey Pophin gave me the contact information for the Rio Bravo. The ranch foreman, Ken Gould, said our odds on the Rio Bravo would be much improved with a night hunt. This indicated to me that the ranch received a fair bit of hunting pressure.

Later, firming up the date and time of the hunt, Ken informed me, "We are running a special on exotics. If you want to pursue exotics we can let you stay over and hunt them for $150 each. I saw four sika deer the day before and three blackbuck today."

This was exciting information. The only introduced big-game species I had previously harvested were pigs and goats. However, the presence of introduced species was puzzling since Mickey Pophin had told me their game was free range.

I queried Ken further. "How did you get all these exotics on the ranch?"

Ken explained, "Our neighbors had a high fence with all kinds of animals: elk, sika, fallow, blackbuck, nilgai, sheep, and so on. A new owner took over and we think they couldn't afford the feed bill, so they cut the fences. Now we want to get rid of the exotics because they compete with the whitetail, which is our primary game animal."

Mike and John were excited to hear about the "exotic" angle. Mike let me know that he was good to go. John called Vincent, who gave a thumbs-up, so John said he could also swing the extra $150. I let Ken know. "Okay. We'll go with the extra $150 on the exotics."

A Texas pig would put me at five states, halfway to my goal. Killing an exotic would be awesome, especially since this was a true "fair chase" hunt. Once the fence was cut, the exotics became free-ranging animals.

About a month before the hunt, Mike's son cancelled on us, as it was homecoming weekend at his high school and he had a date! I called Ken. "Hey, Ken, one of the guys can't make it."

Ken wasn't very encouraging. "You'll still have to pay the full amount owed on the original agreement."

Maybe we could still use that money for something. "Can we use that $120 for an extra couple of pigs?"

Ken was agreeable. "Yeah, that's okay."

Per our original agreement, the winning bid ($120) covered a one-day hunt for two pigs. After adding the exotics option and extending the hunt to twenty-four hours, the total cost was $320 per hunter.

Mike had an appointment in Mobile the Thursday before the hunt. Finishing there, he drove up to the Atmore Police Department and parked in its lot, where I picked him up at 2:00 p.m. Between ice chests, rifles, a bow, and assorted other hunting gear, there was just enough room to inhale and exhale in the "Little Blue Hog-Hunting Mobile." Running I-10 to I-12, and then back onto I-10, Mike and I just made it into Texas before calling it a night, stopping at a motel in Wimberley. The whiskey lasted way too long, though Mike and I had plenty of hunting and work-related stories to catch up on. I just wish we had spread the drinking and storytelling out a bit more. (Note to self: Bring a fifth next time instead of a half gallon.)

John drove from Louisiana to Texas, where he stayed the night with Vincent in Dallas.

The next morning, Mike and I grabbed some coffee and Danishes in the motel lobby and were back on the road a little after 8:00 a.m. There was plenty of time before our scheduled arrival in Dripping Springs, Texas, so we continued west, passing through Houston before our next stop, an appropriately named Mexican restaurant just off the interstate: Cazadores (Hunters).

After a good meal, we pushed to within a few miles of Dripping Springs, where we stopped at a hardware store to pick up some extra supplies. Mike and I were still in the parking lot when John called me on his cell phone. "Hey, man, where are you?"

I answered, "We stopped to pick up some rope for hanging pigs. Where are you?" John and Vincent were just behind us; they pulled in five minutes later.

Of these three amigos, I had grown up with Mike. I had worked, fished, hunted, and partied with John during several of my adult years. I had been on only a couple hunting trips with Vincent, and so far, he was the only one of our group who hadn't gotten me thrown out of a bar.

From the hardware store we drove to Dripping Springs and picked up some extra food and beer. With our coolers well stocked, we drove 8.2 miles to the "white board fence with a green, recessed gate." Ken gave good directions. The gate was locked. There was just enough time to put on hunting clothes before Ken pulled in behind us and opened it. Ken sure looked the part of a ranch manager/hunting guide: tall, gray hair, drooping mustache, cowboy hat and boots. Throughout our stay he never stopped encouraging us, making it sound as if every big-game animal and predator from North America, South America, Africa, or Asia could appear at any moment just around the bend.

Ken explained the hunt as he drove us to our stands. "You'll be hunting over lighted feeders. The pigs won't come out until dark, and most of the exotics are moving from 1:00 a.m. until 4:00 a.m. If you see a mountain lion, please shoot it! We killed three here last year, and there are three more on the ranch at this time. Our neighbors just got a photo of a bear on one of their game cameras, but don't shoot any bears. That's a prosecutable offense."

I asked, "But it's legal to shoot mountain lions?"

"Yes. They are classified as predators in Texas, and you are free to shoot every one you see." Ken continued, "There are five or six elk on the place, including three bulls. What are you all shooting?"

I answered first. "I'm shooting a 7 Mag."

Mike: "Same thing."

Vincent: "A .270."

John: "A .30-06."

Ken instructed us, "If you see a nilgai, shoot it behind the ear. I worked down on the King Ranch, and I can't remember how many we lost when hunters shot a nilgai behind the shoulder with a 7 Mag. I remember one time I was guiding on the salt flats and a hunter shot a nilgai behind the shoulder. It ran clear out of sight like it had never been touched."

Ken's assessment of the 7 Mag was surprising. "You don't think a 7 could break a shoulder?"

Apparently not: "No, it won't break the shoulder. And if it did, it wouldn't penetrate deep enough to get into the vitals."

Whatever a nilgai was, it must be pretty big.

Ken continued with prehunt instructions: "On the pigs, if you shoot a big boar that you are not going to mount, you have to take the meat with you. We don't want the carcass left on the property. If you shoot a boar, plan on quartering it up and packing it out with you. The only pig we ask you not to shoot is a sow with little piglets. If the piglets are too small and you kill the sow, they'll die in the woods." This was a little surprising. While many land managers couldn't care less about piglets dying of starvation in the woods, Ken regarded his pigs as an asset. Or he was softhearted. As I got to know him better, it appeared to be a combination of both.

Mike took the first stand. His elevated shooting house was about one hundred yards from the feeder. Ken told Mike, "If the pigs come in and you can't see them, just get down from the stand and circle around to the left of them. You should be able to walk up on them."

Next, we dropped off John at a stand that was a little closer to his feeder. At each stop, Ken had me scatter three or four large cups of corn around the feeder.

As the only bow hunter, I was allotted the next area, which had a ladder stand directly over the feeder. A shooting house about eighty yards away would be available if I grew too sleepy to maintain my seat on the ladder.

As Ken and Vincent drove around the bend, I organized my gear. In addition to the compound, I'd brought the 7 Mag and the .17 HMR. Climbing nearly twenty feet up the ladder, I hung the rifles on the tree and placed the compound bow in my lap. I attached a red light to the 7 Mag. If an exotic showed one hundred yards out, it would be the 7 Mag. If pigs came to the feeder beneath the stand, it would be the bow. For me, the compound bow had an effective range of twenty-five yards. Depending on the direction, there would be a clear line of sight from as little as eighty yards up to a maximum of about two hundred yards. If there were small pigs and I couldn't get a shot with the bow, I wanted to test the .17 HMR again.

There were no sidebars on the ladder stand. If I fell asleep and rolled out from this height, a few broken bones would be the minimum price. Surprisingly, Ken had not made us sign a liability waiver before bringing us out.

I stood up and went to full draw just to make sure nothing would interfere with my shot. A snort sounded from behind and to my left. Turning and looking over my shoulder, I saw a white-tailed doe bound into the woods. The grass-covered opening supported scattered large live oaks. In this portion of Texas, these are referred to as Spanish oaks.

A long night lay ahead of us. Ken would pick us up around 9:00 or 10:00 the next morning. The first leg of our hunt was fourteen hours on the stand! As much as anything, this was an endurance hunt.

By 8:00 p.m. it was pitch-dark. The first pigs squealed a few minutes later. Not long after I heard the first squeal to my left, another pig grunted to the right rear, which was, unfortunately, downwind. Pigs circled in the darkness for at least thirty minutes, never leaving the cover of the surrounding timber. Eventually, a pig caught my scent downwind and gave an alarm snort.

The first audible shot rang out about 8:30 p.m. Not long after that, my cell phone vibrated in my pocket. It was a text message from John: "Did you shoot?"

I had never sent a text message, so it took me a while to work through the various options and keys. I eventually figured out how to send a rudimentary text message using "predictive text": "no i hear pigs but have not seen any."

A few minutes later, John sent another message: "Vincent and Mike have each killed one. I haven't seen any yet."

Now that I knew the other guys had pigs down, the fever hit hard. My patience for bow hunting drifted away on the breeze.

About 10:30 p.m. a sounder of pigs announced its position to my right, then another group to my left rear. When I put the bow down and picked up the 7, the effective range of my weapon was multiplied severalfold. I waited for the pigs to wander into the range of my light, judging distance by sound, finally turning and shining the area to my left.

It was too early. The pigs were still hidden in the trees, but one snorted in alarm as the beam passed over the area. This was unexpected. Could a pig detect the red light? Perhaps the pigs had just winded me again.

A pig squealed to my front. Excellent! This sounder was upwind and there was no danger of being scented from that direction. With the red light pointed forward, I saw eyes glinting in the distance! Then black shapes appeared! There were several in the group, and the sounder was on the road that led past this stand. The distance was too far for a guaranteed kill, so I turned off the light and waited.

The pigs were grunting and squealing while moving in my direction. I flipped the switch on the red light, but the pigs were mostly obscured by tree limbs. It looked like three medium-sized black pigs and perhaps five smaller pigs. The sounder was about a hundred yards out now and still moving my way. Turning off the light, I concentrated on steadying my breathing.

The first of the medium-sized pigs emerged from the tree limbs about sixty yards out. It was followed by a handful of smaller pigs, then another medium-sized pig. The piglets were big enough to make it on their own and they had two other sows to travel with. It was time to take a pig out.

I clicked the safety off and swung the scope onto the lead pig, the largest in this sounder. The sow stopped to eat corn scattered on the road. The crosshairs settled on the front shoulder and I squeezed the trigger. The 7 knocked me backward, kicking so hard it knocked the red lens out of my gun-mounted light. With white light illuminating the area, I saw the sow roll over, kick a time or two, and lie still. The other pigs ran up the hill and disappeared into the brush.

I crawled down from the stand and walked over to the black sow. She appeared to weigh about ninety pounds. The 7 was shooting 100 percent, with a record of two pigs for two shots, and I had just added my fifth state!

The rope purchased earlier in the afternoon proved a good investment. I cut a slit in the pig's hind leg and ran the rope through the slit. Knotting the rope onto the leg and looping the other end over a branch of a Spanish oak, I hung the sow. With the sow hanging, it didn't take long to eviscerate the carcass. The bullet had clipped both front quarters, punching a hole through the front of the lungs. With the guts on the ground, a bag of ice in the chest cavity helped to cool the carcass down.

That was enough of the ladder stand. The shooting house was well back and downwind from the feeder. Hopefully, the pigs wouldn't pick up my scent so readily there. We still had ten more hours of hunting before our scheduled pickup. The shooting house was about four feet off the ground and the open area was mostly to the front and right. The left window opened to a view of the road. To the rear, a stream bubbled noisily along the bottom of a heavily wooded slope. Except for occasional large clearings, this part of the Hill Country was covered by juniper and oak. Visibility was zilch in the brush and trees, reminiscent of the pinyon pine and juniper mountainsides I've elk-hunted in central New Mexico.

I'd been in the shooting house only a few minutes when a fire ant bit my leg. I shined my flashlight on the floor and saw several fire ants roaming over and through the carpet. This was going to suck.

I watched the feeder. And watched. And watched.

Six hours into the hunt, I left the shooting house and walked toward the wooded ridge to my rear, crossing the stream and entering the thick woods. In the back of my mind, I could hear Ken saying, "There are three mountain lions on the ranch." If this really was lion habitat, then entering the brush at night might not be the smartest thing I'd done in my hunting career.

I fought uphill through the brush with a compass hanging from my neck for directional comfort. At the top of the ridge, visibility was still limited to ten yards or less. There was no point in continuing through this brush. My progress was noisy and any animals would be gone long before I could see them, with the possible exception of a hungry mountain lion attracted by the racket.

I trudged back to the shooting house. It was 2:00 a.m. and the light over the feeder had faded out, but the moon was full. Hopefully, any large exotics would be visible by moonlight if they entered the clearing. I kept dozing off, but the abominable fire ants served as an alarm clock, stinging me at least two or three times an hour.

John sent a text message about every thirty minutes. He had bad news: "I got a shot, but I missed. I think I pulled off the pig."

I messaged back, "I haven't seen or heard anything since I shot my sow."

By 3:00 a.m., I was thoroughly chilled. I retrieved my backpack and pulled a knit shirt over my T-shirt. It helped a little, but the air was damp and cool and a coat would have been nice.

With nothing else to do, I swept the clearing with my red light once or twice an hour.

By 7:00 a.m., there was enough ambient light to see across the clearing. A little later, a flock of turkeys emerged from the brush, the birds pecking their way across the clearing. Besides a few gray squirrels, the turkeys were the first game to enter the clearing since my sow.

Sometime after 9:00 a.m., Ken pulled up and John hopped out of the vehicle. The last we'd communicated, he didn't have a pig. I asked John, "Did you kill anything?"

John answered in a resigned tone, "No. Some pigs came in early. I put the scope on them at fifty yards and they still looked small. I think I pulled the gun off at the shot. I used to have problems pulling off, and I thought I had it whipped but not quite yet."

John provided some additional, pertinent information. "I am pretty sure I spooked some pigs with my red light. I shined it on some pigs after the light at the feeder went out and they snorted in alarm." Here was a second instance of a red light possibly spooking pigs. It appeared that my theory "A red light is invisible to pigs" might have some serious holes.

Ken said, "Mike has already cut up his pig. Let's go get the other guy. What's his name?"

"Vincent," John answered.

It was a quarter mile to Vincent's shooting house. His stand was on the side of a road about fifty yards from a lighted feeder. Except for the road, the only cleared area was around the feeder.

A black pig skin with the head attached lay on the ground next to the shooting house. Judging by the size of the head, Vincent's pig was a little bigger than my sow. Ken and John said Mike's pig was a little smaller than mine. Luckily, all three were corn-fed sows, so hopefully they would prove to be decent table fare.

We helped load Vincent's pig and gear. Vincent described his hunt as Ken drove to the skinning station. "I heard pigs moving in the brush around me. About 8:00 p.m., a group came into the feeder. There were ten or fifteen and they were fairly small, but I decided to go ahead and shoot one. I put the gun up and found them in the scope. Then they spooked and disappeared. I thought I had blown my opportunity."

Vincent continued with the story. "About thirty minutes later, there was a crunching noise. It was the pigs eating the corn. I got my gun up and I could see some small pigs through the scope. Then the sow walked out. I didn't hesitate that time! I put the crosshairs on her head and pulled the trigger. She dropped in her tracks."

That wasn't the end of his pig action. "They came back a few times, but I never saw them beneath the feeder again and I never had another opportunity for a shot."

Ken asked how many pigs I'd seen.

I replied, "I only saw one group of about eight pigs. I heard several other groups, but they never came close enough for me to see them."

Ken told me, "A girl hunted that stand last weekend with a rifle. She shot two pigs and told me she saw nearly 125."

That is an astounding number of pigs, but it was possible. I explained, "Because I was in the ladder stand right over the feeder, the wind was carrying my scent toward a part of the woods where many of the pigs were coming from. I bet my scent scared off several groups. If I had been in the shooting house, those groups may have come in."

Ken changed the subject. "I saw an elk earlier, when I was with John in the truck. And I forgot to tell you: just after I dropped Mike off, a mountain lion ran across the road."

Letting that sink in, I wondered, "Ken, in your years of trapping, shooting, and catching pigs, have you ever seen a pig act aggressive unless it was in a trap or bayed up? Have you ever seen a pig that looked like it would come after you if it wasn't already bayed or trapped?"

Ken thought a minute, then answered, "I've only seen that one time. I was walking the edge of a big field, circling around on a big boar feeding out there. The edge was wooded, and when I got up to that boar, he was pissed that I was between him and the place he wanted to be. He bristled up and came straight at me. It took three shots from a .30-06 to stop him."

This account strengthened my views on dangerous pigs. Given a clear path to escape, 99.9 percent of the time a pig will take it.

Ken pulled up to the skinning station. Mike and I unloaded my pig. Ken told us, "When you get done with that pig, you can turn on the AC in the camper and catch some sleep. There's no point in getting back on your stands before 6:00." All of us agreed with the plan.

Ken took John and Vincent to retrieve Vincent's truck while Mike and I hung my pig and went to work. Mike told his story. "When the first group came in, it was small- and medium-sized pigs. I picked up my rifle. As I set the rifle down on the windowsill, I brushed the window latch and it rattled just a little. Those pigs were gone in a blink of an eye.

"Within an hour, another group came in and I shot my sow. After that, another group of small pigs came in. The light had dimmed considerably but I thought I had them centered. I shot and they all ran off. I went up to look and I found a bone chip like that we found when John shot that boar at Heart's Bluff, but that was it."

John and Vincent pulled in just as we finished the sow. We loaded our coolers full of meat and returned to the camper to wash up a bit. John led the way to the north end of Dripping Springs, where we stopped at a barbeque place to wash down sliced brisket sandwiches with Shiner Bocks.

Everyone was dragging ass as we rode back to the Rio Bravo for a sorely needed nap. My eyes were closed for about three hours. When I woke up, the other guys were already outside getting ready.

Ken picked us up. Everyone felt like going to new surroundings, so we rotated stands. Ken dropped off the other guys first before letting me off at the stand Mike had hunted the night before. Ken would pick us up in a few hours, after the sun went down.

I no longer harbored illusions of multiple shots with multiple weapons. The most likely scenario was no shooting at all. The next most likely scenario was a fleeting opportunity eighty to a hundred yards out. The .17 HMR and the bow remained in their cases.

With little chance of seeing pigs in the early afternoon, I opened a novel, *The Terror* by Dan Simmons. It was an excellent read, holding my attention even with a sleep-deprived and addled mind.

I was thinking that the odds were pretty good that the Saturn would be making the trip back east with one pig for each hunter. The trip had been a learning, if grueling, experience. At least my cooler held Texas pork.

Just after 8:00 p.m., the sound of a truck slowly rolling down a gravel road told me, "Time's up." Ken was on his way. But he never came around the bend. After about ten minutes, my cell phone vibrated. It was Ken. "Anything there?"

There wasn't. "No. It's all quiet here."

The pigs were over by Ken. "I've got three or four pigs right here beside my truck. If you want, crawl down from your stand. Walk toward the intersection. Turn left. The truck is about a hundred yards down the road. One of the pigs is huge."

I opened the door to the shooting house while answering, "I'm on the way." I started down the ladder with the 7 Mag and the gun light, jumping from too high up and landing on my ass. I was up in a flash and jogging for the road. This was my last chance to put more meat in the cooler.

A pig snorted as I approached the intersection. Was it one of the pigs Ken had just seen? Or was it a different pig or group of pigs?

I stepped into the road and swept the area with the red light. Nothing. I walked toward Ken and the truck, approaching on the driver's side. He asked, "Did you see anything?"

The stand had been a bust. "No. But I heard one snort back at the intersection."

Ken pointed. "They were over there to the left."

The red light illuminated the field, but it was fruitless.

Ken wasn't ready to give up. "Let's go check out a couple of feeders."

Ken drove with his lights off, telling me, "If you replace that red lens with a green lens, you won't spook the pigs." I knew red was better than white, but I hadn't heard about green being the color of choice.

Ken stopped the truck near a brush line on the left that ran perpendicular to the road, with an open field on our front left. Ken said, "Follow the brush down until you hit the road. The feeder will be on your left. There should be some pigs on it. If you shoot, I'll come. If you don't see anything, step out and flash your light three times."

Per Ken's directions, I followed the brush line, hitting the road about fifty yards from the feeder. Two or more deer immediately snorted and bounded away. There may have been pigs there earlier, but it was doubtful they were still there.

There was nothing at the feeder, so I stepped back to the road and flashed the light three times. Ken picked me up and I let him know, "The corn was still on the ground. Some deer spooked away from the feeder, but I didn't see any pigs."

Ken drove back to the skinning station, where Vincent was loading his gear in his truck. Ken asked, "Did you do any good?"

Vincent answered, "I was walking to my truck from the stand and I heard some pigs in the brush. I shined my light in there and saw three pigs. If I had had my gun up and pointing in that direction, I might have gotten off a shot. I didn't see anything down at the feeder."

Ken said, "We'll be right back. Mark's going down to kill a pig at that feeder." Ken just wouldn't give up!

He drove a short distance and stopped with the headlights off as I exited and approached the feeder as silently as possible on the dirt and gravel road. Nothing had disturbed the corn. This just wasn't my night. Ken was trying hard, but nothing was paying off. He had given me three more opportunities to shoot pigs, and nothing had panned out.

Ken picked up John, who hadn't seen anything either. It was the same story for Mike. On the ride back, I quizzed Ken about the resident hog populations. "You all have got a lot of pigs. Do the surrounding properties have the same numbers?"

Apparently, they had plenty. "Our neighbors have more than they want. So they trap their pigs and give 'em to us. We bring those hogs over here to the Rio Bravo and turn them loose. I think some of the pigs are back on our neighbors' property within twenty-four hours."

Ken continued, "They talk about how fast hogs are spreading across Texas. It isn't the pigs spreading over long distances. It's the hunters moving the pigs around!"

Ken drove us back to the camper and front gate. After unloading our gear from his truck into the Little Blue Hog-Hunting Mobile, I collected the money from the guys and tipped Ken. He had done the best he could for us.

Rio Bravo had plenty of swine, but these were educated pigs. Still, three out of four hunters had made a kill, so it hadn't turned out that bad.

Five states down, five to go.

10 BLUE PALM

A lust for wine, women, song, and good writing had been his undoing—
that, and Bobby Long.

—Ronald Everett Capps, *Off Magazine Street*, 2004

Blue palm (*Sabal minor*): The dominant native palm in southern bottomland forests. Blue palm is largely replaced with saw palmetto in Florida. During an early-afternoon summertime thunderstorm, it would be difficult for the casual observer to differentiate between a mature southeastern bottomland forest with a blue palm understory, and a tropical rain forest of Brazil or Hawaii. Of the three low-growing southern palms, blue palm is the most innocuous. Needle palm, true to its name, has dozens of dangerous, one- to two-foot-long needles upon which one should avoid impaling oneself. Saw palmetto, with its serrated stem, is very abrasive to skin and clothing. For reasons completely unknown to the author, on the stillest of days, without a hint of a breeze, a blue palm frond will occasionally wave quickly back and forth, as if guided by unseen hands.

Five states down and the finances were starting to get ugly. Was this going to pay off in the long run? Surely it would be worthwhile, if only for the memories and the trophies. But neither memories nor trophies were worth much in the eyes of my wife and coworkers. Tangible results were needed. Perhaps, just perhaps, a book would sell enough copies to recoup at least some of the costs incurred in a ten-state odyssey.

Fall was crunch time. The Texas trip took place from September 27 to October 1. The next weekend was an off week. The second weekend in October was the Bayou Cocodrie, Louisiana, hunt with John. Then another week off. The last weekend in October was a Mississippi hunt. And the week after Mississippi was my Florida black-powder hunt.

Four states over a six-week stretch, from the last weekend in September through the first week in November. If the hunts went well in Louisiana, Mississippi, and Florida, I could potentially have eight states under my belt. If a hunt or hunts zeroed out in Louisiana or Mississippi, there would still be time for return trips during or after deer season. If north Florida didn't produce again, there was an auction for a south Florida airboat hunt on eBay that looked promising.

After these eight states, South Carolina was still a possibility, and there was a reasonably priced Arkansas hunt that looked pretty good. Kills in the last two would add up to a total of ten states. But the odds were pretty good that one or two of the ten states on this list would not yield a pig, even with repeat trips.

California had lots of pigs, and one or two ranches offered hunts that as good as guaranteed a kill. But a California trip would be expensive, and the hunt would have to be paid for with borrowed dollars if I made it that far.

Missouri was another "last resort" state: there wild hogs are few and far between. For the majority of my adult life, there had been no known feral hog populations directly north of Arkansas. It was only in recent years that hunters had reintroduced feral hogs to some southern and western portions of the state.

John Dickson called me the Saturday morning before our Louisiana hunt, asking, "What's the plan?"

I replied, "Well, I was thinking of coming over Friday, possibly in time to get a little hunting in, then a full day on Saturday. Can you get off Friday?"

John answered, "Yeah, it's no problem for me to take off. The place we'll be hunting is way back in the refuge, and we'll need to take a boat to get there. But I don't think we'll be able to do much on Friday if you drive over the same day. It just takes too long to get back to the area we will be hunting."

I got the hint. "In that case, why don't I come over Thursday night?"

That's what John wanted to hear. "That would be better. Our best bet would be to leave well before light and take the boat to the back of the refuge. There are lots of pigs back there. I talked to a guy who hunted there on opening day [of squirrel season]. He didn't kill anything, but he saw sign everywhere."

John continued, "Make sure you bring rubber boots, preferably ones that reach your knees. We have used hip boots back there, but they wear you out too quickly. We'll need to cover a lot of ground."

Vincent (who had gone with us to Texas) had recently hunted with John on the refuge. John relayed the story. "We saw some small- to medium-sized pigs out in some mudflats. I gave Vincent my .22 Magnum and told him, 'Shoot it behind the shoulder.' Vincent took the rifle and said, 'I've got a head shot.' I told him, 'I don't know about that.' But he insisted, 'It's a good shot.' So I relented. 'Okay, then shoot him.'

"Vincent shot, and the pig went down, squealing loudly. We thought it was dead. Then it jumped up and ran a little way. It fell down again next to some palmetto. When we got there, it was gone, and there was only a drop or two of blood where it had lain down. I've never liked head shots because I've lost too many pigs with similar hits."

John concluded, "After we lost that one, we were walking out when a sow jumped up right in front of us. I shot it with the .22 Magnum. She had nine little piglets so we killed them too. It was a cold-blooded massacre."

John was looking at these kills with the eyes of a biologist. One of the primary missions at Bayou Cocodrie is to provide habitat for threatened and endangered species. One species of special concern for Bayou Cocodrie is the Louisiana black bear. Hogs compete directly with the Louisiana black bear (and white-tailed deer, for that matter) for hard mast (acorns) and other food sources.

Feral hogs are an invasive and destructive species in bottomland hardwoods, and if it were up to biologists and many other land managers, all pigs would be eradicated. Since eradication is virtually impossible, they rely on hunters to help reduce or control hog populations.

John laid out the battle plan for the coming hunt. "I've got several locations picked out. I'll go out this week and do some more scouting with my GPS. If I find some more hot spots, we'll work them over when you come. Do you remember me telling you about the honey hole where I killed those last two pigs?"

John was surprised that I remembered the story. "That's it! That's one of the few spots I've killed pigs twice in a row, and the second time was in the middle of the day! That place gets a lot of action. I'll hold that spot until you get here so it will be good and fresh."

This Louisiana trip had been planned as a hog hunt, but John corrected my terminology. "Squirrel season opened up this week and whenever I tell my co-workers, 'I'm going out to kill some pigs,' the game wardens tell me, 'No, you are going squirrel hunting. Pigs are considered "incidental" species on this refuge.' So remember that when you buy your Louisiana license: you are going squirrel hunting."

Because it was squirrel season on the refuge, the only legal calibers were rimfire. My gun cabinet held two .22 semiautomatic rifles and my little bolt-action .17 HMR. Having already taken down a nice red boar, the .17 was a proven hog killer. It would be nice to repeat with another one-shot kill. I told John, "This is going to be another serious test for the .17 HMR."

John replied, "I had a guy come in and tell me his friend shot a pig with a .17 HMR and he couldn't even tell that the pig had been hit. So I asked him 'How big was the pig?' He said, 'About two hundred pounds.'"

Most ammo for the .17 HMR is the smaller seventeen-grain "varmint" rounds. I remarked to John, "It's going to make a big difference depending which round you're shooting." If you were using a seventeen-grain bullet, the bullet might blow up completely in a squirrel or dove. If you shot a pig with one, it would fragment right beneath the skin. I don't think that round would kill a pig over twenty pounds. "How big do you think the average pig on the refuge is?"

The pigs tended toward the small side on Bayou Cocodrie. "I just don't see many big pigs here. Most of the pigs I see weigh forty to eighty pounds," John informed me.

I had just the thing for pigs that size. "I'm going to be shooting Hornady twenty-grain XTP rounds. A twenty-grain XTP should kill most pigs with a behind-the-shoulder shot up to sixty, maybe even eighty, pounds. If we see a big pig, and there's time to switch out rounds, I'll load a twenty-grain full metal jacket and go for a head shot."

The conversation turned back to John's missed shot at the Rio Bravo in Texas.

John said, "I've noticed that whenever I can keep the animal in the scope [after the shot is fired], then it's a good shot. Sometimes I even see the bullet hit. Whenever I look in the scope after the shot and I can't see the animal, then there's a good chance I pulled off."

John continued, "I've found that if I focus on squeezing the gun hard, I don't pull off. It's probably not a good way to get pinpoint accuracy on the range, but it works for me."

Adding my two cents, I said, "Whenever the shot surprises me, when the gun goes off unexpectedly, there's almost always a dead animal."

The next day John called me. "I know it hasn't been long since we talked, but I had to give you a report." By the tone of his voice, good news was coming. John was excited. "I went to that same area where Vince head shot the pig that got away. I've only been there a couple of times. There was rooting everywhere. I said to myself, 'I'm going to work real slowly through here.' Just then, there was a snort to my right. I looked out to see pigs about fifty yards away. At first I thought they had spotted me, but a couple of pigs were coming straight at me. I sat down as a black pig quartered in toward me. It stopped behind some brush. Then it came out and stopped broadside. When the crosshairs settled on him, they were steady as a rock and I thought, 'Game on!' I squeezed hard on the gun like we talked about yesterday and shot just behind the shoulder. I didn't hear the bullet hit like I normally do, and the pig ran off right after the shot."

John continued, "When I shot, most of the pigs ran straightaway. There was a spotted pig and several others making their escape, but one brown pig ran into some nearby brush and stopped. It took two steps forward, exposing its shoulder. I put the crosshairs on the shoulder and pulled the trigger. It rolled over and went down hard. The brown one was a sow.

"Next, I walked to the last place I'd seen the black pig. The black pig only ran about thirty yards before going down. I had thought they were about forty pounds each, but they went through 'groundswell' and they each weighed eighty pounds by the time I dragged them out.

"The brown sow was pregnant. She had four little ones in her. A lot of the old-timers have told me the pregnant sows taste the best. When I tried a pregnant sow one time, I had the same impression. It was the best-tasting pig I've ever eaten. It's not something I tell girls when I cook them up some fresh pork. Like, 'That roast you're eating came from a sow with six fetuses inside it.'" Picturing John and his date, I broke out laughing.

John made a generous offer. I had previously told him that some friends of mine in Ponchatoula, Louisiana, wanted to cook a feral hog for an event they were holding, and I had volunteered to bring the pork. John said, "Your friend in Louisiana can have the quarters off the boar. She can also have the front shoulders off this sow. That would give her six quarters. Does she want the ribs too?"

I thought she would. "Yeah, save them for sure. And if you have room in the freezer, don't bone out the quarters. I think they would prefer 'bone in' based on how they want to cook these pigs. With the quarters off these Texas pigs, we should be in pretty good shape. That gives us ten quarters in all. With another one or two Louisiana kills there should be more than enough for her shindig."

John asked, "What kind of event is this?"

"She is hosting some forestry event on her property, and they want to feed sixty or so people." Later, I learned that it was actually a birthday party.

John was a little worried. "That's a lot of people."

The number didn't bother me. "Yeah, but we're starting to get a lot of pork."

At the house, I packed my gear into the little blue Saturn, including four coolers. This time there would be plenty of space for pork, even if John and I killed a whole passel of pigs. Beryl, my friend holding the shindig, was counting on us to deliver meat for her upcoming event.

I kissed Joseph and Katia good-bye and was on the road by 4:45 p.m. I sent John a text message from Andalusia. A few minutes later John texted back, "Hey, hog killer!"

Although I was feeling rundown and worn out from several days of travel and presentations, a smile crossed my face. "Hey, John! I just left Andalusia. I'm going to be a little late getting over there."

John was raring to go. "Will you be okay with a 5:00 a.m. wake-up?"

It was doable. "Oh, yeah! Don't worry about me. With five hours of sleep, I'll be good to go."

John was relieved. "All righty, then! I am excited about this hunt. I think we're gonna stack them up!"

Considering how many pigs roamed the refuge, I was in agreement. "Me too! I'll give you a call when I get a little closer."

I drove west on U.S. 84. The drive took about six hours. I pulled into John's driveway at 11:05 p.m. John helped load my hunting gear straight into his pickup to save time in the morning.

The next thing I knew, it was 5:00 a.m. and John was yelling up the stairs, "Hey, pig hunter! Rise and shine."

I smiled in the dark, calling back, "I'll be right down."

First I took a quick shower with unscented soap. After the shower I toweled off and applied scentless deodorant. Minimizing odor is important when pursuing animals with a refined sense of smell.

John had some good strong coffee. The smell and taste reminded me of a previous stay with John's parents in north Louisiana. "Is that Community?"

"Yeah, the dark roast." It hit the spot on a cool, early morning.

We were out the door by 5:25 a.m., driving through Natchez, Mississippi, and crossing the state line into Vidalia, Louisiana. The next community was Ferriday, a somewhat notorious little town. During Hurricane Katrina, the local police stopped hurricane evacuees, handing out numerous tickets. This and other matters eventually led to a feud with the Louisiana State Patrol, which had come in and pulled some of their speed limit signs out of the ground, or so I was told.

John pointed to a store at the side of the road. "Sometimes I come by and their sign says, 'FRESH COON & GOO.'"

I was unfamiliar with the latter commodity. "What's goo?"

John explained that it was a Cajun term. "'Goo' or 'gasper goo' is what they call freshwater drum around here."

John entered the refuge and pulled up to the boat launch on the north end of Brook's Brake. It was still dark at Bayou Cocodrie. A friend of John's, Larry, was waiting for us. John introduced us, then we shook hands and loaded Larry's and my gear into John's boat.

John later explained that his boat was a "Lake Sport" type and a 15-51 model, meaning it was fifteen feet long and fifty-one inches wide. It had a trolling motor in the front and a twenty-five-horsepower motor.

John took the driver's seat, and Larry took the passenger seat. John handed me a spotlight to shine the way from the bow. The warm water and the cool air (Larry said it was forty-eight degrees) caused fog to roll off the water, reflecting the light back in our eyes. I turned the spotlight off. It was easier to navigate by starlight.

John kept the throttle down since occasional boat-sinking stobs protruded above the water's surface. John throttled up as the sky lightened. Herons and wood ducks arose from the water in front of us. There had to be alligators in this water, but they were hidden in the darkness.

John banked the boat into some cattails three and a half miles from the launch. The three of us hopped out. The pig sign was marvelous. At least ten feet of the bank was stomped to mud from the water's edge up.

We took our guns out of our cases and loaded them. My .17 HMR was the small gun. John was shooting a lever-action .22 Magnum, and Larry carried a brand-new .22 Magnum purchased for this pig hunt. Or rather squirrel hunt. As John said, "We are squirrel hunting and pigs are incidentals."

Another hunter pulled up and banked about ten yards away. The guy jumped out and walked up the bank carrying a rifle. He was also going squirrel hunting, but squirrels really were his primary target. When he heard we were looking for pigs, he said, "I was hunting here yesterday, and I heard some pigs working through the palmetto. I got out in front of them, and when one came into the trail, I shot it and dropped it in its tracks. When I walked up to it, I saw it was a boar and it had nuts like this," holding up his fists to show the size of the testicles. He finished, "I just left that boar laying there."

If a person shot a deer and left it lying in the woods, he would be shunned by any sportsman with a conscience. But many hunters find it acceptable to blaze away at any pig crossing their track, leaving the carcass or carcasses to rot. They see the feral hog as a nuisance species to be exterminated.

The four of us paralleled a large privately owned field to our right (south). Bayou Cocodrie was to the west of us, and Brook's Brake was to our left (north) and front (east). Reaching the far corner of the field, the squirrel hunter peeled off to the right. Larry took a trail toward a brake straight north. John and I followed the main trail east.

This was the old-growth area of Brook's Brake. The timber was beautiful, with plenty of large overcup, water, and Nuttall oaks, but the real giants were mainly willow oaks. Besides the oaks, other common hardwoods included cottonwoods, honey locusts, sugarberry, and red maple.

Beneath the canopy of mature bottomland hardwoods, the understory was a nearly solid layer of blue palm, or "palmetto." "Palmetto" is a generic term for low-growing palm species. Here in the western part of the coastal plain, blue palm is referred to as "palmetto." In the eastern coastal plain, south Georgia, and most of Florida, saw palmetto (*Serenoa repens*) is the dominant palmetto. [Saw palmetto is used to treat an enlarged prostate.]

Herbaceous species were extremely sparse, with the primary components being scattered lizard's tail and mulberry weed. Grasses were almost nonexistent in the forest proper. As we left the road for a trail, John told me that the soils are classified as alligator or sharky clays. Back in Missouri, farmers refer to similar soils as "gumbo." There were also a few pockets of bottomland hardwoods on similar soils alongside the Conecuh River at the Dixon Center.

The trail led to the brake where John had killed pigs on both his previous visits. Pigs generally aren't very active in the middle of the day, but this brake sounded like a sure-enough hot spot, and John had refrained from hunting it for several months to maximize our chances on this trip. The brakes were some of the few areas where blue palm did not limit visibility in the understory to less than ten yards.

John carried a GPS unit in which he had stored the locations of several previous kills and sightings inside the brakes. John and I turned onto a trail where the squirrel hunter's pig lay. It was a brown boar weighing about a hundred pounds. It wouldn't have been the best eating pig ever, but boars can be used in sausage, and if he was going to shoot it and leave it, he should have at least dragged it off the trail into the palmetto.

John whispered, "Let's slow down and walk in slow and quiet," as we entered the hotspot brake. John led the way, carefully placing each step to avoid sticks and palmetto stems. Hog sign was everywhere.

Each brake was a low area in the woods where water normally stood for long periods of time. The brakes were too low and wet for palmetto. Since the herbaceous layer was almost nonexistent, the ground was wide open nearly a hundred yards ahead and the entire width of the brake. Tiptoeing forward, John pointed to extensive fresh rooting beneath Nuttall oaks. The hogs were tearing the place to pieces but they weren't keeping up with the mast fall. I could see plenty of freshly fallen acorns on the ground.

John and I paused in the middle of the brake next to a fresh wallow with a few inches of water. John whispered, "When the pigs are in the palmetto, you can hear them rustling the leaves. If you watch the area where they are, you'll see the palmetto waving as they move beneath it."

At the far end of the brake, John was crestfallen. "That's the first time I haven't seen pigs in this brake."

It was disappointing, but I was still excited. "The sign was unbelievable. They were in here yesterday and/or today. The rooting is fresh, but our timing was just a little off."

John nodded. "We just need a little luck. This place has pigs everywhere. We just need to be in the same place [with the pigs] at the same time."

The next trail led to a slightly larger brake where Vincent had shot a pig the year before. Near the middle of the brake, John froze and motioned to stop. He whispered, "Pigs!" pointing to our left. The blue palm was rustling as the sounder moved about.

Shortly, a pig went, *Urrrrrrrr,* from twenty to thirty yards away. Then everything was silent. We eased to the edge of the palmetto, but the pigs were gone. The vocalization had been a sow telling her piglets, "Come quick. Danger!"

We stood silently beside the palmetto on the off chance that the pigs would emerge, but they had already moved deep into cover and were beyond sight and sound. After five to ten minutes, it was off to the next brake.

And so it went—one brake after another.

The Nuttall oaks were producing the most mast, but some of the willow oaks had a decent number of smaller acorns beneath them. The water oaks and overcup oaks either weren't producing or they had already been picked over.

Pig rooting was everywhere. In some cases it was older rooting. In some spots everything was fresh. But it was virtually impossible not to see hog sign: tracks, rooting, rubs, or wallows. I've hunted many areas, and this was the most hog sign covering the largest area I'd ever seen. Who knows how many pigs reside within the borders of Bayou Cocodrie?

John and I covered several miles before circling back toward the boat. On John and Larry's advice, I had donned my mud boots. But aside from a few small wallows, Bayou Cocodrie was dry. Rubber boots aren't bad for a while, but walking five miles in them can easily lead to blisters. My feet weren't there yet, but they were pretty sore.

We entered yet another brake. This one stretched much farther than I could see, and the hog sign was as good as any we'd walked through. There were beautiful, huge cypresses in the center of the brake where water would be the deepest. The Nuttall oaks were particularly prolific along this brake. Although the ground was freshly rooted beneath the Nuttalls, the inch-long acorns, obviously prized finds, were still falling.

John and I walked side by side. There was a crash to my left. I froze and whistled to John. A pig snorted. Both of us lowered our backpacks to the ground. We turned to face the palmetto as sounds rose from the right, front, and left. There appeared to be a whole line of pigs in the palmetto across from us. I whispered, "They are all over out there."

John agreed. "The wind is right for us." He pointed to a small opening directly in front of us. "Why don't you ease up into the opening where you can see into the palmetto? I'll angle in to the left."

John went left as I slowly tiptoed to the opening. Soon, blue palm blocked John from view. With the .17 HMR at the ready, I stopped about ten yards into the palmetto and listened. The pigs had moved farther out into the palmetto, but one could emerge at any moment.

After ten to fifteen minutes, John slipped through the palmetto, asking, "Did you see anything?"

"No. They got away again."

John was optimistic. "We didn't spook those pigs. They just worked off into the palmetto. We need to come back to this spot later."

I agreed. "That sounds good to me." I asked John, "Are we meeting up with Larry for lunch?"

"Yeah, I told him we would meet about 12:00. I think he'll want to head out. He's in his sixties and a little over a year ago he had prostate cancer. Since the surgery, he's been working on building up his endurance. He used to hunt pretty hard, but now he can only handle half a day, then he needs a day off to rebuild his strength."

Both of us had passed up squirrels all day long, and it was time to take a couple. I put the crosshairs on the next one I saw, high in an oak tree. At the shot, the squirrel came tumbling out. The sights were dead-on.

As the two of us approached the south edge of the property, a shot rang out to our left. A second later I pointed to the top of a tree and said, "There's the squirrel," as it fell to the ground below.

The hunter who had banked his boat next to ours emerged to pick up the squirrel. John asked him, "Did you limit out?"

"No, I've got seven, but I should have had seven early this morning."

Larry joined us as we walked back toward the boat. John asked him, "Any pigs?"

Larry hadn't done any better than we had. "No, I never got a shot off. I saw plenty of squirrels, some within ten yards looking at me from the base of a tree."

John replied, "We didn't do any better. We got close to two groups. We seemed to be doing everything right, being quiet in the brakes and keeping the wind in our favor. We should have gotten a shot at those pigs."

Larry apologized, "I am sorry you have to haul me all the way back out."

I wasn't sorry. "Man, my leather boots are back at the truck, and I am ready to get out of these rubber foot killers!"

Larry reflected, "This is one of the first times I have been out here with this little water. This might be the driest I've ever seen it."

John agreed, "Some of the brakes we walked through typically have water deep enough to go over chest waders. But today, I am getting out of these boots as soon as we make it to the truck."

The sky was clear and the temperature had warmed into the seventies. It was a very pleasant ride back up the bayou. Small alligators sunned on logs, and larger alligators launched off the bank as the boat drew near. Some quickly disappeared while others stayed on the surface. Bayou Cocodrie was aptly named.

According to some interpretations, "Cocodrie" is an old Cajun name for "alligator."

Back at the launch, John beached the boat. Larry left his cart for us in case we needed to haul out any pigs. He also gave me a cheesecloth carcass bag in case I killed something that could be carried out. We shook hands and Larry wished us luck. John promised him regular reports on our progress.

John and Larry changed their shoes while I cleaned my squirrel and then washed my hands. After lunch, it was back down the bayou, passing alligators as well as great egrets, great blue herons, and many other birds.

John stopped at a different spot, perhaps a half mile short of our previous landing, informing me, "There is one good brake after another as we head east off the bayou. I would like to end up at the last brake where we got on the pigs just before lunch. I think they'll still be in the area."

The bank was just as torn up and covered with hog sign as the morning's landing had been.

John led us through brake after brake. Sometimes there wasn't a clear path leading from one brake to another, so we crashed through the palmetto, occasionally pushing deer ahead of us, their distinctive white-flag tails bounding above the palmetto.

Several miles and hours later, John brought us back to the brake where we'd encountered the second group of hogs earlier in the morning. John led the way down the brake as dusk approached. A pig squealed to the left, freezing us in place. More hog sounds emanated from a wide arc to our left. The pigs were in the palmetto and they weren't far away.

I took a kneeling position about thirty yards from the palmetto and the pigs. A group of cypress knees surrounded me, providing good rifle rests. John stood beside an oak tree, hoping a pig or pigs would emerge before dark.

Pig sounds continued: palmetto breaking, snorts, and squeals. We stood or knelt at the ready. Twenty to thirty minutes passed and our shooting light was almost gone. John eased over to join me. "We need to head out before it gets too dark." He led the way through the palmetto, going a short distance before turning on his LED headlight. With his GPS unit and headlight, it didn't take long to make it back to the boat.

As John drove us back toward the launch, I worked the spotlight, sweeping the water ahead for stobs, logs, or stumps. Alligator eyes glowed red as the light passed over their forms.

We had put in about eleven hours of walking and a couple of hours either in the boat or waiting for pigs to emerge from the palmetto. Our take for the day: one gray squirrel.

Back at John's house, he warmed up some ten-bean soup with hog, deer, and turkey mixed in. It went down pretty well with beer and hot sauce. After supper John asked, "Will you be good for 5:00 a.m.?"

"Sure, just holler and I'll get up. At least I'll get a couple more hours' sleep tonight than last night."

With my belly full and my legs aching, sleep came easily.

But 5:00 a.m. came very early. I heard John moving around the kitchen. A few minutes later, the alarm clock—John's reasonably good imitation of a pig squeal—was heard from the staircase.

Maybe our luck would better yesterday's. I let John know I was awake. "Sounds like it's time to get some pigs!"

As soon as the coffee finished brewing, we filled our mugs and loaded the truck—on the road by 5:20 a.m. It was just shooting light as we entered the first brake, and it was as empty as every break we had visited the day before. John slowed down as we approached the second brake. About ten yards from its edge, John stopped, looked left, and said, "Pigs!" motioning me forward. "They are down there on the far edge of the brake, headed this way."

I stepped past John, easing forward to a small hardwood 5 yards out of the brake. There was a spotted pig, then another spotted pig, then another! It looked like there were half a dozen in the herd, with only one black pig. Bringing up the rear was another spotted pig—much bigger than the others. The herd was about 120 yards out and still coming our way. If the pigs paralleled the palmetto on the far side, they would pass within 50 yards of our location.

A four-inch-diameter hardwood provided support for my .17 HMR, allowing me to track the pigs from a steady position. The leading spotted pigs were all good-sized hogs, with weights I estimated at fifty to one hundred pounds. The black pig was a bit smaller. Any one of these pigs would make my trip.

A big spotted pig drew up next to the smaller spotted pigs. This one was twice as big as the next-largest pig. It chased one of the sows in a small circle, sniffing to see if it was in estrous. The boar's quarry wasn't receptive, so it gave up.

The smart thing would have been to shoot one of the smaller pigs, but there was no passing up that boar. I whispered, "I'm taking the big hog."

John lined up on another pig. "Okay."

The group was moving fairly rapidly, and at this range, a head shot was nearly impossible. This boar was moving too much and it was too far out. I put the crosshairs behind the shoulder. The herd turned left toward the palmetto. If the pigs entered the palmetto, this opportunity would disappear. It was now or never.

The boar was out front when it put its nose to the ground and paused, offering a broadside profile facing right. The crosshairs settled as I squeezed the trigger. *Craaack!*

The boar dropped its right front shoulder, stutter-stepped, and ran into the palmetto, with the other pigs close behind. John didn't have time to shoot.

I released my breath as John asked, "How did the shot feel?"

Exhaling, I answered, "It felt pretty good. The boar dropped its shoulder like a deer does when you hit the vitals."

John nodded. "That's good. I am pretty sure I heard him giving the death thrash nearly straight out. I marked the spot but we better give him a long time to bleed out. If we bump this pig, we'll never see him again. I don't expect we'll find much blood."

My watch read 7:25. Counting my paces to the spot where the boar had been standing, I found that I had overestimated the range at about a hundred yards, while John correctly called the shot at seventy yards. We agreed on where the pigs had been, but there was nary a drop of blood.

We were still in the brake. John suggested, "Let's just wait here. Lots of times when I shoot one pig it lays down and dies, and if I am quiet, the other pigs return to feeding as if nothing has happened."

It would be great to add another pig or two to the tally. "Sounds good to me."

After several minutes of quiet, John said, "I'll loop out into the palmetto and meet you back here."

I wanted to examine the immediate area a little closer. "I'll just wait here and see if anything develops."

John walked down the brake to my left while I repeatedly searched the area for blood, bone, or any other sign of a hit pig, finding nothing. Beyond the occasional Nuttall acorn crashing through the blue palm fronds, the palmetto was silent.

After another thirty minutes, a gray squirrel scampered around the top of a large hollow hardwood about thirty yards away. Taking a rest against another tree, I watched the squirrel enter a hollow stem. It was still visible, but the squirrel would probably fall farther down the hole if I shot it. The squirrel was chewing on the wood inside the tree, enlarging the hole. The squirrel went in and out of the hole, never offering a good shot. Finally, it exited the hole and crawled onto a branch above, pausing a moment too long. *Craack!* The squirrel stiffened and slowly tumbled off the branch, bouncing off the trunk, then bouncing off another branch, and another, before finally thumping to the ground.

I turned around to find John standing behind me. Smiling, with his hand John imitated the squirrel bouncing down to the ground. My confidence in the shot at the boar increased. "I didn't miss that pig."

"I know you didn't!"

After retrieving the squirrel, we returned to the spot where the boar was last seen. A pig squealed from the palmetto to our front. John's face lit up. "Oh, baby! We may get another shot here."

John led us into the palmetto. We slowly picked our way through the minefield of palm fronds, begging the question: With the pigs making so much noise, why do they freak out and haul ass every time a human brushes a palm frond? How in the world do they tell the difference between pig noise and human noise?

A black pig stood up ten yards in front of us. It ran a short distance to the left and stopped in the palmetto. The center of the pig was visible, but John was between me and it. He raised the .22 Magnum, aiming but not shooting. After three or four seconds, the pig disappeared into the palmetto. John shook his head. "I had the scope turned up on high power from looking at a squirrel. I saw black, but it wasn't a good shot. I probably should have just pulled the trigger on him."

There were still pigs to our right, but they never offered a shot. It had been an hour and ten minutes since the boar had run into the palmetto. I told John, "It's time to go look for my pig."

Back at the brake, John entered the palmetto on the left, aiming for the spot where he thought he'd heard the death thrash. I paralleled John to his right. Ten yards in, he held up his hand. I held my breath as he stared forward. After a few seconds, he shook his head and the search moved forward.

Fifty yards farther in, slowly working back and forth, John waved at me again, smiling. "Mark, come get your pig!" John was standing over a very, very nice boar. My knees were almost weak as I yelled in triumph, "Woohoo!"

High-fiving me, John said, "That's one big pig!"

The boar had run about sixty yards before stopping. John had correctly heard and identified the spot where the pig went down. The thrashing had indicated the pig's final moments, occurring seconds after my shot. There was no blood trail leading to this spot. But once the boar had gone down, a puddle of blood collected from its snout and mouth. I rolled the pig over to expose the side I'd targeted. There was no blood or visible hole.

This boar had a long head and good tusks. John said, "He's got good cutters and whetters!" This boar would have made a good mount, but the money wasn't there. After snapping several photos in the palmetto, we dragged it to the brake for some pictures of the boar on a log. With a pig like this, there is no maximum number of photos.

Our celebration ended when John grabbed his .22 Magnum, saying, "Squirrel on the ground. I have to get this one."

The squirrel was going up a small tree with a mouthful of Spanish moss. I observed, "It's building a nest." Sure enough, the squirrel entered a nest of twigs, leaves, and moss, where it deposited its mouthful. Emerging from its home under construction, the squirrel took a fateful pause on the side of the tree. *Pow!* The .22 Magnum was louder than the .17 HMR and the squirrel went flying off the trunk of the tree, landing with a thud.

After we had discussed our options, John went to get the cart from the boat while I gutted the boar. Before leaving, John cut the boar's head off, placing it and our two squirrels in the carcass bag Larry had given us. Most people don't bother saving the head or skull from a pig, but I was boiling out all the skulls I harvested in the Year of the Pig. The skulls would be mementos from the most intensive year of pig hunting I'd probably ever experience.

As a young child on the farm, I saw Grandma Hainds keep pig heads in a tub covered with cheesecloth before she removed the brains for "head cheese." The thought repulsed me at the time, but with age, well . . . it still sounded pretty disgusting.

John trundled off while I gutted the boar.

Gloves would have been a good idea. With numerous scratches, pokes, and nicks on my hands, any break in the skin was a potential entry point for the bacteria that cause undulant fever. But my gloves were in the backpack I had forgotten on my bed in Pleasant Home, Alabama.

The intestines rolled out as I cut away the diaphragm before reaching in to extract the heart, lungs, and liver. The heart was intact. The bullet had entered the right side behind the shoulder, passing between two ribs, a little too high for the heart. The bullet had centered the lungs and the body cavity contained a large pool of blood where the pig had bled out internally.

The bullet had expanded while passing through the lungs. Looking at the opposite side of the carcass, I noted that the bullet had exited the body cavity, again passing between two ribs. There was no exit wound. Digging between the ribs, I extracted the bullet from the area between the ribs and the shield on the left side of the carcass. It was astounding that the .17 HMR retained enough energy to nearly effect a through and through shot on a pig this size.

About an hour later, John returned and helped load the boar onto the cart. I showed John the lungs and the other wounds. John was impressed, but we still agreed that his .22 Magnum was probably a better gun for this type of hunting.

We went back to John's house to quarter the boar and dress the squirrels. Pulling the skin off a squirrel, John told me, "I used to put all my duck wings in the pond. Then one day I came home and found a note from my neighbor saying, 'John, there has been a large, unexplained waterfowl die-off in our pond. Could you check into it?' It was a very polite way of telling me to quit dumping my shit in the pond!

"I started putting my deer heads and hides beneath those pine trees over there, and before long I had my own little buzzard colony. Then the wind would shift and it was like, 'Ugh.'"

This was classic John, but I had plenty of skins hanging in my own attic, literally.

John finished, "So I have been trying not to leave so much carrion around. That way I keep peace with the neighbors. On the other hand, there's only going to be the skin from this pig. It won't have the head or the guts, so it shouldn't smell too bad." I agreed, so John dragged the skin down to his pine trees. The buzzards were thankful.

With the meat on ice, we went inside to shower and change. My ass was dragging, but Louisiana State was playing Kentucky, so we drank a few beers while watching Kentucky pull off a big upset. It would have been nice to watch the Missouri-Oklahoma game, but John couldn't get that game with his channel selection. The results were depressing enough, with Oklahoma ending Missouri's unbeaten streak.

John had done as much hunting and fishing travel as anyone I knew. But John also had professional experience: guiding quail hunts in Texas; turkey hunts in Louisiana, Mississippi, and Texas; and salmon fishing in Alaska. Some of his guided hunts had been televised on various sporting shows. I asked him, "What did you consider a good tip for guiding?" I was paying for several hunts and I wanted do right by my hunting guides.

John considered the question. "It really depends on what type of hunt it is. If you are talking about something like our recent Rio Bravo hunt, where Ken just drops you off in the morning and picks you up several hours later, I would tip less in that case."

John described some of his experiences. "When I was guiding a quail hunt, I was working my butt off from dawn until dark. There was a lot more interaction with that type of hunt, and the success of the hunt was largely determined by the ability of the guide, using dogs that were well trained to put the hunters on birds.

"Of course, turkey hunting was the ultimate one-on-one. The hunter was not going to kill a turkey unless I got them to the right spot and successfully called the bird into range."

Moving his description north, John switched from hunting to fishing. "Up in Alaska, we weren't paid squat, so we were really dependent upon tips to make any money up there."

John described different types of hunters. "I was often amazed at how much variation we got in tips and who tipped what. Lots of times, the guys I really enjoyed taking out on the hunt and I really liked, those were often the guys who could barely afford the hunt and didn't leave much of a tip.

"On the other hand, some of the rich lawyers we guided were complete and total dickheads. We'd get back from a hunt where they had given me hell all day long, and they would hand me a several-hundred-dollar tip. I think they knew they'd been dickheads and this was their way of making up for it."

Human nature is an amazing thing.

Before we called it a night, John talked me into staying for another morning hunt. I am weak-willed when it comes to matters of fur, fish, or game, and John has no difficulty leading me astray. From Ciudad Juarez to the toughest juke joints of Louisianna, if you follow his lead, there's no telling where you'll end up.

This time 5:00 a.m. didn't come quite so early when John sounded his pig-call alarm clock. Rolling out of bed and putting on my overalls, I resolved to put the hurt on some squirrels if the opportunity arose.

On the drive to Bayou Cocodrie, John explained the plan of attack. "Let's go to Brook's Brake. It's the biggest of the brakes in the woods and we saw tons of sign in it. We'll get there early and I think there's a good chance that if we go opposite directions, one of us will catch them in the open."

John cruised up the bayou, slowing to an idle as the boat passed a stump. The boat died. John repeatedly started the boat in idle, only to have it die each time he put it in gear. After a dozen or more tries, he threw the motor into gear while opening the gas to full throttle. It took.

Fifteen minutes later, we were in Brook's Brake, entering the low ground beside some huge, hollow cypress trees. John explained that bears and some rare species of bats used the big cypresses as den trees. We would rendezvous at the big cypress trees at 10:30 a.m.

John turned left and I went right. One hundred yards in, there was movement in the palmetto to my left, so I took a seat. Noises emanated from a fairly wide arc. There were several animals moving through the palmetto. I held my position for nearly thirty minutes before the pigs moved out of hearing.

Squirrels scampered everywhere as I moved down the brake, but I wanted to reach the end of the brake before giving up on the pigs and shooting the little gray, or "cat," squirrels. Although hog sign was fresh and ubiquitous, the pigs were silent and invisible.

As I reached the end of the brake, squirrels barked from three or four directions. Choosing the squirrel that sounded closest, I moved that way. High up in a tree, there were two squirrels, one on top of the other. They were adding to the squirrel population!

I put the crosshairs on the bottom squirrel, about fifty yards away. I squeezed the trigger, and both squirrels tumbled from the tree. The female squirrel was added to the game bag while the male squirrel escaped with no visible injury, but who knew how this event would affect his future sex life?

Retrieving my first kill and then working slowly back up the brake, I had gone only another fifty yards before another squirrel was barking ahead. A few minutes later, squirrel number two joined the first in my game bag. After that, the hunting slowed down, and the rest of the morning was rather uneventful. The brake eventually led me back to our meeting point, where John leaned against a huge cypress tree with his rifle pointed up.

A large woodpecker flew from the area he was pointing toward. Was he trying to identify the woodpecker? It looked like a pileated, but the ivory-billed woodpeckers were all the news lately. A good friend was participating in an organized search in the Florida Panhandle, hoping ivory-bills were still around, but the researchers were having trouble getting photographic proof. Seeing an ivory-billed woodpecker would be a once-in-a-lifetime experience, but I was afraid this species had been extinct for decades.

John told me he had spotted pigs twice, including a sow with a string of piglets. They had been over a hundred yards away and moving quickly, so he didn't take a shot. Our hunt was drawing to an end, and I had taken the only shot at pigs in two and a half days of hunting.

Back in Natchez, John volunteered, "I'll clean the squirrels. I know you've got a long ways to go." I thanked him profusely for a wonderful hunt and for being a great guide. We loaded three coolers of meat in my car. The boar almost filled two coolers by itself, and John kicked in an extra four front shoulders from the two pigs he'd killed the week before, figuring that would be enough for the party in Ponchatoula.

A few hours later, I pulled up at Beryl's house in Tangipahoa Parish, south of I-12. Her property had gotten whacked by Hurricane Katrina. Beryl had salvaged most of her downed timber, and she was in the process of converting back to longleaf pine. It was sad to see the devastation wreaked upon mature stands of timber. But if she got this land back into a fire-maintained longleaf pine forest, it would be a net gain environmentally, aesthetically, and for some landowners, economically.

Beryl's friends and neighbors, Brian Beter and his son, were working on the edge of the driveway. They took me to Beryl's cabin. I showed them the bullet I had recovered from the boar as I told them about our hunting trip. Brian said, "We used to kill wild pigs around here. We'd get down in the swamps and walk until we heard them rooting around. Then we'd sneak up on them and shoot them with buckshot. When we'd shoot, about half would run and about half would turn back on you."

While his assessment was consistent with stories I had heard from other hog hunters, neither John nor I had witnessed aggression from pigs that had just been shot.

Brian told me he had taken a very big pig. "I killed a 450-pound male hog that had been cut. He had this much fat on him." He held his hands at least four inches apart.

Although I still hadn't killed a "cut," "bar," "barrow," or "barred" hog yet, I kept getting the same report: castrated boars grow to be the biggest pigs in the woods. In their book *Wild Hog Hunting: Everything You Need to Know to Get Your Hog!* Dave Sturkey and Craig Marquette write, "Truly big boars that are killed in the wild are usually castrated by man or something has gone wrong with their testicles naturally. Their energy is conserved and their attention is focused primarily on food, not sex!"

John Dickson's biggest pig was another good example. It was an exceptionally old barred hog that he shot on Sandy Lands, one of Temple Inland's big land-holdings in East Texas. Consistent with Brian's story, John told me, "It was just dripping fat."

With my gift-meat obligations fulfilled, I shook hands with Brian and his son and drove just up the road to my favorite Louisiana restaurant, the Spot.

It was going to be a long drive home, but the drive would have been a lot longer if I hadn't killed that big spotted boar.

Feral pigs "captured" by remote motion-activated game cameras: *top,* the sounder of shoats caught snuffling through a muddy seep indicates the broad color and pattern variations seen in populations of wild hogs; *bottom,* the "family" in an upland forest illustrates the variation possible in siblings of the same litter. (Photographs courtesy of Steven S. Ditchkoff.)

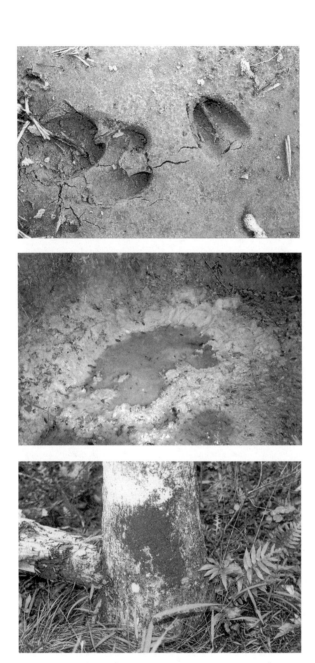

Sign of feral pigs: *top,* characteristically rounded pig tracks on the left, with a single pointed deer track on the right, for comparison; *middle,* a fresh hog wallow in a muddy ditch; *bottom,* a tree rub composed of dried mud.

A Dixon Center wild boar shot with the author's .17 HMR demonstrates
the long, erect hairs on the spine that give many feral hogs a
"razorback."

Ravenous, rooting feral hog populations can do severe damage to general agriculture, as shown in this trampled cornfield (*top*) and in a peanut field (*bottom*) where the animals have uprooted and consumed entire plants.

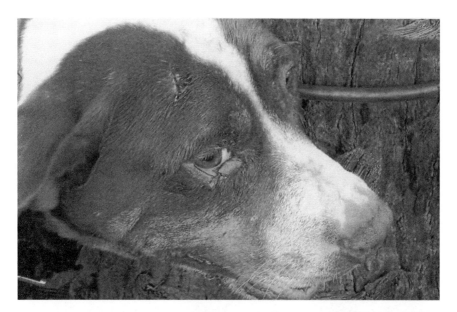

Top, bay and capture dogs are often used successfully in hunting wild pigs. This hunting dog shows the wounds and scars on his head and eye from recent and former encounters with feral hogs. *Bottom,* airboats can provide one of the few feasible methods of pursuing pigs in the swamps and wet flats of Florida.

This mother-daughter team (Deedy and Karin) of expert hunting guides helped the author bag a California boar that shows definite Russian/European ancestry.

Two contrasting southern ecosystems: *top,* a native, healthy stand of fire-maintained longleaf pine/wiregrass in the Conecuh National Forest of Alabama; *bottom,* a fire-excluded slash pine plantation showing no herbaceous layer but rather dangerous "fuel laddering"—a sure recipe for wildfire.

The largest feral hogs killed during the Year of the Pig were both taken in Lower Alabama: *top,* the author with the boar he tracked through a privet thicket; *bottom,* the author and the sow he took during the last week of the challenge.

11 CHUFAS

They live among the lost forests.

—Janisse Ray, *Ecology of a Cracker Childhood,* 1999

Chufas (*Cyperus esculentus*): Sedges native to the Old World. Chufas look like just like the closely related yellow nutsedge, which, as a weed, drives bare root (tree seedling) nursery managers to distraction. Chufas produce an edible tuber beneath the soil surface. These tubers have a sweet flavor and they can be used to make *horchata*. Chufas are planted in some areas to fatten hogs or, in the southeastern United States, as a food source for the wild turkey. Raccoons, deer, and squirrels will also dig and eat the tuber. One of the quickest ways to determine if feral hogs are on your property is to invest several hundred dollars an acre planting chufas. If the chufas take and pigs are there, the planted area will come to resemble a bombing range.

October 20, 2007. I had fallen asleep in a chair while listening to the Auburn–Louisiana State football game over the Internet. When I woke up, the game had taken a turn for the worse for the Orange and Blue, so I switched the line back from the Internet to the phone and went to bed. I'd just lain down when the phone rang. It was my coworker Larry. He asked me, "You want a pig?"

The clock said 11:00 p.m. I asked Larry, "What have you got, a boar or a sow?"

Larry answered, "It's a red sow and it's a big one."

There was no reason to let fresh pork go to waste. "I'm on the way."

Larry was waiting in his driveway. He hopped into my truck and told me to drive behind his house along the field's edge. "If you've got four-wheel drive, you may as well lock it in now." The last two days had brought a long, soaking rain that provided relief from an extended drought that had stretched almost two years.

As we passed his hog trap, Larry said, "Those pigs are not going into the trap. I think they came down here from the Dixon Center, and they ate about $100 worth of my chufas this week. I shot a big black pig first. I am pretty sure it was a boar. Then I shot this big red sow. It knocked her down and she got back up so I shot her again. I ended up shooting at her three times."

"Where did you hit the big black pig? Do you think it's worth trailing him?" I asked Larry.

Larry shook his head. "Not where he ran."

The brush on the field's edge was thick yaupon and blackberry. I felt no obligation to look for a big boar shot by someone else. If Larry hit the boar hard, it was probably a goner. And butchering a big sow would give me plenty to work with over the weekend.

Larry's sow was lying on the edge of the field. It was indeed a big pig. I'd never seen a sow quite like this one. "Holy cow! That is one fat hog." The legs were short and the body was almost round.

Larry asked, "You think she's over two hundred?"

"This sow is closer to three hundred than two hundred."

I jumped into the back of the pickup and reached down to grab a hind leg. Larry stayed on the ground and tried to lift from below. We strained hard enough to herniate ourselves, but the sow's hindquarters wouldn't get up and over the tailgate. After a couple of minutes, we gave up.

Larry asked, "Have you got a rope?"

There was a long section of climbing rope in my truck bed. Larry tied the pig to a tow ball on my rear bumper, and we dragged the sow to a terrace. I untied the sow, pulled around, and backed in from downslope. With half the height between the tailgate and the ground, we finally got the tub of lard into my truck bed.

Back at his driveway, Larry hopped out. Before he shut the door he asked me, "Are you taking it to the Dixon Center?"

That was the best place to work this pig up. "Yeah, I'm just going to gut it and put it in the walk-in cooler until tomorrow."

Larry said, "I'll see you there."

What could I say? "Man, you've already done enough. I appreciate your calling me and helping me get it in the truck, but I should be able to handle it."

Larry explained, "I want to see what it weighs."

That was understandable. "Okay. I'll see you at the scales."

At the Dixon Center, I backed my truck beneath the hanging rig on the concrete pad. The 300-pound scales were just big enough for this sow. They read its live weight at 280 pounds! What a hoss!

Larry posed with the sow as I snapped a few photos before gutting the pig. Out of curiosity, I put the scales back on and cranked up the carcass again. It weighed 250 pounds with the guts removed. I'd killed taller and longer sows, but I hadn't seen anything with this much fat or this much weight. The sow had a good three inches of fat layering its body.

On the way home, I stopped to check our peanut field. Entering the northwest corner of the field, I shined the area with a red light, walking as quietly as possible. Halfway across the field, eyes glared back. I turned off the light and tiptoed forward, my progress silent except for the occasional popping of peanut hulls. Two-thirds of the way across the field, I again turned on the light. A coyote was standing at a distance of a hundred yards. Just behind the light-colored coyote was another set of eyes but no apparent body. This would be the first one's mate, the black coyote I'd seen about a week ago. There were two more sets of eyes on the west edge of the field. It was a mature gray fox with a smaller pup following close behind her. The leftover peanuts sure drew the wildlife. Leaving the foxes and the coyotes to their peanut scavenging, I drove home and went to sleep.

The next day, Sunday, Joseph and I drove to the Dixon Center, where I dragged the sow out of the cooler and cranked it up to a comfortable skinning height. Joseph was mesmerized by the huge hog, repeatedly asking or stating, "Pig? Pig? Pig!" Each time, I assured him, "Yes, that is a pig."

After skinning the pig, I cut enough fat from the carcass to completely fill a forty-eight-quart cooler. Carolina Custom Meats could grind and blend the fat with frozen venison and pork to produce some of the best smoked sausage links around. There was no need to purchase any extra fat this year!

12 COLLATERAL DAMAGE

Taking fire out of the longleaf forest is like taking rain out of the rain-forest.

—ROBERT J. MITCHELL, "Silly Shit I Say All the Time"

Hollies (*Ilex spp.*): There are several hollies in the southeastern United States. The American holly is commonly found on shaded, north-facing slopes and fire-excluded bottomlands. Other hollies, such as gallberry, yaupon, and tall gallberry, are native shrubs or small trees, but they are very invasive in the absence of fire. Hollies will form walls of green brush in fire-excluded longleaf and/or slash pine forests. Their waxy leaves are highly flammable, and large stands of hollies at the rural/urban interface are recipes for disaster. A headfire moving through a pine overstory with a dense holly midstory may produce flame heights of one hundred feet or more. Since many practitioners of prescribed fire are barely closeted pyromaniacs, they secretly smile when given the challenge of using fire to knock down a dense growth of hollies. In prescribed burner terminology, this practice is referred to as "reducing the fuel load."

The meeting in Virginia wrapped up late on a Thursday afternoon, and I was looking forward to a Mississippi hog hunt scheduled for Saturday morning. As I crossed from North Carolina to South Carolina on I-85, I set the cruise control at two miles above the speed limit. The police had stopped cars every three to five miles. I passed a woman standing in front of a police cruiser as the officers searched her vehicle. Then a black man signing a ticket. Then a

Hispanic gesticulating as an officer stood listening. Then another Hispanic, spread-eagled on his car as the cops frisked him.

Now driving the exact speed limit, I continued down the interstate, seeing the exit to Bob Jones University while a young white man went around me in the passing lane. The back glass of his white sports car sported a sticker: "South Carolina is GOP Country." I'd have never guessed.

Nothing would be gained by delving into South Carolina politics, but it is hard to say enough good things about the state's forestry and natural resources community. The South Carolina Association of Consulting Foresters has invited the Longleaf Alliance to its meetings and received our message with tremendous enthusiasm. Clemson Extension Service has two forestry specialists (Bob Franklin and Beth Richardson) who have educated hundreds of landowners about *Pinus palustris*. The South Carolina Forestry Commission sent dozens of its foresters to longleaf academies. The South Carolina Natural Heritage Program has an inspired biologist and preserve manager, Johnny Stowe, who works tirelessly restoring fire, longleaf, and the native herbaceous community to South Carolina's many Natural Heritage Preserves. The list of agencies working to restore longleaf in South Carolina goes on and on. Over the next fifty years, hundreds, perhaps thousands, of off-site, fire-excluded loblolly and slash plantations should be converted back to longleaf across South Carolina. With the restoration of its native forests and prescribed fire, South Carolina will be better off economically, aesthetically, and ecologically.

When I got home, my Mississippi contact, the recently retired Chester Hunt, reported zero hog sign in the WMA we had intended to hunt. Already exhausted from the Virginia trip, I decided to drop Mississippi and catch up on work before the next weekend's Florida trip.

My good friend Mike was accompanying me on the next Florida hunt. I called his cell phone a few days before the scheduled trip and updated him on the coming hunt. "I talked to Jerry, the guy I bought our Florida hunt from, and he is driving to his lease on Thursday. I'm thinking about joining him Thursday evening and hunting all day Friday."

Mike would join me later. "I should be able to get over there Friday afternoon." We had our plan.

It was late Thursday when I finally got away from the Dixon Center. Passing through Milton, Florida, I called to touch base with Jerry, the guide, and then Mike. Jerry was at the lease and Mike was already at a hotel in Tallahassee, where I would join him. Mike had appointments in the state capital before he could join me later for the hog hunt.

It was 1:30 a.m. by the time I got to Tallahassee, met Mike, and got to bed. The alarm went off at 4:00 a.m. After getting dressed, I grabbed my gear and Mike's black-powder rifle. He had just purchased the .50-caliber rifle and hadn't had time to work with it, so it was up to me to get it sighted in after the morning hunt.

Traffic was sparse and I made the Madison exit by 5:15 a.m., forty-five minutes early. Jerry arrived at 5:35. A deputy sheriff in south Florida, he was a heavyset man with very short hair.

After shaking hands, we made a short drive to the lease, but after we passed through a gate it was another six to eight miles in on dirt roads. This was a big property. The drive began in thinned, relatively open slash pine plantations. The farther back we went, however, the thicker the brush. Jerry told me, "When we get back on our lease, the brush is so thick the hogs and deer will run a quarter mile down the road before they can find a hole to duck into!"

Jerry drove past numerous signs along the road with names and years. He explained, "The terms of our lease are: if you hunt by yourself, you get two stands. If you are married and your wife hunts less than five times a year, you get three locations. If your wife hunts more than five times a year, you get four stands. When you select a location that has not already been claimed, you put up a sign to claim that spot."

Baiting was legal in Florida (though, unlike in Texas, night hunting was not). There were dozens, if not hundreds, of feeders scattered across thousands of acres on this lease.

Jerry stopped beside a sign with his last name. We exited the truck. I extracted my black-powder rifle from its case, dropping two pellets of powder into the barrel followed by a 250-grain sabot, forced home with a ramrod. A #209 primer would be inserted on the stand. To fire the rifle, I would cock the hammer and pull the trigger. The hammer would fall, pushing the firing pin into the primer. The primer would explode, shooting fire through a small orifice called the nipple. This would ignite the black-powder pellets, propelling the sabot out the barrel.

Jerry led me to the stand in the darkness, with only a sliver of a moon and the stars providing ambient light. About fifty yards off the road in the slash pine plantation, Jerry located a ladder stand attached to a small slash pine. He told me, "The feeder is about forty yards to the front. You can't miss it when the sun comes up. Good luck; I'll see you about 9:00 a.m."

I climbed the ladder stand as Jerry shined a flashlight for me. Once I took my seat, Jerry went to hunt from another feeder. It was 6:38 a.m.

By 7:22 a.m., there was enough light to see the open sights on my rifle.

At 7:38 a.m., the time trigger on the feeder went off, throwing my heart into my throat. It's shocking to go from silence to the whirr and clatter of the motor throwing corn kernels off the stand's legs and surrounding tree boles, much like a covey of quail exploding beneath one's feet. A minute after the feeder threw its corn a stick broke to the left. Were pigs on the way?

Three wood ducks lifted off water to my right, flying overhead as the sky lightened. Cypress trees were visible a few hundred yards to my left. There was plenty of water in the neighborhood. With the temperature in the fifties and a light breeze in my face, my scent was being carried away from the feeder. There was food, cover, and water. The layout looked ideal.

To pass time, I tracked shots. 7:55: a distant shot to the right/east. 8:05: a close shot to the west. 8:24: a distant shot to the front/north. 9:00: a very far shot to the right front. 9:01: a distant shot to the left front.

True to his word, Jerry pulled up a few minutes after 9:00. Riding back to camp, I gave my report and asked Jerry if he'd seen anything. "Yes, I put the sights on a black pig, pulled the trigger, and got the 'pop' of my primer going off. The nipple must be clogged."

As Jerry exited the hunting lease, I saw that the roadway was lined with large live oaks and water oaks; such trees were entirely absent from the thousands of acres we'd just driven through that morning. I had watched carefully, and I couldn't remember seeing a single mature oak tree on over six miles of dirt road. It was as if the foresters were completely focused on destroying any potential wildlife value on their landholdings. In the southeastern United States, oaks are a natural component of all but the wettest bottomland forests, and oaks should be in every upland forest. Their acorns are referred to as hard mast, and they are an essential food source for almost all our major southeastern game species (deer, turkey, squirrels, quail), while countless nongame species dine on the fall/winter acorn crop.

Back at hunting camp, there were thousands of acorns beneath the oak trees on the road edge. If the foresters who managed this hunting land had just left some strips or islands of oaks in the huge blocks of land to our west, the mast production would have benefited the hunting, nongame species, and even the hogs.

At the camper, Jerry warned me, "I killed a couple of snakes under or around the trailer on the last trip."

This did not surprise me. "What were they?"

"I don't know. If I see a snake, I kill it." How many times had I heard the same story? I had just about given up trying to convince people not to kill snakes. Jerry's opinion was similar to the belief, "If they are Muslim, they are terrorists." The world of such people is black and white. They have decided what is right and what is wrong, and no fact or contrary opinion will change their minds.

Resigned to failure but obligated to make the attempt, I remarked, "I have a tree nursery, and if I find a nonvenomous snake, I take it to my greenhouse. They help control the rats and mice, and prevent the loss of expensive seed." By providing a true example of the positive aspects of snakes, I try to add another dimension to people's thinking.

Jerry set up a target behind the camper while I retrieved Mike's rifle. Mike had mounted the scope but that was as far as he'd gotten with it. From ten yards, the first shot was about five inches low and to the right. Successive shots and scope adjustments walked the bullets closer to the bull's-eye. After about nine shots, the rifle was still hitting one and a half inches low and slightly to the right. That was acceptable at the range we were shooting. With the scope mounted on top of the rifle, one to one and a half inches low at ten yards should be nearly dead-on at eighty to a hundred yards.

I backed up to Jerry's truck for one last shot. The target was about fifty yards out. I pulled the trigger and the primer fired. Repeated shots had clogged the nipple and it was almost a full second before the black powder discharged. Jerry and I inspected the target. The sabot had struck level with the bull's-eye and about two inches left. Although I wasn't entirely comfortable with the sighting in, the rifle needed cleaning before any more shots could be taken, and there were only ten loads remaining for Mike and I to hunt with.

Jerry cooked up some smoked sausage while I cleaned Mike's rifle. Having had less than three hours of sleep the night before, I faded quickly after lunch. Jerry pointed to the back of the trailer, and I crashed on a twin bed, waking to my cell phone a couple of hours later. Mike would be joining us soon.

Mike pulled in and parked, stepping out in full investigator regalia—shirt and tie, pistol, and badge. He is a special agent in charge of the southeastern region of the U.S. Department of Housing and Urban Development. After introductions and a few minutes for Mike to change his clothes, it was time to head back to the stands.

Jerry drove us through the gate onto his lease at 3:45 p.m. A quarter mile back, a dead snake lay in the road. Jerry ran over it again, just to make sure he added to the dead snake tally. He told us, "The last time I was up here we killed a rattlesnake crossing the road." In this part of Florida, diamondbacks are probably the most common rattlesnake, but there are other species. I asked, "Was it a timber rattler or a diamondback?" Jerry's herpetological skills were pretty limited. "I don't know. It was a snake so I killed it."

It was a long drive back to our stands. Jerry explained that he supplemented his meager deputy's income by transporting mental patients on his off days. Come to think of it, this *was* one of Jerry's "off days," and he was driving Mike and me back into the woods. Hmmmmm.

Because Mike and Jerry were both in law enforcement, the conversation moved to drugs and cop stuff. One of Jerry's relatives had found a more lucrative calling. "My uncle just got busted the second time for cooking and selling meth. He was out on probation, awaiting trial for his first arrest. This time, they won't let him back out, and he'll be going away for a long time."

Jerry dropped Mike off at the stand I'd hunted in the morning, while I got the stand Jerry had hunted that morning. The surrounding vegetation was composed of the same species present at my earlier stand. The groundcover was an occasional patch of broomsage and bracken fern: nothing for wildlife to eat there. The midstory was choked with waxy leaf shrubs, primarily holly species like gallberry and tall gallberry. There was also lots of titi and wax myrtle, all laced through with catbrier. The overstory was slash pine.

Hogs are frequently cited as destructive forces when introduced into fragile intact ecosystems. For instance, in a pitcher plant bog, their rooting behavior can wreak havoc. In this forest, however, their presence was relatively benign. The damage had already been done by two or three rotations of high-density, fire-excluded plantation forestry. The forest floor was rooted all around me, but there were no fragile endemic plants and animals left to remove. The pigs were just turning over pine straw.

This ecosystem had been destroyed by shortsighted foresters. Pacing trees, I put the spacing at ten feet between rows and six feet in the row, or 726 slash pines per acre. When trees are planted that closely, they rapidly achieve "crown closure"—their branches and needles cast enough shade on the forest floor that most herbaceous species cannot prosper or even survive.

Secondly, the land managers were not using prescribed fire. Periodic fires remove pine needles that accumulate on the forest floor, choking out the herbaceous layer. Frequent fire could potentially add dozens of species to the herbaceous layer, and if fire was combined with thinning the overstory, the foresters could manage for timber, wildlife, and aesthetics. Apparently, the decision makers on this property were indifferent to every forest value except volume production.

This is the type of forest management that nearly wiped out the native longleaf pine ecosystem of the southeastern states. It is a type of forestry that put dozens of species on the threatened and endangered list. Would forestry, my profession, ever redeem itself? E. O. Wilson describes this exact scenario in a chapter from *Naturalist* entitled "Biodiversity, Biophilia": "[T]he loss of genetic and species diversity by the destruction of natural habitats. This is the folly our descendents are least likely to forgive us."

The afternoon was a bust. Pigs were neither seen nor heard from my stand.

Mike's luck wasn't much better. Pigs came in on Mike shortly after the feeder went off. Resting the black-powder rifle on the stand, he squeezed the trigger, firing the rifle. All the pigs ran off. Mike got down and checked where they had been standing but found no sign of a hit pig. Mike's a pretty good shot. Either I screwed up the sighting in, or the scope wasn't holding.

On Saturday morning, Jerry dropped me off at the back of the lease. I was impressed when the sun came up, illuminating the ground beneath the feeder. The pigs had moved so much sand that the roots of the slash pine were exposed four inches above the soil surface. Unfortunately, when the feeder went off, only five to ten kernels of corn hit the ground. The feeder was clogged, and the pigs had already learned that this feeder was not spreading corn.

Mike's morning on the stand was also a bust.

The day before, Jerry had pulled over at one of his stands after our morning hunt. He scattered corn along the road and over the trail to the feeder. The pigs responded quickly; they had rooted up everything in the area by the time we returned that afternoon. The stand looked fantastic, but Jerry dampened my enthusiasm. "We haven't killed a pig off this stand in three years. We've killed some deer here, but the pigs are mostly nocturnal." Nevertheless, there wasn't any corn on the ground. This indicated that the pigs had visited the site and cleaned up the corn during daylight hours.

Saturday afternoon rolled around and Jerry dropped me off at the stand where they hadn't killed a pig in three years. He carried Mike to the back of the lease. They had another twenty to thirty minutes of driving before reaching the back stand.

Over lunch, Mike and I had picked up three one-gallon bags, each about half full of live oak and water oak acorns. When I scattered the acorns in a line to the right of the feeder, the nuts covered an area with a clear line of fire from my stand.

I climbed my ladder stand and took a seat, making myself comfortable before opening the book *Looking for Longleaf* by Lawrence Early. Time passed quickly. The book was an interesting read. Corn-fattened gray squirrels provided some early entertainment. By 6:30 it was getting darker. The witching hour was upon us.

As the temperature dropped, I added another flannel shirt and sprayed DEET on my hands, rubbing the repellent on the exposed skin of my hands, face, neck, and forehead. I hadn't used DEET the afternoon before and had paid the price with dozens of bites.

My rifle sights were still visible at 7:00 p.m., but there was little time remaining. At 7:06, a pig squealed to my right rear. I thought, "This is going to happen!" Less than a minute later, a pig squealed to my right front. How many groups of pigs were out there? The pigs had made their presence known, but they weren't coming to the feeder.

The sun went down, but the pigs stayed in the brush. This last afternoon hunt was another bust, but at least I'd heard some pigs.

Although Jerry's family hadn't killed a pig off the stand for three years, I believed it was due, and I asked Jerry to drop me off there for our last hunt on Sunday morning. Just before dawn, following the trail in, I walked out to shine the ground beneath the feeder. All the corn was gone, as were the acorns that I had scattered the afternoon before.

As I reached the ladder stand, a pig snorted in the brush to the left of the feeder. A herd of pigs walked into the feeder, snorting and grunting. The pigs were only twenty yards away but invisible in the darkness. After a few minutes they went back into the brush and I climbed the ladder stand.

It was nearly an hour before the sun came up, but the pigs did not return. The feeder went off, but no pigs showed. Counting mornings and afternoons separately, I now had seven consecutive fruitless Florida hunts under my belt.

On our way out, Jerry stopped to talk to another hunter emerging from the woods. Jerry asked him, "Did you do any good?"

The hunter answered, "No, I didn't see anything and I haven't killed a pig since Thursday. But I did have a four-hundred-pound Yogi [black bear] about ten yards away. A couple of more steps and I would have plugged him!"

Jerry didn't need the threat of imminent harm to shoot a black bear. He told us, "If I see him, I have something for him. He's torn up my feeders one too many times." Jerry had explained earlier that two or three bears were wreaking havoc on the many feeders scattered throughout the woods, and that his patience was about worn out with this threatened subspecies. The black bears had become dependent on the corn, and the bears wanted more than the pound or two distributed twice a day. Jerry told us, "We called Fish and Game [the state wildlife agency] and asked them if they could move the bears, but they said no."

I asked Jerry, "Are some feeders more or less bear proof?"

Apparently so: "Yes, but they probably cost a good $100 more than our typical feeder."

How many feeders are currently operating across Florida? Thousands? Tens of thousands? What does this mean for bear populations across the state? How many bears become dependent upon this supplemental feed? How many bears are shot by disgruntled hunters?

My opinion of baiting had been neutral to negative on deer, and positive when it came to feral hogs. This was an argument against baiting that I had not previously considered. Later, a biologist friend of mine told me that baiting was actually "a boon for bears in Lower Alabama." Although hunting over bait is illegal in Alabama, it is a common practice, and another biologist attributed recent increases in Alabama bear populations to deer hunters putting out bait and refraining from shooting bears that raid their corn piles. This same biologist changed his mind about the benefits of baiting in Alabama when several carcasses of bears were found, shot over illegal baiting stations.

From an ecological viewpoint, this Florida property was a disaster, largely because of abysmal forestry practices. Beyond that, when a bit of the native fauna emerged, it was run over or beat to death with a stick. The one threatened and endangered contingent remaining on the property, the Florida black bear, was soon to become a little bit rarer.

There was one minor league success story. Alligators inhabited the ditches and ponds scattered across the property, and feral hogs probably provided a relatively steady source of protein for this formerly threatened reptile.

Back in Alabama, I read an e-mail from the obviously excited Hard-Luck Jimmy (see chapter 6). Jimmy had been hunting feral hogs on the Okmulgee WMA in west Alabama. Owing to the season and regulations, he was carrying a lever-action .22 LR rifle and a twenty-gauge pump shotgun with #4 shot. Both of these firearms are pretty small for feral hogs. After he had located a large group of pigs, Jimmy stalked in close and shot a large sow with his .22 LR before charging in with both guns blazing. He hit four piglets, killing three. One wounded piglet and the sow escaped, along with the rest of the herd.

There are few, if any, animals more damaging to our native herpetofauna (amphibians and reptiles) than are wild hogs. Since Jimmy is a herpetologist, he is justified in his animosity toward feral pigs. Thus, Jimmy didn't feel the slightest bit guilty about wounding two wild pigs that subsequently escaped. Many, if not most, biologists would agree with Jimmy's sentiment that "the only good pig is a dead pig."

While my streak of bad luck in Florida was holding strong, Jimmy had finally broken his eons-long dry streak, finally killing his first feral pigs or, to be more precise, piglets. I guess there was some justice in that.

13 OLD GROWTH

We came to break the bad.
We came to cheer the sad.
We came to leave behind the world a better way.
　　　　　　　—AVETT BROTHERS, "Salvation Song," 2004

White oak (*Quercus alba*): Although most hunters' tree identification skills range from weak to nonexistent, they can almost certainly identify a white oak. Although many foresters in the Southeast have little concern for anything that is not a pine tree, they will go out of their way to leave a white oak during a timber harvest. White oaks are beautiful, long-lived, graceful oaks that produce occasional heavy mast crops (acorns) that draw deer, turkey, squirrels, and all matter of wildlife. When the wood is cured, it is so hard that nails cannot be driven into the dry lumber.

Mississippi had fallen through and Florida was a bust . . . again. Hopefully, things would turn around in Missouri and Arkansas. My sister had a game camera set up on the family farm, and she'd gotten pictures of some decent bucks. Since it is a danged long drive to Missouri, it made sense to combine the trip with an Arkansas pig hunt. If time allowed, some Corps of Engineers property around Lake Wappapello, Missouri, was also worth investigating for hog sign. The year before (2006), one of Lake Wappapello's personnel gave a presentation at the First Conference on Feral Pigs in Mobile, Alabama, describing how feral hogs had become a serious problem on Corps of Engineers lands in south Missouri, so my interest was piqued.

The trip north from Pleasant Home began at 5:00 p.m. on November 8. Because I have been reseeding the home place for years, I made frequent stops along the way to pick up acorns and other tree seed: three thousand northern red oak in Tennessee, thirty pounds of sawtooth oak, red oak, and basswood in Kentucky, and ten pounds of cherrybark and black oak in Illinois.

It was 8:45 p.m. on the 9th when I finally turned off Highway D onto the farm property in Chariton County, Missouri. After almost twenty-eight hours of driving and nut harvesting, my middle-aged body was saying, "Please don't do this anymore."

But after a decent night's sleep, I was up early, settling into the tree stand by 5:55. Comet Holmes was visible in the night's sky.

The morning hunt didn't produce much so I wandered out to check my trees. A profound depression settled over me as I surveyed plantings from the last three years. Mom had hired a couple of people to mow between the rows of planted trees. The rows were laid out perfectly straight and exactly twelve feet apart. In the first three fields I examined, the tractor operator had cut down thousands, perhaps tens of thousands, of two-year-old trees. Sometimes, large blocks of the field were mowed clean. In these areas, there were no unmowed strips and every single sapling had been cut off.

Such is the nature of tree planting. It's basically a long-term gamble. In this case, hundreds of hours and thousands of dollars invested establishing these plantations were devastated by an uncaring or ignorant tractor operator.

A neighbor pulled into the field with his son and a friend while I was still tallying the carnage. They had three deer in the back of their truck: two does and an illegal six-point buck. Rudy (I've changed his name here) told his friend, "Don't worry about Mark. He's done his share of poaching."

Rudy was right. I was a bit of an outlaw as a young teenager. But experience, knowledge, age, discretion, and a conscience helped clean up my act. Over the last couple of decades, my concerted effort to help the environment and many wildlife populations has, I hope, outweighed my youthful indiscretions.

I addressed all of them. "No, I don't care what you kill, but I wouldn't drive around too long with that buck in the back of your truck."

Rudy explained his rationale for shooting the six-point buck. "We're finally starting to get some good bucks around here because we've been thinning out these 'scrub bucks.'"

Rudy's reasoning was not uncommon. Many hunters lack a basic grasp of biology and how deer develop. Other hunters have told me, "I shoot every spike I see because I don't want them passing on their genes."

Rudy's little six-point was either a big one-and-a-half-year-old or a small to average two-and-a-half-year-old. If it had lived another year, it probably would have sported a decent eight- to ten-point rack. Had it survived another two years, it may have been worthy of mounting and hanging on the wall.

Mike Powell, my best friend, who had accompanied me on the Texas pig hunt, also made it up for Missouri's deer season. He called on opening day from his family's home place a couple miles down the road. "Did you do any good?"

I hadn't. "One came by too early for me to tell what it was. How about you?"

Mike's voice had a satisfied ring to it. "Come on over. We got a couple to show you."

Mike had killed a nice eleven-point buck. Slim, Mike's older half brother, had taken a small "basket" eight-point with his bow. And Slim's younger sister, Rachel, had killed a decent eight-point.

I helped load the bucks into the back of a truck. Slim hauled the three deer to a neighbor's slaughtering shed where six of us, two on each deer, went to work caping the bucks. They'd work up the carcasses later.

While Mike and I were caping out his deer, the knife slipped and sliced my left thumb. I held the thumb against my left thigh to stem the bleeding. "Did you cut yourself?" Mike asked.

I nodded, not wanting to admit my gaffe out loud, but the cat was already out of the bag.

Slim gave his opinion. "Knives are sharp."

Mike concurred. "Mark's knife is." He paused a moment, assessing my skinning ability, then pronounced, "Rookie!"

Did I mention that the "smartass gene" runs in their family?

Over the next several days, my sister, Billie, and I harvested several antlerless deer from our hills, pastures, fields, and creek bottom. The deer hunting wasn't bad, but the scenery was great. The farm has been in our family for nearly two centuries, and our hill ground has some of the last remaining old-growth white oak and post oak stands in the area.

After dark one evening, I was skinning and quartering a couple of does when a cousin pulled up. Several years back, Jerry used his bow to kill a white-tailed deer with the largest typical rack ever harvested by bow in Missouri.

When I told Jerry about my ten-state goal, he said something that surprised me. "They killed two wild hogs over in some nearby bottoms!"

I had never heard of feral hogs in this country. "What?!"

Jerry explained, "Yeah, some guys brought a pair of wild pigs up from somewhere down south. They put them in a pen and then claimed that the pair 'escaped.' A farmer saw the pigs out in his fields and shot them a few days later." It wasn't going to take long for pigs to become established in all fifty states if this type of incident repeated itself on a regular basis.

After a week of hunting, I'd taken a few antlerless deer and missed a good opportunity for a large, mature buck. This, combined with the tree-mowing massacre, had caused my mood to sink considerably since I'd arrived in Missouri. It was time to try my luck in Arkansas.

14 OZARKS

I turned with growing concentration to Nature as a sanctuary and a realm of boundless adventure; the fewer people in it, the better. Wilderness became a dream of privacy, safety, control, and freedom. Its essence is captured for me by its Latin name, solitudo.

—E. O. WILSON, *Naturalist,* 1994

Ozarks: An eroded plateau region comprising large parts of Arkansas and south Missouri. Ozarkian topography is big hills or small mountains, generally covered in the oak/hickory forest type. The region is known for its fine wines, haute cuisine, and attractive cousins. Major industries and occupations of the past were hunting and fishing for sustenance, charcoal, and shine. These have largely been replaced by hunting and fishing for sport, cannabis, meth, and Boer goats.

I left the farm at 8:00 a.m. on November 15, heading south to Arkansas for another eBay hog hunt. The day before, Mark Martin of Wrangler Up Outfitters had told me to check in by 2:00 p.m.

After missing the required turnoff a couple of times, I finally pulled up to the hunting lodge at 2:20. Mark introduced himself and invited me to sit at the kitchen table to discuss the particulars of the hunt and sign a release form.

Of the states I've hunted, Arkansas has the loosest regulations regarding pig hunting. No hunting license is required to shoot or catch pigs. Baiting is okay. Hunting at night is okay.

Mark had already told me there wasn't much chance of seeing pigs while the sun was up. I asked him now, "What do you think my odds are of seeing some pigs tonight?"

He answered, "The odds are pretty good. There are two groups of pigs working the stand you'll be hunting."

Was this going to be a repeat of my Rio Bravo endurance hunt in Texas? "What time are the pigs coming through?"

Mark said, "There is one group coming in right after dark and another group coming in about midnight to 1:00 in the morning. You'll be hunting in a two-person ladder stand with a blanket around it. If the pigs come in and you get a shot, wait at least forty-five minutes before you get down. Often, if you don't make any additional noise, they'll circle out and come back in about forty-five minutes. They don't care if a dead pig is lying next to the corn."

Mark wished me luck, and his son Justin brought a four-wheeler around for me. I strapped down my two-gun hard case with the black-powder rifle and the 7 mm Remington Magnum inside. The temperature was in the low fifties. It was going to get pretty cool when the sun went down, so several extra layers of clothing went on the four-wheeler. Since there hadn't been time for lunch on the way down, I filled the front basket of the four-wheeler with food and drink: two cheeses, some elk summer sausage, and two cans of carbonated beverages picked up just south of Branson.

With the four-wheeler loaded, Justin and I left the lodge at 3:00 p.m., stopping to pick up a bag of corn on the way to the hunting site. As we left a pasture and entered the timber, a covey of quail scattered ahead—a good sign. As we entered another small pasture, a large doe and four fawns ran out the other side. Justin pointed at them. "Have you ever seen a doe with four fawns?"

"I've heard of does with triplets, but I've not seen nor heard of four at a time," I answered.

Justin explained, "A couple of years ago this same doe had four fawns. This makes the third year in a row she's produced quadruplets."

That was some amazing breeding capacity.

We entered the timber again. A nice eight-point buck ran a short way and stopped. Justin pulled up, asking, "How big is that deer?" It was deer season in

Arkansas, and Mark had explained back at the lodge that their bucks needed to score at least 120 points for harvest on this property.

Justin was asking the wrong person. "It looks pretty nice but I am not a good judge of how many points it would score."

Near the end of the trail, three more deer ran off as we stopped on top of a hill covered with oaks and hickory trees. This place was filled with wildlife!

Justin scattered a bag of corn while I unloaded and carried my gear to the base of the two-person ladder stand. The baited area was surrounded by two strands of barbed wire to keep cattle from reaching and eating the corn.

With the area baited and my gear on-site, Justin asked, "Can you find your way back out of the woods?"

Picturing the road in my mind, I tried to remember all the twists, turns, and gates. "I can make it out."

Justin drove back down the trail as I carried my gear up the ladder, settling in by 3:30 p.m. It was lunchtime for all of God's critters. I downed my sausage, cheese, and carbonated beverages while wildlife gathered at the corn. In no time, there were six squirrels, one mourning dove, and a woodpecker consuming the bait.

At 4:40, two does and a yearling ran past in the woods, followed by a larger deer farther back, probably a buck. Deer wandered around behind my stand until dark, occasionally snorting and looking down the hill. What did they see? A bear, another hunter, a revenuer?

At 5:30, it was too dark to see the iron sights on my muzzleloader. Hooking the red light to its battery, I practiced switching it on and pointing the light with my left hand while swiveling and aiming the black-powder rifle on the ladder stand's rail with my right hand. The skies were exceptionally clear and the comet was still visible. The temperature quickly declined to the high thirties, with more room to drop.

At 5:46, a pig squealed to my right. This was the first sign of pigs. Two minutes later, there was another squeal about a hundred yards out, still to the right. They were nearing rapidly. Cocking the .50 caliber, I oriented my body to the right. The pigs were close enough that their progress was marked by the rustling of dry oak leaves. Would they go straight to the corn? Now the rustling sounded in a line, with several yards between the lead and the trailing hog. If they got any closer, the pigs might hear my heart thumping. But they angled to the rear, passing from hearing without stopping.

My fingers were getting numb as I uncocked the rifle and settled back. I turned the collar up around my neck and pulled the stocking cap over my ears. Next, I donned gloves and put my hands back in my coat pockets. It was time to conserve as much body heat as possible.

Looking up at the star-filled sky, I saw one star fall away to the right. An inner peace settled over me, dispelling the funk that had followed me all the way down from Missouri.

A few years back, I was hardcore into coon hunting, going three or four nights a week for months on end. It was fun to take people along on those coon hunts, but it was the solo hunts that brought true peace of mind. Many times, my hair stood on end when old Babe, my best bluetick hound, struck a trail or voiced a long tree cry just before she started a chopped bark, announcing a treed coon.

The solo out-of-doors experience is even more intense underwater. Several times I've solo spearfished at night in the Gulf of Mexico. The last couple of trips, I descended sixty to a hundred feet below the surface. Once on the bottom, I rested on the seafloor, or wrapped my legs around a rail on a shipwreck, listening to my breath through the regulator, letting the current rock me back and forth while phosphorescent plankton danced in the inky blackness.

These are the moments when the body relaxes and the rest of the world goes away. It may be similar to what a person would feel floating in space.

A few minutes passed, and another shooting star passed behind the oak limbs to my left. Half an hour later, yet another meteor lit up the sky. If the pigs came back, they were going to die.

I watched the sky for falling stars and listened to animals walk though the woods. Time passed quickly despite the frigid temperature.

From my right, there came the steady *crunch, crunch, crunch* of a large animal walking toward me. Removing my gloves and orienting on the sound, I switched on the spotlight, freezing a large doe in the red beam. I turned the light off and the doe resumed walking a straight, steady line, with no alarm snort.

Several minutes passed, and once again there was rustling in the leaves behind my stand. Was it deer or pigs? Soon enough, I recognized the rapid advance, pause, advance, pause characteristic of small- to medium-sized pigs. For fifteen minutes, the pigs rustled the leaves behind the stand. Then one grunted, confirming my preliminary identification.

When it sounded like the nearest animal was about forty yards away, I aimed the red light to my right and illuminated the area. The rustling stopped as a pig froze, still invisible beneath the tree limbs. This was followed by the patter of running hooves a short distance away. I turned the light off. There had not been an alarm snort, but it was worrisome that the pig had turned around and left shortly after the light was pointed in its direction.

In a few minutes, the rustling resumed as the pigs slowly moved toward the baited area on the crest of the hill. This time I resisted the temptation to activate the light. The pigs worked beneath the surrounding canopy before moving back out of hearing.

Another thirty minutes passed and the pigs circled back again. At least one pig was directly in front of me. Surely they would go to the corn any minute. But they moved off again.

Enough was enough. The next time a pig walked in front of my stand I was taking a shot.

The pigs came back in a fourth time, but not close enough. The herd turned around and moved off the hill. It was 8:00 p.m. and my increasingly frozen butt had been sitting quietly for several hours in sub-thirty-degree weather.

The pigs started back a fifth time. My pulse quickened as one approached to my right. It was time to make a move. The pig was in front of me. I had the .50-caliber black-powder rifle resting on a padded rail, pointing toward the noise. I switched on the light with my left hand, immediately finding a small black pig twenty-five yards away. The rifle was already cocked, so I targeted the pig's front shoulder as it took two steps and froze broadside. *Kapow!* Flames shot out the barrel and a cloud of smoke obscured my view. There was rustling on the other side of the smoke. Was it running away? When the smoke cleared, I saw that a pig was lying on the ground. The rustling was its final reflexive kicks. I remained still and listened while breathing a deep sigh of relief.

The other pigs were out of sight, but not out of earshot. They moved off without an alarm snort. This was a group of little ones without an adult escort, and they weren't aware that one of their littermates had just departed this world.

When the pigs were out of hearing range, it was five minutes before my next move. Mark had instructed me to wait forty-five minutes, but my extremities were numb and movement was necessary to get the blood flowing. I set the black-powder rifle to the side, attached the spotlight to the 7 Mag, and climbed down the ladder to examine my kill. The sabot had struck a couple of inches high, but it was a solid hit to the vitals. Good enough. It was 8:30 p.m.

I heard rustling in the leaves downhill. Mark was right about the pigs coming back. Easing forward into the timber, I searched for a spot with better visibility. It seemed like the pigs were more comfortable on the side of the hill than on the top of the hill where the corn was scattered. Each time the pigs rustled the leaves, I took two or three steps forward. When the pigs were silent, I held still. Visibility was better from the ground, beneath the midstory of oak and hickory branches that had blocked the view from the elevated stand.

The rustling continued, but the pigs were still out of sight. Every few minutes, I flicked the light on, scanning the woods for eyes, finding nothing. Eventually, the rustling drew closer, down the hill to my front and right. There was sound from at least two directions. The pig to the front was closest. Nearly an hour had passed since I had shot the first pig, and my toes were in the early stages of frostbite. Having frozen two of my toes as a youngster, I knew these appendages were the quickest to go numb.

The pig to the front was getting pretty close. Flicking on the light, I saw an eye in the brush, but the shot was obstructed by branches. Quickly turning off the light, I waited until the pig moved again before switching the light back on. Another small black pig walked out and turned broadside, facing left. The crosshairs settled on the vitals. *Powww!* There was a flash, but no cloud of smoke. The pig flipped over and lay still.

No need to wait for the 1:00 a.m. pig traffic. There were two pigs in the bag by 9:30 p.m.!

15   A LONG WALK

I would be sad
Because I got left by a girl that I adore.
I would be sad
For all the love I had before.

—Avett Brothers, "I Would Be Sad," 2007

Red oak (*Quercus spp.*): Oak timber in the United States is marketed as "red oak" or "white oak." Although there is considerable variation among the dozens of North American oak species, all of them, once sawn, will be sold in one of these two categories. Red oak is generally more attractive and valuable than white oak lumber. As an undergraduate forestry student in the late 1980s, I saw mixed white and red oak sawtimber sold off the Mark Twain National Forest in south Missouri for as little as $60–$70 per thousand board feet. That equates to $.06 or $.07 a board foot. Twenty years later, I visited a forester selling veneer grade logs from north Missouri for $6–$7 a board foot, or one hundred times the price. A good forester will act as a middleman, helping the landowner obtain maximum value for timber. A typical logger, unsupervised, will ensure that the landowner gets the absolute minimum.

The sun was shining through the windshield, waking me. I had been so exhausted from the previous night's hunt in Arkansas that I had just barely made it into Missouri before taking the first exit off the highway. I had parked my truck on the shoulder of an onramp, reclined the seat, and fallen asleep with the engine running to provide some heat in the subfreezing temperature.

Now, at about 7:00 a.m., having secured a few hours of sleep, I scraped the cobwebs from my eyes, sat up, and got back on the interstate, driving to the first exit that promised coffee. It would take another three to four hours of driving to reach the day's destination—Army Corps of Engineers property surrounding Lake Wappapello in south Missouri.

During my drive across south Missouri, I listened to a couple of CDs by the Avett Brothers. While listening to NPR a few months earlier, I had been struck by a song titled "I Would Be Sad" and I sought out the CD—*Emotionalism*. In short order, I also bought *The Gleam* and *Mignonette*. Their music formed a soundtrack to my travels during the Year or the Pig.

My introduction to Lake Wappapello had been about sixteen years earlier when I was a forestry student at the University of Missouri, Columbia, during summer camp. During the day, I was occupied with forestry courses. At night, I fished the rapids beneath the Lake Wappapello dam.

There were no feral hogs around Lake Wappapello in the 1980s. According to John J. Mayer and I. Lehr Brisbin Jr.'s 1991 book, *Wild Pigs in the United States: Their History, Comparative Morphology, and Current Status,* there had been no feral pigs in the entire state of Missouri at that time. The situation has changed. Feral hogs either have moved up from Arkansas, or they have been released by hunters on Corps property and/or the bordering Mark Twain National Forest. At the 2006 Mobile, Alabama, pig conference, an Army Corps of Engineers employee gave a presentation on the organization's efforts to control feral hogs on Lake Wappapello. Hunters were being encouraged to kill pigs all year long and a volunteer trapper had reportedly removed several dozen pigs over the previous year, keeping the population somewhat in check.

A few weeks before my trip to Missouri and Arkansas, I had called the Corps office for Lake Wappapello. A helpful employee sent me a map of its holdings with highlighted areas showing where hogs had been shot, trapped, or spotted. If that map was accurate, the highest concentration of pigs was south of the lake, where the map showed a section of the Corps property separated from neighboring private property by a dirt road.

I stopped beside an old cemetery, where a couple of deer hunters were taking a midafternoon break. I showed them the map, seeking to confirm my location. They told me, "You're where you think you are, but we've been hunting here for twenty years and have never seen a pig in this part of the forest."

Oops! It looked like the pigs weren't quite as populous as the presenter had made out at the Mobile conference.

The hunters invited me to join them for lunch and a beer, which I gladly accepted. Still studying my map, one of the pair pointed to a spot a little farther east and north, where he had seen a hog trap and what looked like fresh rooting.

I told them about my quest, describing my Arkansas hunt that had just ended a few hours earlier. After hearing my story, they extended an invitation to an evening meal with all their hunting buddies. They even offered to let me sleep on the couch of their camper.

After the three of us ate lunch, one of the pair escorted me to their hunting camp, where I quartered the two black Arkansas pigs, giving him three front shoulders for the evening barbeque.

With the pigs dismembered and iced down, I turned my thoughts elsewhere. It was only a few miles to the place where the pig trap was supposed to be located. I parked on the side of a gravel road and walked a trail into the forest. A few miles in, the trail crossed a creek near a series of oxbows. The pig trap was on the other side of the creek. Examining the surrounding fields, I saw a fair amount of rooting, but not a single fresh hog track since the last rain three days before.

I worked out the creek bottoms and sloughs bordering the lake. There was old rooting but no fresh sign. After a few hours, I went back to the truck and drove a couple of miles, to another highlighted area with a large food plot planted in soybeans. I saw only a scattering of fresh deer tracks and old hog sign in the miles I covered before dark.

As the dusk gathered, I took a seat on the forest floor beneath a solid canopy of mature white and red oak timber. Of the red oaks, the majority appeared to be black oak, northern red oak, and scarlet oak. The timber was open enough that I could see a couple of hundred yards downhill. Gray squirrels and orange fox squirrels foraged for acorns on the forest floor. As dark approached, they climbed the trees, scampered from limb to limb, and disappeared down holes in hollow trees for their night's lodging. I exited the woods well after the sun had set. Back at the parking area, two deer hunters told me they had heard people talk of pigs, but neither of them had seen a feral hog on Corps property.

It was dark, and I was exhausted and in no mood to stay up half the night telling pig-hunting stories. Under normal circumstances, it would have been nice to hang out with the guys I'd met earlier in the day. And a free couch would have been appreciated, but an undisturbed night's rest was what I really needed. I secured a hotel room in a nearby town, bedded down early, and didn't get up until ten hours later.

The hunt commenced where it had left off. After driving back to Wappapello, I stopped at every highlighted area, working my way around the lake. After lunch in the field, I scouted a very large food plot on the northeast edge of the lake. Several dozen acres of soybeans and corn had not been harvested, and most of the grain was still on the stalks! The food plots were in a low bottom area, bisected and bordered by thick brushy streams that fed into Lake Wappapello. If there were pigs anywhere within several miles, they would be working these food plots.

I parked the truck and uncased the 7 Mag, circling around the fields, watching for sign in the muddy soil. Five or fewer deer had entered and exited the fields in the four days since it had rained. As for pigs, there were no tracks, rooting, wallows, or rubs—fresh or old. The entire northern edge of the lake was devoid of hog sign. The search continued southward along the east edge of the lake, where I parked my truck and entered the woods two or three more times before dark.

With the sun going down, it was time to admit defeat. Two days of searching and about twenty miles of walking had failed to turn up a single hog track less than three days old. If there were still pigs in the neighborhood, they had moved somewhere off Corps of Engineers property to the Mark Twain National Forest or surrounding private property.

Missouri had delivered some deer, but the Show Me State would have to "show me" its pigs at some later date.

16 FOOD PLOT

We have just one word for it: "fire," but fire can mean a billion things, and in the hands of a knowledgeable forester, it can be a delicate and precise tool.

—BAILEY WHITE, *Quite a Year for Plums*, 1998

Broomsedge (*Andropogon virginicus*): Portions of the native longleaf range are identified by the dominant grass component of its understory. Southeast Alabama is known as the "Wiregrass," even though ninety-nine out of one hundred residents of the Wiregrass would not recognize the long-extirpated bunchgrass that once covered this area. Wiregrass (*Aristida stricta* and *A. beyrichiana*) covers much of the Carolinas, Georgia, Florida, and Alabama. But the northern portions of Alabama, Georgia, and the rest of the longleaf range—Texas, Mississippi, Louisiana, and Virginia—were dominated by bluestems. Bluestems are warm-season bunchgrasses that provide vital cover for quail and other wildlife but, more important, they provide fuels for prescribed fire. When wiregrass and/or the hardier bluestems are destroyed through agricultural practices or intensive forestry site preparation, broomsedge is one of the few native bluestems that readily recolonizes these ruderal sites. In the fall and early winter, broomsedge provides an attractive palette from which young rocket-stage longleaf emerge like bright beacons of green. These longleaf saplings are ready to burn, and a backing fire will just creep through a thick stand of broomsedge, but if the wind switches, the fire moves fast and hot, so that a forty-acre burn scheduled for several hours is done in a matter of a few minutes. In these cases, it is recommended that members of the burn crew be up-to-date on their CPR skills, as the burn boss may require them.

I got up at 4:50 a.m., and that was a little late. It was 6:03 by the time I climbed the ladder stand over the Sheep Field at the Dixon Center in my home state of Alabama.

Auburn University was on Thanksgiving break. On our last day at work, Punky, one of the university forestry technicians, told me a contractor had seen a big black pig in the Sheep Field. According to Punky, the guy had said, "It was so big that I thought it was a bear."

Since my return from the Arkansas and Missouri hunts, I had seen plenty of fresh tracks and rooting in the Sheep Field. The woods surrounding this field had already produced three pigs for me, but the peanuts were still drawing them in.

Now that it was deer season, this was a combination hunt. Fair game included all pigs, does, and mature bucks with at least four points on one side and a fifteen-inch inside spread.

Shortly after taking a seat on the ladder stand, I watched a large flock of kill-deer circle the field, bank hard, flash their white bellies, and sing *Keedee, Keedee!* By 7:00 a.m., dozens, then hundreds, perhaps thousands of redwing blackbirds and robins flocked to the peanut field. The robins also fed heavily on red yaupon (a type of holly) fruits along the field edge. A flock of turkeys walked into the peanut field. There were eleven hens of varying sizes. Two of the hens had beards. While this may be uncommon in some areas, a sizable percentage of hens on the Dixon Center sport beards. Mourning doves and flickers joined the cacophony. Although it was now misting rain, it was a beautiful morning to be in the woods, and I counted myself lucky for the experience.

No pigs showed that morning, and I returned in the afternoon to hunt a nearby slash pine plantation that pigs and deer transit on their way to the peanut field and a nearby food plot.

My climber was mounted to a tall longleaf on the edge of a slash pine plantation of three- to four-year-old trees. The climber provided a good view of a fire lane through the middle of the plantation. The fire lane had been heavily rooted earlier in the fall. A cold front was coming in and the wind was ripping. Despite the abundance of recent deer sign and slightly older pig sign, no animals appeared in the three hours before dark.

A couple of days later, I moved the climber to another spot about a quarter of a mile away. As I walked the climber up the tree and settled into the seat, a six-point buck and another deer jumped from the tall broomsedge and plume grass to my front. The two deer had been bedded down. They were able to hold still for the fifteen minutes it had taken me to carry the climber in, attach it, and work it up the tree.

The sun was out and the wind had died. Forty-five minutes into the hunt, two deer bounded toward me through open longleaf. I picked up the lead deer in my scope. It was a small fawn, perhaps forty to fifty pounds—too small to shoot on the Dixon Center.

Maybe the second deer was a tasty doe? No, it was a twin to the other fawn. I lowered my rifle and the pair walked beneath me. The second fawn's spots were barely visible. These two were recent orphans. The hunters on the Dixon Center had already harvested seventeen does this season and that left plenty of unescorted fawns in the woods.

It was the same cycle every year. Most of the mature does on the Center produce two fawns, and many of these does are harvested each season. Additional does emigrate from surrounding properties where landowners do not focus so intensely on controlling their deer population. In a typical season, seventy to ninety deer are harvested on six thousand acres, and about two-thirds are mature does. Yet, the overall population remains steady.

The following afternoon, I worked in our tree nursery until almost 2:45 p.m. before breaking away to do some hunting. Three hunters had signed in to blocks adjacent to my climber, so I relocated to a ladder stand overlooking a small food plot, about half a mile east on Reed Break Road.

It was 3:15 p.m. when I took a seat on the stand. The sky was overcast, the wind was light, and the temperature was pleasant. I had finished Larry Earley's book *Looking for Longleaf,* and now I was reading *Forever Green* by Mr. Chuck Leavell, a tree farmer and keyboardist for the Rolling Stones. I'd met Mr. Leavell a few years back at a Tree Farm meeting on his property. He talked about putting longleaf back on his property, and I followed up with a short lecture on the technical aspects of artificial regeneration and prescribed fire in young longleaf. (Many people do not realize that longleaf seedlings can be burned as early as one year post-planting.) Our photo was taken together and used in several articles that my wife proudly forwarded to many of her friends.

Reading books in tree stands or shooting houses probably leads to some missed animals, but it beats the heck out of watching a static food plot for two or three hours. It's thoroughly enjoyable: sitting, reading, and looking over a food plot or stand of timber after every page. When wildlife walks, runs, or flies into view, the experience is that much better.

Several pages and thirty to forty minutes later, I looked over my right shoulder and spotted a deer in a field road behind me, about 120 yards out. I picked up my rifle and pivoted, quickly identifying the deer as a doe just before it slipped into some brush and disappeared. The same location had produced a mature doe the year before. That doe had two fawns at the time, and this deer could be one of those fawns from 2006.

After I'd stood and watched the area for about ten minutes, it appeared that the doe had given me the slip. Tall broomsedge covered everything on the far side of the road, concealing her presence or passage. I glanced over my right shoulder and froze in place. A deer had snuck into the food plot behind me! Was a reversal of position possible without alerting it? Was it another doe or an immature buck? After a slow-motion turnaround, I retook my seat and raised the 7.

Now there were two deer! The lead deer was a little bigger than the one in back. The deer closest to the timber was clearly a fawn. The deer in front was larger and a close look revealed the elongated head of a doe. They were only fifty yards away. This shot was a "give me." I decided to shoot behind the shoulder, expecting the 7 to lay the doe down right there. *Powww!* The doe dropped its front shoulder and ran into the woods to my left with the fawn close behind. On the one hand, she was going down quick. But on the other hand, I regretted not sacrificing the paltry meat of a front shoulder and dropping the doe in its tracks.

Before I could stand up, another deer entered the plot on the left. Cycling in another round, I cranked the scope up to nine-power and looked at the deer's head. It was a small spike with antlers right at the hairline, perhaps a couple of inches long. It was a legal deer off the Dixon Center but prohibited on this property. Either way, it was not a deer I would intentionally shoot.

The spike watched from the other end of the food plot as I climbed down the ladder and stepped into the plot. Young bucks are the most foolish deer of all, predisposing spikes and fork-horns to disproportionately high harvest rates on unmanaged properties.

The doe's fawn reentered the plot. A nondiscriminating hunter could have shot a pile of deer out of this food plot.

It was about 4:40 p.m. and it was already getting noticeably darker. There was no time to wait on the deer to bleed out if I wanted to follow the blood trail without a flashlight. But the shot had felt good and the doe was almost certainly dead.

Both the fawn and the small spike allowed me to approach within bow range before running back into the timber. At the edge of the food plot, a heavy blood trail led straight to the doe. She had made it only about twenty yards into the trees before expiring. Standing over the doe, I noticed an unusual growth over its left eye. Interesting! I grabbed the doe by a hind leg. There was something wrong with its hooves, too! Spreading its legs and examining the belly, I saw that there was another, much larger warty-looking growth there. This deer had problems.

Back at the Dixon Center, I took photos of the growths and hooves to our director, Joel Martin. Both Joel and his wife, Carmen, are knowledgeable biologists. They could diagnose this doe's afflictions.

In the office Monday morning, Joel told me the warts were cutaneous fibromas and the hooves were evidence of epizootic hemorrhagic disease. Joel explained, "When deer get epizootic hemorrhagic disease, they often go through a high fever that causes the hooves to slough off. In extreme cases, there is almost nothing there. They are basically walking on bone."

I questioned further, "So this deer was afflicted with this disease but survived. Would it recover completely and become asymptomatic?"

That was the case. "Yes. Actually, you want your deer to have some immunity to this disease. It is always out there, and many herds are resistant until the virus mutates and sweeps back through the population."

Joel went on to explain that neither disease was communicable to humans. The meat was fine to eat if I could just disassociate taste from appearance. Still, there was no giving this deer away! If people ever found out I was giving away diseased deer, they may never eat my food again. I'd have to eat this one myself.

17   SLASH PINE

These plants have stories to tell. Some are quiet, gentle tales of our be-
loved wildflowers. Others, like the historic yellow pines, roar like thun-
der out of the pages of our pioneer past. Through their stories, I believe
we can forge new connections with our collective past, and, on a more
personal level, with our own ancestors.

—FRED NATION, *Where the Wild Illicium Grows,* 2002

Slash pine (*Pinus elliottii*): One of four species that may be sold as
"southern yellow pine," the others being shortleaf, loblolly, and of
course, longleaf. Compared to its weedy northern neighbor loblolly,
slash pine is superior in almost every characteristic: disease, insect,
and fire resistance, wood quality, form, pinestraw, and lifespan. Compared to its immediate neighbor longleaf, slash is inferior in virtually
all of these same characteristics. And yet, slash is a vital and native
component of many Florida and Gulf Coast landscapes. In natural
fire-maintained forests of the lower Coastal Plain, longleaf dominated the uplands while slash gained the upper hand on wet soils
near drains, swamps, and flatwood sites. In south Florida, the two
trees are so similar in appearance that early explorers mistook them
for the same species.

To review my attempts at killing a pig or two in Florida: the first
two afternoon hunts in July took place near Florala, Alabama, where I may have
possibly heard one pig squeal in over seven hours on the stand. The next three

morning hunts and two afternoon hunts were the first week in November, an hour east of Tallahassee. Pigs had come within twenty yards of my stand, but only when it was too dark to see them. After seven hunts, Florida still hadn't put a pig in front of my stand during daylight hours.

I called Dan, the landowner near Florala. Dan would let me hunt for the same deal worked out previously: $25 for corn to pre-bait the stands and $50 for each pig shot. It would be a cheap deal if I ever saw a pig.

Dan was baiting the same stand I'd hunted in July. Plus he had put up an automatic feeder on another part of his property. He suggested hunting the new feeder. "I went over this morning to change out the spinning unit and the ground was torn up. Some of the biggest hog tracks I've ever seen were beneath the feeder. If you don't do any good there, you are welcome to go back and hunt the other spot. I don't have other hunters coming in until next weekend."

I decided to follow Dan's advice. I took off early on a Friday afternoon, November 30, stopping by his house for directions to the new spot, a little west of the previous stand. From the edge of Dan's property it was a short walk through a slash pine plantation on what looked like old agricultural land. Terraces were evident on the recently established food plot. Entering a low shooting house, I was pleased to see a padded chair that was every bit as comfortable as it appeared.

The shooting house was on the edge of a shooting lane/food plot that had been cleared out of the fire-excluded slash pine plantation. An automatic feeder on a tripod stood a little less than a hundred yards downhill. The whole food plot had been planted to a green cover crop of rye, oats, or wheat.

Excepting wet drains, all this area would have been longleaf pine forest a hundred years ago. As in most of Florida, the longleaf in this area had been cleared decades before. Most areas have been replanted to slash pine and deprived of fire, seriously degrading the longleaf ecosystem. In the absence of fire, the herbaceous layer disappears rather quickly, replaced by a shrub layer. The soils and native species on this site were very similar to those on the Solon Dixon Center and the Conecuh National Forest. Luckily, only a small percentage of the Dixon Center had gone this long without fire.

The two big winners in this forest were yaupon and Chinese privet. The yaupon, at least, was a native species. Another big winner was Japanese climbing fern, an invasive species from Asia whose vines were tying the privet and yaupon together in an impenetrable jungle. Owing to their low, stocky forms, hogs can push trails through brush that would stop a human cold.

Was this forest the future of Florida? A forest dominated by a handful of weedy Asian species? If so, it was a horrendous deal for the Sunshine State: trading the open, beautiful, diverse, longleaf pine forest for this mess. Absent a dedicated and coordinated effort, the native ecosystem—and the wildlife that depended upon it—was the clear loser.

I settled down to wait. I was still reading Chuck Leavell's *Forever Green,* a book that reminded me why forestry is my chosen profession. It is a bit idealistic but a good read.

At 4:14 p.m., the feeder went off. It spun only for a few seconds, distributing perhaps a pound or less of corn. About 4:45, I put the book in my backpack and focused on the surroundings. A doe entered the food plot on the left and proceeded slowly and cautiously before disappearing into the brush on the other side. The deer had not stopped to graze. Had I not been watching carefully, it would have passed unseen and unheard. By 5:30 p.m., it was dark and the woods were still quiet. I headed back to Dan's house, where he told me, "You're welcome to try it again in the morning."

So the next morning I was up at 3:45 a.m. to make some coffee and take a shower. Fully dressed and alert, I was back on the same stand by 5:05. But my arrival was unnecessarily early. It was nearly 6:00 before there was enough light to shoot. All was quiet until the feeder went off at 7:00. Sometimes the sound of a feeder throwing corn draws the pigs in, but I was disappointed again. Three hours after daylight, I finished Chuck's book and called it quits for the morning.

Before leaving, I examined the ground beneath the feeder. There was quite a bit of corn on the ground, indicating that the pigs had not come during the night. There was, however, plenty of reasonably fresh rooting and the tracks of an enormous pig. This pig would equal or perhaps exceed my best boar. The sign was impressive, but you can't shoot or eat sign. You've got to see the pigs.

Back at Pleasant Home, I worked in our tree nursery until 1:00 p.m. After a quick lunch, I drove to the Dixon Center to skin and quarter a doe I had killed a few days earlier. With the meat iced down, it was back to Florida.

This was my fifth hunt on Dan's property. He had done a lot of work to improve the hunting possibilities, and there was plenty of sign to whet a hunter's hopes. He'd added an automatic feeder on a tree with a new ladder stand mounted nearby. A little farther down the road, he'd added a new shooting house.

Hunting with the 7 Mag, I felt no need to climb the ladder stand directly over the feeder. The new shooting house was even more comfortable than Dan's other ground blind. It had an easy chair and a footrest. I dozed off within ten minutes. Birds, squirrels, and the shooting house's resident mouse woke me frequently over the following hours. The last twenty minutes of light were spent intently watching and listening, but this hunt ended as had my previous nine Florida hunts—without me seeing a pig.

This was an amazingly dry stretch, and it was discouraging but not unexpected. My good luck in other states was being balanced by my bad luck in Florida.

There were only three hunts remaining on my schedule. Next Sunday was south Florida, for an airboat hog-hunting trip near Mims. A California hunt was scheduled the weekend after that. And my final hunt was scheduled for December 28–30 in Oklahoma. To accomplish the goal of killing at least one pig in ten different states, I would need to score a trifecta with those forthcoming opportunities.

18 SAW PALMETTO

At the core of this idea [ecosystem management] is the belief that the best forest management maintains the full diversity of an ecosystem's organisms—trees, grasses, herbs, fungi, wildlife—as well as their multiple and complex interconnections.

—LAWRENCE S. EARLEY, *Looking for Longleaf,* 2004

Saw palmetto (*Serenoa repens*): A more abrasive, aggressive, and flammable version of the blue palm—*Sabal minor.* Fires get out of hand quickly in saw palmetto. In the late 1990s, the USDA–Forest Service went to great expense installing a huge Fire and Fire Surrogate Project at multiple locations across the United States. One study site was at the Solon Dixon Center, where we have a bluestem understory. Another study site was at Myakka River State Park in Florida, where they have a saw palmetto understory. At the Dixon Center, our burns went as planned. At Myakka, a small prescribed burn quickly became a large uncontrolled burn, and much of the project at that location went up in smoke.

Florida, the land of broken hearts and dissipating dreams. This state had punished me with ten consecutive strikeouts. It was well into December, and if I wanted a kill in ten states, it was time to bring back some pork-filled coolers from the Sunshine State.

Back in the spring, a search on eBay for "hog hunt" had turned up an airboat hunt in south Florida that seemed pretty cool. Even so, I passed it up, looking for closer and cheaper hunts. After ten north Florida hunts without seeing a single pig, it was time for a south Florida airboat hog hunt. It had been several months since this seller had listed his airboat hunt on eBay. Luckily, I had saved his contact information, just in case my other Florida hunts didn't pan out. Which they certainly had not.

The seller's name was listed as David Watson. I called the number from the eBay listing and explained the reason for my call. "I saved your information from an earlier listing on eBay. I would like to book a hog hunt if you are still guiding." David said he could take me the following weekend. It was perfect timing. After I explained my quest and writing project, David surprised me by extending an invitation for me to stay over at his place, so we could get an early start on Sunday morning.

What was needed for an airboat hunt? David suggested knee-high boots or, "Really, your ideal footwear is tennis shoes if we enter deeper water. If you're going to get wet you might as well be comfortable, and wet tennis shoes are a lot easier to walk in than wet boots."

I knew exactly what he was talking about. I used to noodle (fish by hand) and work nets in lakes and creeks where there were numerous hazards to bare feet. Tennis shoes were standard wear on those water adventures.

David's airboat hog hunt cost $300. My wallet already held a Florida nonresident hunting license, so no additional money there. But the drive was going to be another doozy. MapQuest said Mims, Florida, was five hundred miles from Andalusia, Alabama. But an airboat ride would be an exiting new adventure, and if it delivered a pig, all my travails in Florida would prove worthwhile investments on the way to the final payoff.

The Solon Dixon Center still had me in its clutches at 6:00 p.m. on Friday, December 7. I was wrapping up loose ends before my weekend airboat hunt when an e-mail popped up. It was "Supermee," another eBay seller from Florida whom I had previously contacted about hog hunts in south Florida. Supermee also had a hunt available for the upcoming weekend! Considering my record of extreme bad luck in Florida, was this some sort of sign? It was pretty unusual for me to be sitting in the office at 6:00 on a Friday evening. Would Supermee help me break the Florida drought? Supermee's phone number was in the body of the e-mail so I called him. I told Diego—his real name—about my Sunday hunt in south Florida, and he encouraged me to come on down. "No problem. I can take you hunting in the morning."

It would be challenging to travel so far down the peninsula on such short notice. Was this a chance worth taking? "What are the odds we'll see pigs?"

Diego responded, "I see and kill pigs on 95 percent of my trips to this ranch."

Perhaps it was meant to be. "Where can we meet and what time should I be there?"

Diego explained that Lake Wales was the closest town to the place we were hunting. Lake Wales was near Florida's west coast, while Mims was on the east coast.

Diego requested, "Let's meet a little after 5:00 a.m. if possible." MapQuest put the drive at 480 miles from Andalusia to Lake Wales. It was possible I could do that, though I certainly wouldn't have any sleep that night.

But it was fate. Diego would meet me at the Lake Wales Super Wal-Mart parking lot at 5:15 in the morning. I ran back to my house and packed my gear as rapidly as possible. The drive south started at 8:30 p.m. in the Little Blue Hog-Hunting Mobile. It took an hour to make Crestview, Florida, pick up some coffee, and catch I-10 East. A few hours after that, I dropped south on I-75, stopping every couple of hours for another large cup of convenience-store caffeinated swill. As I pulled into the Lake Wales parking lot at 5:30 the next morning, my body hurt from an acid-filled stomach, an aching lower back, and an overfilled bladder.

Earlier in the year, a jealous female astronaut had made a similarly long trek, from Houston to south Florida, seeking to intercept her boyfriend's other lover. I thought, "It sure would have been handy to use some of those adult diapers like she employed for her long-distance Florida run under similar time constraints."

A quick survey of the parking lot didn't turn up any potential hog hunters so I went inside to get rid of some coffee. If this guy didn't show up, it would be very disappointing.

But Diego pulled in at 5:45 a.m. He had driven two hours northwest for our rendezvous in Lake Wales. There was little time to waste as I followed him toward the River Ranch, which covered about fifty thousand acres and was owned by hundreds of people who had purchased lots on the property. These owners were allowed to bring guests on hunts. The River Ranch had a manned check-in station, where Diego showed his membership card and signed me in as a guest. From there, it was a short drive to "the South Side," where we parked on the edge of the highway and walked in through a gate on a dirt road.

The dirt road passed through a stand of scattered mature pines with a dense saw palmetto understory. Locating Diego's feeder, I noticed that a nearby ladder stand was propped against an old, flattop longleaf pine. The first glimmers of light tickled the horizon as we climbed the ladder and took our seats, with Diego on my left.

About forty-five minutes after light, the feeder still hadn't gone off, which was puzzling. "What time does it throw the corn?"

Diego surprised me. "It is set for 5:15 a.m. It has already gone off. Do you see any corn on the ground?"

Some cardinals hopped around beneath the feeder, but there wasn't any surplus of corn down there. This didn't make any sense as 5:15 a.m. Eastern time was a good hour before shooting light. If the pigs timed their arrival by the feeder, they would have cleaned up the corn and been long gone before light.

An hour into our hunt the sun was up. I turned to Diego. "Wake me up if any pigs come," I said, then promptly leaned against the railing and fell asleep with my head resting on crossed arms.

About 10:00 a.m., Diego crawled down and checked the feeder. It was clogged. With Jerry's feeder (on my earlier hunt near Tallahassee), the culprit had been cheap, weevil-ridden corn clogging the feeder. In this case, the problem was a powder attractant that Diego had added to the corn. Diego manually turned the spinner, scattering a few kernels. Breaking off a stick, he poked a hole through a clump of corn and powder blocking the hole in the bottom of the drum. If this feeder had gone off automatically at all, it probably hadn't thrown more than a few dozen kernels of corn.

And if the feeder hadn't worked for the entire week, most likely, the pigs had stopped coming to this stand. If nothing else, my Florida luck was consistent.

For me to kill a pig in Florida, I would need global warming to melt the polar icecaps, submerging most of the Florida peninsula, thus concentrating Florida's pigs onto a few small islands where they wouldn't be able to hide from me!

Our ladder stand was leaning against a mature longleaf pine on a flat, sandy ridge. In south Florida, three feet of elevation over the surrounding area qualifies as a "ridge." The understory was nearly solid saw palmetto, with holly species and greenbrier woven throughout. A scattering of mature longleaf pines stood on the sand ridges. Judging by these old but stunted pines, this area had a very low "site index"—that is, should these trees be cored and the rings counted, they would probably age out at seventy to a hundred years, yet they topped out at less than fifty feet in height. Less than a hundred yards to our right the elevation dropped off a few feet into a wet flatwoods site, transitioning to a slash pine and sweetbay magnolia overstory.

It had been decades since fire had touched this forest. The telltale black on the bark of the longleaf or slash pines was missing. The herbaceous layer was almost completely gone, but there *were* a few surviving sprigs of wiregrass among the saw palmetto.

Surprisingly, an active gopher tortoise burrow gaped open not far from the feeder. The gopher tortoise is a protected species in Florida, but it is not listed as threatened or endangered (T&E) in this part of its range. The gopher tortoise is considered a "keystone" species in the longleaf pine wiregrass ecosystem. Its burrows provide homes and safe zones for several other T&E species. When the gopher tortoise disappears from an area, the gopher frog, the gopher cricket, and the indigo snake are not far behind.

This gopher tortoise was probably eating wiregrass and greenbrier, and possibly palmetto seed. It was surviving, but a prescribed fire would turn this forest around, bringing a bounty of low-growing herbaceous species for the tortoise to browse. But as in all the other sites I had hunted in Florida, negligent landowners or managers didn't appear to be making an effort. Three of the most important components of this ecosystem were present: longleaf pine, wiregrass, and gopher tortoises. But this ecosystem was choking and dying from fire exclusion.

Diego realized that our morning hunt was over, at least from this location.

Having unclogged the feeder, he motioned for me to climb down the ladder. He led the way down a trail cut through the saw palmetto. The trail led toward some slash pine and sweetbay. The elevation dropped only two or three feet, but the soil conditions changed dramatically. On the higher ridge, the soil was white, coarse sand. Beneath the slash and sweetbay, the soil was a black, organic muck.

There were plenty of pig tracks on the sandy trails, but very little rooting. As we approached another feeder in the wet flatwoods site, I saw that the ground was torn up in all directions from fresh pig rooting. Wallows were scattered beneath the dense overstory. The bases of many trees were black where pigs had rubbed after wallowing in the muck.

Stalking through the palmetto would be impossible. The saw palmetto was as noisy and difficult to push through as the blue palm had been in Louisiana. But the abundance of sign beneath the feeder indicated that pigs were using this area on a regular basis. Diego said, "We'll come back here later this afternoon."

Diego and I followed the trail out to a larger, better-maintained trail, looping out and back, mostly passing through upland longleaf overstories with a solid saw palmetto understory. We passed an occasional showy shrub with red fruit. I asked Diego, "Is this a Brazilian pepper tree?"

Diego confirmed my suspicions. "Yes, it is a big problem down here." Brazilian pepper is one of the more aggressive woody invasives in south Florida.

Diego explained that he was an immigrant from Brazil, and that he had lived in the United States for several years. Knowing that hunting is largely illegal in Brazil, I asked him, "How long have you been a hunter?"

Diego's answer surprised me. "I've been a hunter nearly all my life. We hunted many type of animals in Brazil." He ticked off a list, using sometimes the English name and sometimes the Portuguese: "Deer, pigs, *anta* [tapir], and capybara."

I remembered another small mammal I'd seen in the Pantanal and the Orchidario in Santos, Brazil. People had told me it was very good to eat. "How about agouti?"

Diego shook his head. "I don't know that."

That was the English name. I switched to Portuguese. "*Cutia?*"

Diego knew that one. "Oh, yeah. Those too."

Diego had even pursued wild cats. "We also hunt two types of jaguar there:

the big jaguar and the small jaguar." I guessed that he meant ocelot when he said "the small jaguar."

Diego explained how he was able to hunt in Brazil. "I have an uncle who is a policeman. We go to a large property where he knows the game warden, and we pay $20 or $25 a day to hunt, mostly with shotguns. We hunt many animals there, including the small jaguar."

Diego constantly monitored the trail for tracks, pointing out fresh hog tracks and meticulously examining every deer track he found. He told me he shot pigs on this tract and another site in the Everglades, but he was really a whitetail fanatic.

Back at the highway, we decided it was time for lunch. Diego drove to a nearby town, and as we ate at a cheap Chinese buffet, he told me a little more about himself. He'd lived in the United States since his family emigrated from Recife, Brazil. Diego was twenty-three years old, married, and he already had two children. His son was a little older than my boy.

After lunch, Diego drove us back to the River Ranch while I fought to keep my eyes open. Despite the better-looking stand, I just couldn't get excited about staying for another afternoon hunt. I asked Diego, "What's your pricing for an afternoon hunt?" Earlier, we had agreed on $100 for a morning hunt, and an additional $50 for an afternoon hunt. If he stayed with his prior pricing, I was going to pay him the $100, call it a day, and go find a place to park and sleep for a while.

Diego saw that I was ambivalent. "Since we didn't see anything, you can hunt the rest of the day for the flat $100."

He had persuaded me. "Okay, but I really need a nap."

Diego took me to the end of a trail, where I lay down beneath some palmetto fronds. Diego was concerned for my welfare. "You should probably lie in the middle of the trail to be safe from snakes."

I mumbled, "Don't worry. Me and the snakes have come to an understanding."

Diego asked, "Have you been bit before?"

I was already almost asleep. "Yeah. A rattlesnake bit me and I spent a couple of days in the ICU." Diego didn't answer. He probably didn't believe me. But I would rather sleep than elaborate.

Diego woke me up at 1:30 p.m. We were back on the ladder stand by 2:00, and we stayed there until 4:45. The afternoon was shaping up just as I thought it would—pig free. Diego motioned for us to get down. He wanted to check the stand in the slash pine where we'd earlier seen the fresh rootings.

We stalked in as silently as possible. There were lots of palm fronds to step over and around and, much to my annoyance, Diego pushed through in front of me. If there were pigs beneath the stand, it would take a snapshot to get one, and the person in the front would be the only one with an opportunity.

Twenty yards from the stand, my fears were realized. A nice spotted pig woofed and ran to the right, disappearing into the palmetto. Diego and I knelt side by side with our guns raised. He was on the right.

A small black piglet and a little blond piglet dashed from the palmetto, crossing the trail to our right. I tried to pick them up in my scope. After eleven fruitless hunts in Florida I was ready to take a ten-pound piglet and say, "To heck with this state!" But Diego had other ideas. "Let them go. The sow will come back. They always do."

I wasn't so sure. But the ploy had worked in Arkansas, where I had shot one pig and the others circled back within a few minutes, allowing me to take a second pig from the same stand.

Sure enough, a sound emanated from the woods to our right. I brought my rifle up and waited, but nothing stepped out. I lowered the rifle, and both of us kept our kneeling positions.

The pigs were close, and a few minutes later they approached again. My rifle was already up when a nose and ears emerged. Then the head appeared in my scope, and still I held my fire. The pig took a step forward, exposing its left front shoulder. Moving the crosshairs onto the shoulder, I squeezed the trigger. *Powww!* The sow dropped in its tracks and piglets scattered into the surrounding palmetto.

After a few seconds Diego asked, "How many piglets did you see? I saw at least five."

The sow had captured most of my attention. "There were a couple of black ones and a blond one. There may have been more."

Should a piglet step back into the trail, I was prepared to send a bullet in that direction, but Diego said, "No. Let them go. You will separate a piglet if you shoot it with that rifle."

This was the first time I had heard the word "separate" referring to shot game. But Diego was probably correct; there wouldn't be much left if a piglet caught a projectile from the 7 Mag.

I dragged the sow to the trail, where Diego and I left the pig and walked the road in a circle to an open grassy field. It was deer season and Diego was hoping to get a shot at a buck. Doe harvest was prohibited on the River Ranch.

Minutes later, it was too dark to shoot so we walked back to the sow. The 150-grain bullet had entered the left front shoulder, blown through the vitals, and exited through the right shoulder. The bullet and the pig had done just what I wanted. The sow had dropped in place, necessitating no tracking and/or searching through palmetto in the gathering dark.

I dragged the sow about a quarter of a mile to our automobiles while Diego walked beside or in front of me. Diego didn't want to put the sow in his SUV so I put the sow in my big cooler. Diego did help me load the cooler into the backseat of my little blue Saturn. I was learning that Diego was what one might call "a minimal service guide."

Back at the check station, a young couple ahead of us had a long, lean, black boar. It was the young lady's first feral hog. The scales put her pig at about 120 pounds. Retrieving my video cam, I took two minutes of video of her boar and my sow. My sow wasn't big in stature but it was fat—and after I'd dragged it a quarter mile and more, it had gained about twenty pounds. But looking at the girl's boar, I decided I had overestimated my pig's weight. The scales put its live weight at ninety-four pounds. We snapped a couple of photos of the sow on the scales before loading it back in my cooler.

It was time to gut the hog, but field dressing at the check-in station wasn't allowed. Diego didn't have any ideas on how or where I should field dress my pig, so I called David in Mims. "Have you got a place to clean a hog?"

"Sure, bring it on over."

I shook hands with Diego and paid him $150. Diego and the River Ranch had delivered. What the River Ranch lacked in size, it made up for in sweet success.

Judging by photos on the wall of the check station, the best bucks harvested at the River Ranch would be passed over in Lower Alabama as too small. A "trophy" buck on the River Ranch would be a small "basket" eight-point on the Dixon Center. The soil and browse here were simply too poor to grow big deer.

They did have some nice pigs, however. They were a little small on average, but their boars were capable of growing tusks just as long as our best pigs in LA.

The land management was obviously conducive to invasive pigs, but an occasional prescribed fire could do wonders for the herbaceous layer. It may not double the "carrying capacity" or number of deer, quail, and turkey the land could support in a given area, but it would improve browse for deer and the number of insects that quail and turkey depend on, while simultaneously benefiting gopher tortoises, indigo snakes, and the hundreds of other animals and birds that need an occasional fire to perpetuate their survival.

The River Ranch was the third location I had hunted in Florida. A central theme was emerging from my Florida hunts: the devastating effect on the southeastern environment from an absence of fire.

On two of the three Florida sites I had hunted, the landowners favored high hog populations. On the closest site, just forty miles from my house, the landowner was more or less indifferent to an increasing hog population. He was a farmer, so he didn't like the damage they inflicted on his crops and deer plots, but he was happy for the extra income the hogs generated from hunting leases. Although there were highly concentrated hog populations on all three ownerships, the pigs' impact on the herbaceous layer and the ecosystem was minimal in comparison to the effects of fire exclusion and, to a lesser extent, invasive species.

Hogs can be destructive, but first there must be something to destroy. On all three of my Florida hunts, there was no longleaf regeneration to worry about. Fire exclusion was preventing longleaf regeneration on the part of the River Ranch where I hunted, and longleaf had already been wiped out on the other two ownerships, along with virtually the entire native herbaceous layer. Wiregrass and gopher tortoises do persist on the small portion of the River Ranch I visited, and it is possible that pigs will be detrimental to these few survivors, but both Keystone species will eventually disappear with fire exclusion, with or without feral hogs.

With my hunt concluded at the River Ranch, it was a tremendous relief to finally have a Florida pig in my column. The Sunday airboat hunt was sure to be exciting, but the experience would be even more fun now that the pressure was off. Also, I was looking forward to hunting pigs in a south Florida wetland ecosystem, which would be a totally new environment for me.

19 DOG FENNEL

A giant piece of ground too deep for a human to wade in, too shallow for a boat to draw. Too tangled for passage. Full of mosquitoes and yellow flies. A place that holds the world together. A natural feature full of natural features. Some of the last real wilderness in the South.

— JANISSE RAY, *Pinhook: Finding Wholeness*
in a Fragmented Land, 2005

Dog fennel (*Eupatorium spp.*): There are several species of dog fennel in the genus *Eupatorium,* the most common of which is *Eupatorium compositifolium.* These are "ruderal" plants in the aster family. "Ruderal" means these are pioneer plants that thrive on disturbed sites. There is little dog fennel in a diverse, fire-maintained longleaf understory community. Over time, hundreds of long-lived, fire-adapted competitors reach an equilibrium in which there is no room for the ruderal-weedy dog fennel. But cut the trees, skid the logs, harrow and root-rake the soil, thus wiping out this community, and dog fennel will explode. Dog fennel seed is everywhere. The plant may be seen sprouting and growing from neglected gutters and even cracks in walls or foundations. When humans eventually settle the moon, erect a dome, pump in water, oxygen, CO_2, and heat, dog fennel will spring from the moon dust.

From the River Ranch, it was two hours east and a bit north to Mims, Florida. It didn't take long to find David's house; it was the only one on

Panther Lane with an airboat parked in the driveway. David came out to meet me. After shaking hands, David had me drive behind his house to a cement pad with pulleys and winches. It was a great setup for cleaning large animals.

David's "buggy" was parked to the right of the cement pad. These swamp buggies are a common sight in south and central Florida: jacked up, four-wheel-drive vehicles on giant mud tires, these custom-made trucks and jeeps are designed to provide an elevated viewing and shooting platform while cruising through the swamps, tall grass, palmetto, and low brush that cover much of south Florida. To the right of the swamp buggy were dog pens containing both bay and catch dogs.

David invited me inside for a drink, introducing me to his girlfriend, Patty, from Indiana. David, who was my age (thirty-eight), worked as an electrician for NASA, spending much of his time wiring the crawler that carries the space shuttle back and forth to the launch pad at Cape Canaveral. He was also a big guy, and it didn't look like much of his mass was fat.

A couple of glasses of iced tea did much to revive me. Then David helped me hang and skin the sow. As we spilled the guts out into a container, David observed, "Pigs are nasty, but they sure are fun!" With the smell of rotting entrails inundating my nostrils, I agreed that the "nasty" part was dead-on.

When David had first walked out to greet me, I noticed that he had only nine and a half fingers. Was this from his work as an electrician? Or was his finger a pig-hunting casualty? David explained, "A boar bit it off with one snap. Besides my finger, it gutted one of my bay dogs." Later, David showed me the offender's tusks hanging from the rearview mirror of his truck. Payback!

With the sow quartered up, David let me put the meat in a dirty but functioning refrigerator that had housed plenty of animal parts over the years. Everything about this place said "serious hunter."

Patty showed me to a bedroom with a nearby bathroom. I took a much-needed shower and changed my clothing. Patty had also prepared a fresh, delicious salad. Finishing supper, I was in bed and asleep by 10:30 p.m.

A few minutes later, or so it seemed, dishes were clinking in the kitchen. Rolling over and checking my watch, I saw that it was 4:00 a.m. I dressed, putting on my brand-new $10 swamp-walking tennis shoes. After a cup of coffee, I helped

David put two catch dogs and two bay dogs in the airboat, asking David, "Do I leave the rifle here?"

David told me, "If we get on the pigs today, all we'll need is this knife." He was carrying a KA-BAR-style military knife.

With our gear loaded, David drove to a gas station and topped off the airboat's gas tank. From there, it was a short drive to Sovereign Land. David explained the term: "This property goes back to the original Spanish land grants from the king of Spain. After that, the French owned it until they sold it to America. This area was and remains swamp ground, so nothing has ever been done with it." He continued, "We'll be meeting a friend of mine named Jimmy. He'll be coming in through the 'Super Highway.' That's an airboat trail that cuts through the Sovereign Land."

It was still dark when David stopped on the edge of a vast wetland. The land in front of us was between the east and west forks of the St. John's River. Jimmy was waiting for us with his airboat. Jimmy was built more like me than David— on the slender side. And whenever there was a pause in the action, it didn't take him long to light a cigarette. After David introduced us, Jimmy told us he'd already had a bit of excitement.

In the fog and dark, he'd been cruising along when he saw a herd of pigs on the edge of the trail. Jimmy ticked off a list of pigs he'd seen, listing their color, sex, and weight. While he was tallying the pigs to his left, a big silver boar materialized out of the fog in front of him. The boat ran up and over the pig, but the boar powered out from beneath the boat, circling around to the trail behind the boat. Jimmy said, "He was really pissed off!"

After a brief conference, Jimmy and David decided to return to the spot where Jimmy had run over the silver boar. They fired up their airboats. Jimmy flicked his cigarette into the fan on the back of our airboat, where it exploded into a shower of sparks.

Other airboats headed into the marsh. David said they were duck hunters. David had me climb up to the airboat's seat, handing me a pair of earmuffs. He revved up the motor as the fan pushed the airboat across twenty yards of dry land; then we hit the water and rapidly picked up speed.

The Super Highway alternated from a few feet of water to a few inches to dry land for as much as a hundred yards at a stretch. The temperature was in the fifties, but several layers of clothing kept the cold, wet wind at bay. The sun wasn't quite up yet when Jimmy pointed to the right, indicating where he'd seen the pigs. Jimmy and David both drove past the spot before turning the boats around and stopping. Jimmy checked the wind direction. The bay dogs would enter the marsh downwind of the pigs' suspected location.

David and Jimmy parked their airboats on the bank of the Super Highway. The worst part was stepping off the boat with dry tennis shoes into the water. After the initial shock, it only took a moment to forget I was wet from the knees down.

The dominant cover was grasses, rushes, or sedges, stretching to the horizon in all directions. Most of peninsular Florida was in an extended drought, and water levels were way down. The surrounding ground was mostly mud or a few inches of water beneath the grass. The water was only a few inches to a foot deep in the Super Highway. The main channel was slightly lower than the surrounding grasslands, which would typically have been underwater. One or two feet of elevation allowed trees and shrubs to become established, highlighting islands in the sea of tall grass. A couple of acres of bald cypress stood to our left.

Even though this was a hot spot for pigs, pig sign was sparse. How were pigs affecting this type of environment?

David explained how our hunt should play out. "We want the dogs to run silent until they are looking at the pig. That's when you will hear them bark. Hopefully, the pig will back up in some grass or cover, and the bay dogs will stay from me to you away [about ten feet]. We want that pig to be as comfortable as possible. If the dogs go in and start nipping at him, the pig will break and run, and that can lead to a long chase. When you get thirty or forty yards from the pig, you turn the catch dogs loose. You want the dogs to come out of nowhere and be on that pig"—smashing his fist into his palm–"before it knows what hit him!"

The dogs strained at their leashes, whining and begging to be turned loose. David and Jimmy unclipped Jake and Cowgirl, two blackmouth curs. The catch dogs stayed leashed. One catch dog, named Scrappy, was half pit bull. The other, Son, was a pureblood pit. After a few quick circles, the blackmouth curs ran ahead, springing into the air with their noses pointed into the wind.

The wait was short. About two hundred yards in, Jake and Cowgirl bayed to the right. David and Jimmy ran straight down the trail until we were perpendicular to the dogs. Breaking right, they charged into six- to eight-foot-tall switch grass while I followed closely behind, promptly falling on my face. The base of the switch grass formed hidden hummocks or humps one to two feet higher than the surrounding mud. David and Jimmy were experienced at traversing this habitat, so they remained upright. I soon learned to navigate the uneven surface, but not before falling down a couple more times.

Twenty yards from the bayed pig, David yelled to Jimmy, "Turn 'em loose!" The pits disappeared into the switch grass ahead of us, where a melee erupted. We heard the squealing of a pig mixed with the snarling and barking of four dogs. David, judging by the pitch of the squeal, yelled back to me, "It's a good one!"

David reached the fight first, diving into a hole in the grass and grabbing a large brown boar by the hind legs while Jimmy seized one of the catch dogs. David shouted, "Stick him!"

I unsheathed the KA-BAR knife as I closed in. One pit and the bay dogs were still latched onto each side of the boar's head. Stepping up to the pig, I plunged the knife into its side, pushing down on the blade and stepping back. The blade hit a few inches farther back than intended and the pig was still fighting hard, so I hit it a little farther forward. This time the stab produced a gush of blood. Stepping back, I asked for their assessment. "Is that good?"

The pig was still fighting, but Jimmy assured me, "That did the trick."

It took the boar about fifteen seconds to expire. Perhaps it was a less than ideal "stick." Or boars are made of a little tougher material than sows. It was probably a little of both.

David asked me, "What did you think about that?"

"That was awesome!" I high-fived David as Jimmy gave a thumbs-up while smoking a cigarette.

David and Jimmy asked if it would be okay to leave me with the pig while they walked the catch dogs back to the boat. "Sure, I'll stay here and gut the boar." I gutted the boar then, having a little extra time and energy, dragged the carcass toward the channel.

With the boar lying on the bank of the channel, there were a few minutes to contemplate my kill. This weekend had brought more than I expected. After eleven straight strikeouts, my first Florida pig had come the day before. That tan sow was followed by this large brown boar. The sky was clear, but my pig drought was over.

David and Jimmy pulled up, beaching the airboats across from the boar. After a few photos beside the channel, we tied the brown boar to a rack on the front of Jimmy's airboat. Jimmy looked at the brown boar, saying, "That's the brown one I thought was a sow this morning. There is still a big silver boar out there somewhere. There are also a bunch of fifty pounders in the area."

David and Jimmy decided to run the dogs a little farther down the channel in hopes they would strike the scent of the silver boar. Silver is an uncommon color in most feral hog populations. I remember killing only one silver pig, an attractive silver sow a couple of years back at Heart's Bluff Ranch in Texas. They worked the dogs through the area for another thirty minutes. With no other hits, Jimmy suggested we check an island that was used as a fish- and duck-hunting camp on Lake Cane.

It was a thirty–minute run through the marsh to get there. David and Jimmy parked the airboats at the camp and we walked into a grove of willow trees and wax myrtle. I saw scattered rooting, but the dogs didn't strike and we circled back to the airboats. I walked over to an outhouse, but before I could step inside, a dog barked. David yelled, "They've got one!" Running back to the boats, David told me, "Hop in with Jimmy!"

Jimmy fired his boat up as I jumped in. Jimmy ran the airboat about 100 to 150 yards, then shut the motor down so we could listen. The pig was squealing to our right front. Jimmy ran the boat motor another 50 to 80 yards and cut it off again.

The blackmouth curs were latched onto a black pig to our right. Jimmy yelled, "Jump off! Let's get him." Jimmy beat me to the melee, where he grabbed a fifty-pound black pig by the hind legs. I got ahold of Jake, pulling him off the small boar. Real catch dogs weren't needed for pigs this size; the bay dogs were fully capable of holding this one.

David pulled up and joined us, asking me, "What do you want to do with the pig?"

There would be more than enough pork between my Lake Wales sow and the brown boar we'd just killed. "What do you normally do with a pig like this?"

David said, "Normally, we 'bar' a small boar and turn it back loose, but this is your hunt. Whatever you prefer."

If that was their usual practice, I could live with it. "I already have a ton of pork; let's castrate this one."

David pulled out his knife and asked me, "You grew up on a hog farm; do you want to cut him?"

I declined. "I've cut quite a few pigs, but it has been twenty-five years since the last one. I'll just watch how you do it."

David made a small incision, popping the testicles out the hole before cutting them loose. Back on the farm, these were saved for "mountain oyster fries." David dropped the testicles into the sulfur-smelling mud and turned the semi-lucky pig loose. At least it was escaping with its life. It could have ended up on the barbeque grill!

We were now two for two on locations and hogs caught. David suggested, "Let's run over to 'Catfish' and plan our attack." Cruising farther down the Super Highway, David and Jimmy pulled up to some buildings beside a highway with several airboats parked in the yard. David explained, "We [the Electricians' Union] were on strike for four months so I ran airboat rides to make a little money before the strike ended." This was the location where his customers were picked up and dropped off.

With the airboats parked on the grass, we stretched our legs and had a drink before loading up and idling beneath the highway. The river widened on the other side of the road. Cattle dotted the landscape, and several more boats powered by Go-Devils were coming in with duck hunters and their retrievers. I asked David, "How much water do they need for those Go-Devils?"

David said, "They run pretty well in straight mud." That's American ingenuity.

Jimmy and David pulled up to another high spot, where Jimmy lit a cigarette and checked the wind direction with the smoke. We walked inland with the wind in our face. This was totally different habitat. For a while, we pushed through solid dog fennel. Grass cover was sparse and the land was much drier. David led the way with Scrappy on a leash and the curs running ahead. Jimmy ran his airboat and the other pit (Son) around to the other side of the high ground. David kept us on the high ground. I saw some old rooting and an occasional hog or deer track but not much fresh sign from either species.

David and I were ten minutes in, with the dogs checking back regularly. With no advance warning, the curs cut loose straight ahead. This area had cattle, and David was worried that it may not be a pig they were on. Just minutes before, David had explained what could happen if the dogs bayed a cow. "The curs just stand back and bark, but this meathead [nodding at Scrappy] will catch a cow as quick as a pig. We need to be certain of our quarry before we unleash him."

David pushed through the ten-foot-high growth at a fast jog. The dog fennel was mature and clouds of light, fuzzy fennel seed enveloped us. We emerged into a small opening to find both curs latched onto the throat of a bony old buck. The deer wasn't putting up a fight. It was evident from its emaciated condition that this deer was on its last legs. Its hip bones protruded from the hind quarters and the ankle of a front leg was ballooned with swelling. With its long head and graying muzzle, this was a very old deer. Its antlers were two long spikes, with a smaller point about midway up each spike. The buck was a four-point, using eastern scoring.

David grabbed Jake, saying, "This buck is done for. Do you want to go ahead and put it out of its misery?" Nodding, I unsheathed the knife and buried the blade behind the front shoulder. The buck died almost immediately.

It is unusual for dogs to catch deer that haven't been previously shot. I asked David, "Have you ever caught a deer like this before?"

David shook his head. "I am pretty sure this is the first time. It looks to me like it was snake bit and got so poor that it just laid down to die."

Neither of us had any interest in meat from this buck. Old bucks are typically gamey and tough, even when they are in good health. Meat from an old buck in rut is best suited for summer sausage or some other heavily processed and seasoned product. Although it looked like a physical injury had led to this deer's poor health, it was also possible that it was suffering from some other ailment, making the meat questionable to consume.

I cut a ring around the deer's neck and twisted the head off. It would make an interesting European mount. After removing the hide and flesh, I would clean and whiten the skull.

We continued our transit through the dog fennel until the grass transitioned to large palm trees, beneath which the cattle had grazed everything to short stubble. Earlier, Jimmy had pointed toward the palms, saying, "The deer hunters have been running feeders up around those palms." Smiling, David added, "That benefits all of us!" I could see some ropes where feeders had been hanging, but no corn or other bait on the ground.

Could one consider this a "degraded" environment because of the hogs and/ or cattle? It would be hard to make a case that pigs were having much of an effect on this area. It appeared that, given free rein, the hunters were keeping pig numbers in check. As soon as concentrated sign became evident, hunters with dogs, like David and Jimmy, moved in, capturing, culling, and castrating. All in all, the pigs appeared to be having little effect on this environment.

What about the cattle? It appeared to me that cattle had had a significant impact on the surrounding landscape. Cattle grazing and cattle tracks obscured virtually all pig sign in the area.

Before the first Native Americans arrived in Florida, there were many large herbivores, including bison, giant armadillos (actually an omnivore), mammoths, camels, and other large grazers. Many paleontologists and ecologists believe that Native Americans hunted these large prey species into extinction, leaving the smaller and more elusive whitetail as the only large herbivore in the state, not counting the manatee. It is possible that cattle are playing the same role in this landscape that wooly mammoths did twenty thousand years ago.

Pigs could fill a niche once inhabited by the giant armadillo. Both dig or root for their food. Sure, they have widely differing diets and habits, yet an argument could be made that an absence of large herbivores or omnivores is every bit as unnatural as the presence of the recently introduced ("recent" meaning centuries instead of millennia) cattle and pigs.

Circling back to the main channel, David and I met with Jimmy. David said, "Why don't you ride back with Jimmy and I'll walk the dogs back." Jimmy ran us back around to David's airboat. Parked on the bank, Jimmy told pig- and deer-hunting stories, while I kicked back. The temperature had risen to the seventies and this was probably our last stop of the day.

Ten minutes later, David's voice sounded in the distance, yelling at the dogs. Jimmy yelled out a "Woooo" to let David know where we were. Then Jimmy returned to telling stories.

About five minutes later, I remarked, "He's been out there quite a while." Jimmy nodded, but he didn't deviate from his story line.

A couple of minutes later, I sat up. "I hear dogs barking!" Within seconds Jimmy's cell phone rang. David yelled, "They're bayed up! Bring the other catch dog!" David had Scrappy. Son, the other pit, was in Jimmy's boat. We jumped into Jimmy's boat, but his cell phone went off before he could start the engine. David repeated, "Bring the catch dog! Hurry up! It's a big boar! We're over by the power lines!"

Jimmy fired up the airboat, and we shot into the main channel, banking hard left toward the power lines. Jimmy ran full throttle, cutting across land at large bends in the river, where the mud allowed for shortcuts. He pulled into a channel near the power lines and shut off the motor. I pointed. "There!"

The noise had intensified dramatically. The boar was roaring and the dogs were snarling and barking, yipping when the boar scored a cut with its tusks. David's voice rose above the fray, screaming, "Hurry! Hurry!" and something unintelligible about the catch dog.

It sounded like they were only a hundred yards out. Jimmy yelled, "Take the catch dog! Go! Go! Go!"

Flying off the side of the boat, I landed in a few inches of water over relatively solid ground. I reached back into the airboat and secured the pit's leash. Son jumped out and lunged forward, pulling me into the grass. Plowing into the tall dog fennel, we ran toward the noise. One hundred yards in, I realized that the fight was farther away than I had first thought. Jimmy was coming up behind me when David screamed something that sounded like "Turn the catch dog loose!"

Jimmy yelled forward to me, "Let him go!"

I bent over and unsnapped the dog. It sprang forward as I followed close behind. I broke left to skirt a thick patch of undergrowth as the catch dog disappeared, and Jimmy went right.

The distance I had first guessed at one hundred yards turned out to be several hundred into the dog fennel. Sound and distances are deceptive in these parts.

The continuous noise from the melee kept me oriented in the right direction, but the dog fennel had me choked and gagging, while my side was hurting from the exertion. Each time David yelled, it sounded like he was farther away, and I was beginning to wonder if we would get there before something bad happened.

I finally broke through a wall of dog fennel to find David kneeling on top of a large black boar that was kicking and flexing, lifting David well into the air each time it tried to right itself. Scrappy was locked on the boar's head and David was trying to keep the other catch dog away from the front of the pig while the two curs grabbed and chewed on legs, ears, or whatever other appendage stuck out. David pointed at the pit I'd loosed, saying, "Tie him to a tree!"

I pulled the leash from my pocket, snapped it to the pit's collar, and dragged the dog to a nearby willow where I leashed it. I quickly returned to the fight, leashing and extracting another dog just as Jimmy broke into the clearing. Jimmy helped David hold the boar down while I tied the other dog to a tree. The situation was finally under control.

Pulling my camera out of my backpack, I snapped a few pictures of Jimmy and David holding the boar down. Then Jimmy and I switched positions. Unsheathing the KA-BAR and holding it in both hands, I buried it into the side of the boar. As I pushed down, blood shot onto my face and all over Jimmy, who was standing about six to eight feet in front of us. Laughing, Jimmy said, "That'll do the job!" It was a good stick, and the boar died quicker than the brown one I'd stuck earlier in the morning.

On the ride back to the truck and trailer, I watched the surrounding landscape for wildlife and hog sign. There was an occasional hog trail through the grass, but the cattle were having a much larger impact on the environment. The cows kept the grass grazed short, and their tracks, trails, and manure were ten to one hundred times more prevalent than pig sign on this side of the highway. As we passed beneath the highway, the cattle sign disappeared, and there was only an occasional indicator of hog activity. The hog hunters appeared quite capable of controlling hog populations in the surrounding swamps. Without dogs, though, it would surely be quite different.

Earlier, David had told me, "Unless we are taking someone on a hunt who wants to kill a pig, we rarely ever kill a hog. We cut and release the boars, or we tie them up and take them to a landowner who hunts pigs. Even when I am hunting from a stand, I rarely, if ever, shoot a pig anymore." He added, "Lots of pigs get dumped on the River Ranch, where you hunted yesterday. I know someone who traps pigs on Avon Park [a nearby military base]. Everything they catch goes to the River Ranch."

Back at the trucks, we loaded everything and David drove us off the Sovereign Land. The elevation increased on the public road, and before long I noted extensive pig rooting on the road shoulders. This was more sign than I'd seen anywhere on the Sovereign Land. David explained, "This is a wildlife refuge. They don't allow pig hunting here, so they hire professional trappers to come in and trap the pigs. Whatever they catch, they shoot and leave lying in the woods. But they aren't keeping up with the hog population. But if they find one of our dogs on this refuge, we are looking at a big fine."

It was a remarkable contrast. On the one hand, there was the Sovereign Land, where the pig population was essentially controlled by hunters with dogs. On the other hand, there was the wildlife refuge, where hunters were excluded, the pig population was out of control, and the government was paying trappers to kill the pigs and leave the carcasses lying in the woods to rot.

It was a tremendously powerful argument for hunting and hunters. There are many species of animals that, left unchecked, reproduce to unsustainable levels and wreak havoc on their environments. The two best examples in North America are the white-tailed deer and the feral hog. What would have kept these two species under control before humans were around? The clear answer is—other large predators. In North America the wolf and the mountain lion could have been the two primary predators that kept the native white-tailed deer in check.

Pigs are not native to North America, but to some degree, it is likely that mountain lions and wolves would also prey on pigs where their populations overlapped (as in Europe and Asia). Also, alligators occasionally take pigs. Bobcats and coyotes probably snatch an occasional piglet, but unless wolves, bears, and mountain lions are allowed to spread back across most of the continental United States, hunters will be required to keep pig and deer populations in check.

Although, if hunters are going to control wild hog populations, they'll need to do a lot better than I did on my first eleven Florida hog hunts.

20 VALLEY OAKS

"What are you looking for in a typewriter?" the salesman asked.

"Something more than words," I replied. "Crystals. I want to send my readers armloads of crystals, some of which are the colors of orchids and peonies, some of which pick up radio signals from a secret city that is half Paris and half Coney Island."

He recommended the Remington SL3.

—Tom Robbins, *Still Life with Woodpecker*, 1980

Valley oak (*Quercus lobata*): The valley oak, at least in appearance, is a western cousin to the bur oak *Quercus macrocarpa*, which grows across much of the United States and Canada. Or, if you prefer, the valley oak also closely resembles the live oak *Quercus virginiana* of the East Coast. When open grown, these oaks have relatively short boles and huge spreading crowns composed of large branches that cover much ground. While southern pines are commonly planted at six hundred or seven hundred trees per acre, five to ten mature valley, bur, or live oaks could fully occupy the same space.

In the process of killing my Florida pigs, I'd spent the equivalent of the gross domestic product of your typical west Alabama county, but the Sunshine State was finally in my rearview mirror. Praise the Lord!

As the next-to-last state on my list, California would add both the West Coast and a new style of hunting: "spot and stalk." At the Dixon Center I had killed pigs using a similar method called "still hunting." The hunter moves slowly through good habitat, listening and looking until the pigs give their position away. Most of my still hunts had been in thick cover, where I'd shot the pigs at very close range. From what I'd read, the experience in California would be more like elk hunting in the mountains. This generally requires watching and spotting the animal a long distance away, then stalking to within rifle range. Many shots are taken at longer distances in the wide-open terrain.

Starting in October, I searched the Internet for hog-hunting options in California. It didn't take long to find places advertising hunts, but many of the ranches required a minimum of two hunters.

Trying another venue, I searched YouTube with the keywords "California Hog Hunt." This turned up a few videos, including one of a truck racing across pastures with a shooter in the back. The video shifted back and forth from hunters in the truck to pigs running across valleys and ridges. The truck stopped so that the hunters could jump out and shoot at the herd of pigs. The shooter knocked down at least one good pig, but it was hard to get a final tally with all the bouncing and cutting from scene to scene. At the end of the video, a phone number was provided for Tom Willoughby Guide Services.

When I called the number, I reached the Bryson Hesperia Resort in California where I talked with Deedy: owner, manager, and hog hunter. After I explained my goal, Deedy was enthusiastic and excited to have me try their operation. Although Bryson Hesperia's prices were high by southeastern standards, the fees sounded pretty reasonable when compared to other California hunts. Regardless, beggars were no longer able to be choosers, and it was exciting to find an outfit with open dates and a positive attitude. Without further ado, I booked a hunt and a flight to San Francisco.

The night before the California trip, I logged onto the airline's Web site to find that my tickets had been cancelled! Gritting my teeth, I started looking for new flights. Even if flights were available, I figured, I'd get stuck with an exorbitant fee. But Orbitz turned up another series of flights on a slightly different schedule for $20 more than my original tickets. It was a miracle! The trip was booked and tickets purchased from Pensacola to San Francisco via Houston.

Arriving at the airport in Pensacola at 9:30 a.m., I found I had plenty of time before boarding for a few cups of coffee and to write down an outline of the Florida hunts from the weekend before. I cleared security without incident, which was a welcome change. On a previous flight out of Pensacola, the police had pulled me to the side after my backpack went through the X-ray machine and a Transportation Security Administration (TSA) agent asked, "What's this?" holding up a twenty-gauge shotgun shell.

The first word out of my mouth was "Crap!"—more a reflection of my feelings than an answer to his question.

They were actually pretty cool about the incident. The airport policeman said, "Tell me you are sorry."

I provided a heartfelt assurance: "I am very, very, very sorry that that shell was in my bag!"

Later, the TSA sent me a nasty letter and probably put me on some terrorism watch list, but I was not required to pay a fine or appear in court.

Before this flight, I had unzipped every pocket on my backpack, dumping all the contents. I'd found: 7 Mag, .243, and .17 HMR shells, a pocketknife, a Leatherman, a fillet knife, and a sharpening stone. The cartridges stayed in Alabama, but everything else went into my checked luggage.

The first leg of the flight was delayed, and as the minutes stretched by, I knew the transfer to the second leg was going to be tight. The plane touched down in Houston and pulled up to the gate. According to my tickets, the San Francisco flight was in another terminal, and it had started boarding half an hour earlier. My connection was scheduled for departure in twelve minutes. It didn't look good.

I was the third passenger out the door, running up the ramp, through the terminal, and back down some stairs to the train between terminals. I arrived at the gate four minutes before the scheduled departure. The Houston departure was also delayed, and they were just getting around to the standby passengers. Breathing a sigh of relief, I handed over the boarding pass and got on the plane. The flight had been delayed only by about twenty to thirty minutes, just long enough for me to make the connection.

The second plane landed in San Francisco at 6:00 p.m. Incredibly, my checked luggage and cooler had made the connection in Houston. I picked up a rental car and stopped for supper at a nearby Thai restaurant. After the hectic rushing of the day, I had a little time to think things over during the meal.

What are the important things in life? On a scale of 1 to 10, killing pigs in ten states over a twelve-month period probably didn't rank that high. But this was an adventure, if not an odyssey, that would probably never be duplicated in my life, and memories of this year would stay with me always.

Deedy had e-mailed directions from San Francisco to a twenty-four-hour Super Wal-Mart on the way to Bryson Hesperia. The sporting goods section sold a two-day nonresident hunting license for $38, and a nonresident pig tag was a little over $60. Thus a nonresident hunter was allowed to kill one wild pig for $100 in the Golden State.

To my knowledge, California is the only state that treats wild hogs just like any other big game animal. According to Professor Ditchkoff at Auburn University, "This may explain their rapid population expansion on the West Coast."

My day had started nearly twenty-four hours ago, so the last one hundred miles of my drive were a struggle. To stay awake, I repeatedly rolled down the windows, letting the freezing air rush around me. A coyote and two jackrabbits narrowly missed becoming roadkill during the last twenty miles of the trip. I pulled into the Bryson Hesperia Resort at 12:30 a.m. local time.

Deedy had left the lights on and the door unlocked at cabin number 3. I packed and carried my gear in, and I was fast asleep fifteen minutes later.

There was a knock on the door at 6:10 a.m. I was supposed to have been up by 6:00. Dressing quickly, I grabbed my knives, Leatherman, digital camera, and video camera. I stepped into the resort office at 6:20 and shook hands with Deedy and Tom Willoughby. Deedy's daughter Karin would also be coming along. The three of them would try to find me some pigs.

The sky was just starting to get light and Tom was impatient, saying, "We should have been in the field already." I hopped into Tom's twenty-year-old Chevy pickup, which had four hog dogs in the back. Deedy handed me a brand-new short-barreled Remington .308, informing me, "I just had two shooting instructors from the army check to make sure this is sighted in, so it should be dead-on." She and Karin followed us out of the resort, each in a big, new Ford diesel pickup. The Gods of Global Warming smiled.

Tom drove a curving road that would have qualified as "mountainous" in Lower Alabama or Missouri. I asked him, "What are we hunting?"

"Pigs."

The question had not been framed properly. Now that the blindingly obvious was out there, I clarified. "I mean what type of land? State? Federal? Private?"

His next answer was a little more helpful. "We'll be hunting private land today."

We were making a little progress. "Does the property have a name?"

"No, we'll be hunting two or three different ownerships this morning, but I don't think they are named." Tom turned into a driveway, and I jumped out to open a homemade barbed wire gate, just like those back on the farm in Missouri.

One hundred yards up the side of a steep hill, his radio went off: "Tom! Tom! Tom!" Tom picked up the two-way radio and answered. Deedy's voice came over loud and clear, "I've got six pigs running up a ridge across the highway from you!" Tom did a U-turn, bouncing back down the hill, through the gate, and about a quarter of a mile back up the highway.

Deedy and Karin were parked on the side of the road just ahead of us. Tom pointed up a very steep hill on their side of the highway. "There goes a pig!" he yelled. The ridge was nearly straight up and the pigs were gone by the time I looked. Tom pulled in beside Deedy and Karin.

Deedy said, "There were five to seven pigs and they just went over that ridge." She pointed to the area where Tom had seen the last pig entering the tree line. Tom pulled through an open gate and bounced uphill, circling around to the back side of the tall ridge. He picked up the radio. "Deedy, come in behind us so you can see them if they come down the ridge behind us. We'll circle around and see if we can get ahead of them."

The road followed an open grassy valley, with oak forests covering the ridges above us. The ridge where Deedy had seen the pigs was now above us and to our left. Following the valley, the road curved back to the right. Rounding a bend,

Tom and I simultaneously spotted a large boar standing in the middle of the valley, about one hundred yards ahead of us. The boar was thick in the front end, tapering to smaller hindquarters. This was a good one. Tom immediately stopped, saying, "Get out and get him!"

I opened the door and went as far away from the truck as required to meet California legal restrictions. The boar was standing still, looking at us. I was getting ready to shoot when Tom told me, "Put a bullet in the barrel!"

The bolt wouldn't move. I slipped off the safety, which allowed me to cycle a round into the chamber. The boar started running up the slope to the right. In seconds the boar would enter the tree line. The boar was angling away, moving at a good pace to the right. Tom said, "Aim for the shoulder." He handed out instructions as if I were a first-time hunter.

Moving the crosshairs just behind the shoulder, I had just started to tighten up on the trigger when the rifle fired, startling me.

The first flight, the one that was cancelled, would have gotten me to the resort earlier. An earlier arrival would have given me time to practice with Deedy's rifle. Then I would have known that the trigger pull was exceptionally light, especially compared to my 7 Mag and my .17 HMR.

The boar stumbled at the shot. It recovered and ran into the trees, disappearing before I could get another round in the barrel. Judging by the boar's movement, it had been hit hard, but possibly too far back. Back in the truck, I told Tom, "I may have gut shot him," as he drove up the valley.

Tom pulled up to the timberline and looked up the ridge, saying, "He's down!"

The boar was about fifty yards above us. It seemed that Tom was compelled to order my every move. "Go up to him but have your gun ready." He was really starting to get on my nerves.

I stepped out of the truck and started up the hill. Tom told me, "I'll go get the girls," as he circled around and disappeared down the valley.

The boar started rolling downhill, coming to a stop a mere twenty yards up the slope from where I was standing. There was no need for a follow-up shot on this pig.

This one was special. The heavy front end, the exceptionally long black hair on the back, the overall form, and the coloration identified this hog as having a very high percentage of Russian or European blood. Some of my previous kills had long snouts and other Russian characteristics, but nothing like this. The tusks were a little small, but this was a beautiful boar.

It had taken only about fifteen minutes in the field to score this kill, but that was okay. There had been way too much stress over the last several months. It was going to be really nice, sitting back and enjoying the scenery from this point forward, because there was a fine California hog under my belt.

Tom pulled up with Deedy and Karin. Deedy was very excited when she saw my boar. "Look at that! Look at that long hair! This pig has a lot of Russian!"

It was a pretty boar. "Yeah, this pig has more Russian blood than any I've ever killed."

My boar was harvested in Monterrey County which, according to statistics from the California Department of Fish and Game, leads the state in numbers of feral hogs harvested annually.

Because my boar was more "Russian" in appearance than most of the pigs Deedy encountered, she wondered aloud if it had come from Russian boars reportedly introduced on the nearby William Randolph Hearst ranch. Fortuitously, Deedy knew William R. Hearst's grandson, George Hearst, so later she called him on her cell phone to ask if we had killed one of his pigs. According to Deedy, George Hearst told her, "My ancestors did not introduce Russian pigs onto our land." Mr. Hearst thought that the Russian pigs were descendents of a herd brought into the central coast area by a gentleman farmer (he couldn't remember his name) and released in the Carmel Valley in the 1920s.

Later, I read *Hunting Wild Boar in California* by Bob Robb. Mr. Robb backed up Mr. Hearst's account, attributing the European/Russian characteristics of the pigs in the central coast region to "three boars and nine sows . . . released onto the San Francisquito Ranch in Monterey County in the mid-1920s. This was the first documented release of pure-strain wild boar into California."

Deedy directed the photo shoot like a true professional. She had me drag the boar to a large exposed root where the light was good. Propping up the pig, I knelt behind it, with one hand steadying its back. Deedy snapped away with her digital and mine while Tom paced in the background. Deedy shook her head and smiled. "He hates this type of stuff," she said, meaning the photo shoot.

I offered, "I imagine he's pretty happy with the length of the hunt." It was only 7:15 a.m. and his job was already complete.

After a few dozen photos, we loaded the boar into a truck. Everybody guessed at the pig's weight. Tom guessed 190. Deedy offered 220. I went with Deedy's estimate. Shaking hands with Tom and saying good-bye for the day, I hopped in the truck with Deedy and rode back to the Bryson Hesperia Resort.

Deedy unloaded the boar and located a set of new scales. When she cranked the boar up, we found that it weighed 181 pounds. Tom's guess was only nine pounds off. Deedy and I hadn't guessed so well.

The course of the bullet was easily tracked while we gutted the pig. The 150-grain bullet had entered behind the right front shoulder, traveling through the lungs, through the ribs on the far side, entering and shattering the left front shoulder, and then exiting. It was a devastating blow.

Two activated U.S. Army Reserve shooting instructors, Mark and Russell, walked up to inspect the kill. Deedy introduced us. They were training soldiers to shoot at the nearby Fort Hunter Liggett. Rather than using base housing, they were renting a cabin from Deedy, and they were envious of my pig. Mark said, "I would have that pig mounted, for sure."

If this boar had had larger tusks, I would have considered getting it mounted, but the tusks were only one and a half inches long and my financial situation was already precarious.

When the pig was gutted, skinned, and quartered, we put the meat in a walk-in cooler.

I asked Deedy, "How does your average hunter stack up in marksmanship?"

She frowned. "Not very good. I always try to get them out to the range before we go so I can see how they shoot. Some of them do okay until they see the pig, and then they can't hold it together."

Deedy described a case in point. "I had a lawyer come in to hunt with us. I had trail cameras that showed a really nice spotted boar coming to our barley field every day at 8:45 a.m. So I set this guy up close to where the trail entered the field. Sure enough, we heard the boar coming down the ridge about 8:40. The guy let the pig get to within twenty yards. Then, instead of sliding the safety off, he snapped it off. The boar heard the click, wheeled around, and started running for the brush. The guy didn't have a shot, but he pulled the trigger and blew the front shoulder off. We looked until midnight before we finally gave up. But the pig lived, and I am pretty sure he is starting to work the field again."

I asked Mark and Russell, "What about the soldiers you are training? How is their marksmanship?"

Mark answered, "On average, simply atrocious. These are all people who qualified and most of them have been in the service for several years, but many of them are still scared of their M-16s."

Mark continued, "While it's bad enough with rifles, what's really bad is their competency with pistols. The MPs are worst of all. These guys are like, 'I am an MP. It's a pistol. Don't bother.'"

Deedy explained that Mark had won the "All Army" shooting competition a couple of years back. Mark said he hadn't won the individual competition last year, but his team had won three years' running. So later I joined Mark on the shooting range where he was practicing with an M1 Garand, the standard-issue rifle for most soldiers in World War II.

Mark said, "I've got two rounds left. Do you want to shoot it?"

Of course I did. "Sure!"

He loaned me his earmuffs and I assumed the prone position, aiming one hundred meters downrange. The sun was directly in my face. Mark held his hand out to shade my eyes. The trigger pull was atrocious; I finally pulled it back far enough to fire the rifle. I took the second shot.

The first shot was in the closest ring, less than one inch off dead center. The second shot drifted about four inches high, less than impressive.

Russell uncased a brand-new .204. As Russell fired, Mark watched through a spotting scope, calling correction, "One minute left and two minutes down." But Russell's scope wasn't holding, and the bullets kept drifting off. Mark reminded Russell, "I told you that brand sucked when you were buying it," referring to the scope.

Back at the resort, Deedy offered to take all of us to Fort Hunter Liggett for a pig hunt. Mark wanted to kill a pig with his M1 Garand. Both Mark and Russell are from North Dakota, and neither had killed a wild hog before, although Russell had grown up around pigs. "I've killed dozens of domestic hogs with a .22. Sometimes I had to shoot a hog more than once, but that was pretty rare."

Deedy drove past a couple of large herds of tule elk on the way to Fort Hunter Liggett. Besides elk, black-tailed deer were all over the place. I noticed that their average antler size was pretty modest. Deedy said, "Around here, a fork-horn is about as good as you get."

Deedy pulled up to the front gate, where the security guard checked our IDs and waved us through. She asked me, "Have you seen the mission yet?"

I had heard of the California missions but hadn't seen one yet. So she drove us to the Mission San Antonio, the third mission established by the Spanish in California, several hundred years back. She told me, "Of all the missions I've seen, this one is my favorite."

Deedy stopped so we could read a couple of historical markers before driving deeper into the base. Parking at a trailhead, she let her dog run ahead as we followed her through a pasture of short grass. Steep, eroded rock faces and gullies stretched to our right.

On the property we had hunted earlier in the morning, cattle had eaten every visible sprig of grass. Cattle trails and cow pies were everywhere. Occasional pig rooting was visible beneath the valley oaks, but it didn't appear that pigs were having a significant impact on the environment. Certainly, pigs were impacting the flora and fauna in ways both visible (rooting, rubs, wallows) and unseen (what herpetofauna did feral hogs eat in California?). But as I had discovered during my hunt around Mims, Florida, it was evident here that large numbers of cattle were affecting the ground cover and soil ten times as much as the pigs were.

I asked Deedy, "Are there any areas around here where hogs are a real problem?"

She told me about a nearby county park. "I heard from some of the staff that they trapped and disposed of nearly a thousand pigs last year."

The National Park Service has a long history of excluding hunters, and this is the perfect recipe for exploding deer and hog populations. The Great Smoky Mountains National Park is a good example: professional marksmen are employed to do what hunters could do for free.

The four of us walked beneath some beautiful old valley oaks. Their large, bowling pin–shaped acorns littered the ground. I told Deedy and the soldiers, "Back home the deer and pigs would be all over this mast."

Deedy replied, "We had a really good number of acorns this year." Then she took us to the entrance of a box canyon with a stream flowing out of it. "This is a favorite hangout for pigs, but there is no sign [tracks] going in, so we won't find any pigs here today. In a month or two they should move back. When they are in this canyon, you've got a near-guaranteed shot because there is nowhere else for them to exit. They have to come by this spot."

We walked back to the truck, and Deedy drove off base to a property near the resort. Turning onto a dirt road that dropped into a valley, she told us, "I want to show you some Rio turkeys. They are down here every afternoon."

On the way up the valley some California Gamble's quail crossed the road in front of us. Not much further on, Deedy pointed to a whole flock of gobblers on the right. She shut off the engine and I pulled out my video camera and filmed the flock as the turkeys casually crossed the road twenty yards in front of us. Deedy said, "Listen to this." She started her engine, and several turkeys gobbled. She opened and shut her door, and they gobbled again.

Sunset was approaching and Deedy wanted to chase pigs one more time. "Let's go up the road and watch for the pigs to come out. Mark and Russell might get a shot yet."

Pulling through a gate next to a small farmhouse, she drove up a large, steep hill, stopping on a peak several hundred feet above the road below. The spot allowed for long to exceptionally long shots in several directions. Deedy pointed across the highway. "Generally they come from that direction. The first thing they do when they get up [pigs generally nap in the heat of the day] is go to water, and there is a permanent spring down here to our left."

I asked. "How many are there generally?"

It was a bunch. "About thirty. There is one big old black sow that seems to be dominant. She is continuously sniffing and watching out for danger."

Obviously, Deedy knew this sounder well. I asked her, "Do they follow a pretty regular pattern?"

She answered, "Yes, a lot of these pigs do pick up steady patterns, until a lion [puma or cougar] moves in. When a lion comes into an area, it can change everything, and the pigs may get pushed clear out of their territory for a while."

The four of us watched the surrounding hills and valleys for about forty-five minutes while sitting in the truck. The only animals we saw were a couple of blacktail does just as we drove back down the hill in the gathering dark.

That night, Deedy, Karin, and Karin's friend Shelley cooked us a great meal. Mark and Russell assisted by firing up a grill and browning some pork ribs that Deedy had pressure-cooked earlier.

After supper, I showed them a few of my favorite YouTube clips, including the clip of the Tom Willoughby hunt that had led me to Bryson Hesperia. Deedy hadn't seen that clip before.

Deedy was one of the most interesting hunting guides I've ever met. I wasn't sure how long she had been guiding, but she approached her job with a tremendous amount of enthusiasm, practical knowledge, and experience. She told me that she had been a wrangler/cowgirl. She described one incident in which she was riding her horse up a trail along a steep drop-off when a wild cow charged out of the chaparral. "I'd just had time to lift my leg out of the stirrup when the cow hit the side of the horse, pushing us over the cliff. It killed my horse."

Deedy came across as an independent, tough, warm-hearted, capable cowgirl—and I realize the redundancy of using those adjectives with the term "cowgirl." Finding her and booking a hunt with the Bryson Hesperia Resort had been incredibly good luck.

Nine states down; one to go.

21   INSIDE THE FENCE

But there it is: I enjoyed shooting a pig a whole lot more than I ever thought I should have.

—MICHAEL POLLAN, *The Omnivore's Dilemma,* 2006

Eastern red cedar (*Juniperus virginiana*): The only conifer native to northern Missouri. Eastern red cedar is a widespread, shade-tolerant, fire-intolerant, native evergreen. On the positive side: eastern red cedar yields a beautiful, aromatic, red and yellow wood that can be manufactured into closets, cases, paneling, and shelves. On subzero nights, red cedars may be covered with snow and ice on the exterior, but shine a light into the crown from straight below, and the branches will be filled with cardinals, blue jays, slate-colored juncos, mourning doves, and other birds that brave midwestern winters. Red cedar is readily available as a Christmas tree, and is more aromatic and attractive than the imported and cultivated Scotch pine. On the negative side: there are very few remnants of native tallgrass prairies, and in the absence of fire, eastern red cedar has invaded and dominated many of the remaining fragments. Also, if eastern red cedar is utilized as a Christmas tree, don't let it dry out. Its needles are impossible to remove from carpeting, and a parched cedar is liable to explode into flames if someone lights a cigarette within twenty feet.

I was running out of ways to make my ten–state program. The Mississippi hunt had fallen through when Chester couldn't find recent hog activity on the local WMA. Two or three people had offered to set up South Carolina hunts, but the property owners never came through with a response. Missouri had been a straight-up bust.

Oklahoma was an option I'd been considering for a few months. One outfit had been advertising hunts on eBay for a couple of years, but it was a high-fenced place with "guaranteed" opportunities where the hunters drove around and picked out the hog they wanted to kill. This struck me as patently ridiculous.

A search on the Internet turned up several other ranches offering hog hunts in Oklahoma. I'd forgotten that earlier in the year, Oklahoma had experienced historic floods until the first outfitter couldn't book me, explaining, "Most of our pigs died or were washed away in this summer's floods." An e-mail to a second outfitter yielded a quick reply: "Our hunting guide is out of town but he'll be back on November 22 and we'll let you know if he can take you."

My inquiry to the second outfitter explained my yearlong quest and intentions of writing a book about my experiences. When the guide read the e-mail, he turned me down, saying, "If you don't get a pig, I don't want you to blame me for your failure to reach your goal." This was the first time a hunter had responded negatively to my project.

The second outfitter recommended contacting the Shiloh Ranch, which she described as "a first-rate operation."

I dug a little deeper. "Are they high-fenced?" Earlier in the year I had decided only to hunt areas that were not fenced.

She replied, "It's low-fenced."

This was a conundrum. On the one hand, what was the point of setting a ten-state goal if I went from guaranteed hunt to guaranteed hunt? Where was the challenge in that? On the other hand, a large percentage of the hunts that are sold today are high-fenced hunts or, as in the case of Shiloh, "low-fenced."

Hunts on fenced operations are set up for a different clientele than I represent. They are fashionable among some wealthy individuals who desire a variety of trophy heads on the wall. Fenced operators turn every animal into a commodity. Most buy their game animals or raise them under agricultural regimes. Paying "hunters" are then offered a menu of animals. Different species of sheep and goats have become popular in this regimen because they offer comparably cheap but attractive trophies, with variable coats, beards, and horns. Prices for rams or billies may range from $300 to $600 for a good set of horns.

A hunter may not have the time or financial resources to hunt Asia or Africa, but most people can save enough to purchase the opportunity to kill exotics from fenced operations here in the United States.

One of the highest-priced trophies is our native white-tailed deer, and the value of the buck is directly correlated to the size of the rack. High-scoring bucks can go for thousands, even tens of thousands of dollars.

Pigs are pretty low on the totem pole. But even pigs become valuable trophies when their tusks reach certain lengths. If a boar has long tusks, this can double or triple the price of the animal. The largest boars may be priced between $500 and $1,000.

My one prior experience "inside the fence" had been shared with some friends in New Mexico. They ran some boars with hog dogs, shooting the pigs at near point-blank range in a cattail swamp while I walked the perimeter and stuck a stick in my eye. Having derided this type of hunt for years, maybe it would be better for me to criticize from experience rather than ignorance. Undertaking a fenced hunt would allow me to report accurately how such a hunt played out.

Matt Napper from Shiloh Ranch returned my call on Friday evening, November 24. There had been a few late cancellations and three dates were available in 2007. I reserved the last slot, December 28–30. If I were lucky enough to score in Florida (I was) and California (there too), Oklahoma would be the final stop on my itinerary.

Matt said Shiloh specialized in bow hunting and they tried to book all their stands with bow hunters. The organization's three-day package (one afternoon, one full day, and one morning) cost $295 for bow hunters or $350 for a rifle hunt, if a spot was available. Since this was a fenced hunt, hunting with a bow would add some degree of difficulty, and I felt obligated to give my archery skills another test.

December 28–30 fell in the middle of our Christmas vacation to Missouri. I would need to check for flights out of Kansas City or St. Louis. After a fair bit of searching, I found that the cheapest deal was flying from Kansas City to Dallas, picking up a rental car, and driving north to the Shiloh Ranch in Oklahoma. Compared to Oklahoma City flights, this added a couple of hours' driving, but the cheap flight and very cheap rental car made it worthwhile.

Shiloh guaranteed a chance at pigs inside bow range. Now it was necessary to bring my bow shooting back up to a proficient level. I had been on target in Tennessee, but the situation in Oklahoma might require longer shots. With practice, perhaps my comfort range could be extended from twenty-five yards out to thirty-five.

As will happen with aluminum arrows, several of mine were bent or busted in the weeks of practice before the Missouri-Oklahoma trip. Unfortunately, neither of my sources at home in Andalusia was stocking the arrow size I had been practicing with, so I planned to pick some up either on the way or once we reached Missouri. But of course my luck was such that I discovered Wal-Mart had taken all its archery supplies off the shelves. We stopped at numerous stores on the way north, but none had arrows in stock.

When Mom and Katia went Christmas shopping in Columbia, I sent an arrow with them, asking them to purchase more at the Bass Pro Shop. But they returned empty-handed. The Bass Pro Shop didn't have aluminum arrows in that size. So, crossing my fingers, I hoped to make it through the week without bending or breaking any more arrows during practice sessions.

My flight out of Kansas City International Airport was scheduled for a 5:55 a.m. departure on December 28. Since our farm is two hours from the airport, my good friend Mike, my companion on the Texas and Florida hunts, invited me to stay over at his place in Kearney, Missouri, just east of Kansas City.

Although Mike's house put me much closer to the airport, I still had to get up at 3:30 a.m. It was snowing, so Mike laid out a route choosing roads that were most likely to have been cleared. I was out the door at 4:00. After a slow, treacherous drive, I pulled into the airport at 5:00 a.m.

A long line of passengers already snaked from the ticketing/check-in counter. After checking my bow and a cooler filled with clothing, I cleared security and just made it to the gate as the plane was boarding. I took a seat and looked out the window at several inches of snow covering the plane's wing. Not good!

After everyone had boarded and taken their seats, the captain announced, "The plane needs to be deiced twice." He explained that the first deicing would wash off the accumulated snow and ice, and the second would prevent further accumulation. By the time they finished spraying us down, the flight was forty minutes late.

I was more relieved than normal to achieve a safe liftoff and smooth landing at Love Field in Dallas, where I picked up the rental car and drove north toward Ada, Oklahoma, calling the ranch along the way to let them know I'd be there for the 12:00 p.m. orientation. Matt Napper, one of the co-owners, gave excellent directions, and I managed to arrive fifteen minutes early.

Four other hunters had arrived for the weekend hunt. John, a retired firefighter, was a return customer and Oklahoma native. He was shooting with a modern compound bow. Mike was a local schoolteacher who apparently had a deal worked out with Shiloh whereby he could do some hunting while guiding the paying hunters. Mike had shot two pigs in the morning with his modern compound bow and he would be carrying a camera to the field for the afternoon. Mike was also an author, having written and self-published a book entitled *Class Dismissed, I'm Going Hunting*. The other two hunters were Will (whose name I have changed), an older gentleman from Columbus, Georgia, and his son-in-law, Peter (name also changed). Will would be the only hunter using modern firearms. He was shooting a .30-06. Peter would be shooting a compound bow.

As I unpacked and put on my hunting clothes, Peter took a few practice shots with his bow. That looked like a good idea, so I retrieved my bow and quiver. It had proven impossible to locate new arrows, and my quiver held only three unblemished arrows with 125-grain broadheads. A fourth arrow had a field point and insert forced up into the shaft. Adding to my difficulties, the nock had slipped up the bowstring, and the first practice shot with the field point was way low. Worried that the deformed shaft was affecting the flight of the arrow, I decided to take a couple of practice shots with a broadhead.

Adjusting slightly upward, I let fly, again hitting low, but not as badly as on the first shot. Extracting the arrow from the target, I tried again and aimed a little higher. This shot struck closer to the bull's-eye. When I grabbed the shaft and tugged, the shaft came out but the broadhead stayed in the target. Down to two functioning arrows now, I was up a creek without a paddle. I dug into the target with my Leatherman, fruitlessly attempting to locate and extract the broadhead buried deep in the foam rubber target.

Matt and Cheryl (husband and wife) pulled in to the driveway. It was time for orientation, so all of us walked to the camp office and took seats around a table. Matt explained the rules of the hunt. Hunters in tree stands were required to use tree harnesses. Our price of $295 covered one pig of any size. There were no trophy fees for boars with outsized tusks. Hunters who wanted to shoot an additional pig could do so for $1.50 per pound live weight. The hunting enclosure was four hundred acres, and if anyone got lost or disoriented, he had only to follow the fence, which would eventually lead him back to the front gate.

Matt said, "If you shoot a pig and don't kill it, be honest! If you don't tell me, I will find out, and you will be escorted off the ranch and not allowed back." Hunters were required to fill out an information sheet detailing our arrow length and fletching style as well as colors, brand, and other identifying characteristics of our arrows and points. Presumably, if Matt found a wounded or dead pig with one of our arrows sticking out of it, he could quickly identify the guilty party.

Most of the goats and sheep on this property cost $450 and up to kill. There were also fallow and sika deer for the taking.

Matt recommended that all hunters be on their stands by 3:00 p.m. and stay there until dark. Spotting and stalking was prohibited with firearms, but not with a bow. However, it was clear that the owners disapproved of this method. Cheryl said, "Most of our wounded and lost pigs come about when people spot and stalk."

Matt added, "We have about a 95 percent success rate from our stands, but only about 20 percent success when people get down and walk around."

Matt pointed to shelves lined with small lunch bags that were filled with shelled corn. "I would take at least a couple of bags of corn with you. Scatter some in front of your stand. When they come in, that corn will hold them close. If you have other, exotic animals come in and start eating the corn, don't scare them off. Those are the best decoys you can have to draw the pigs in."

Peter asked about the wind direction and stand selection. Shiloh had eight feeders set to scatter corn at 7:00 a.m. and 4:00 p.m. The wind was moving from the north to the west. Matt recommended stands 1A, 2, 4, and 7. Will from Georgia with the .30-06 wanted stand 1A. It was closest to our cabins, so he wouldn't have to walk far. Peter picked a stand a little farther around the bend from his father-in-law.

John, the return customer from Oklahoma, warned us, "Stand 7 is a haul. It is way back on the east boundary." Earlier, Matt had told me that the walk to the stand was one and a quarter miles. Maybe 1.25 miles was a "haul" to these guys, but it was a short stroll compared to distances I had walked on many of my previous—and no doubt future—hunts.

I volunteered, "I'll take 7."

There were two stands on the northern boundary, 5 and 6. John said, "I would like to work back and forth between 5 and 6."

With his camera, Mike took one of the remaining stands on the south side.

With orientation wrapped up, I had a few minutes to contemplate my sorry arrow supply. Placing the two arrows with broadheads and the third arrow with the screwed-up field point in my quiver, I walked past Mike, the hunter who had killed two pigs earlier in the morning. Mike observed, "That's confidence, only three arrows!" If only he knew.

It took five minutes to reach the north boundary. Passing stand 5, I was walking a ridge along the fence, looking down the trail, when a herd of fifty- to seventy-pounders ran into the woods. A rifle shot would have been possible in the brush, but it would have been a low-probability shot.

A few hundred yards farther up the trail, three larger, black pigs stood up in some grass about forty yards away. Another black pig was still bedded in the grass. I contemplated a stalk for about two seconds before the bedded pig jumped up and followed the other pigs into the woods. It would have been pretty easy to drop at least one with a rifle, I thought.

I was halfway to my stand when a large black sow with a couple of shoats walked into the road about two hundred yards east. This was another good rifle opportunity, but it would be a challenging stalk with a bow. Entering the woods, I paralleled the trail, peeking out after covering half the distance to the sow. The sow and piglets had disappeared into the woods, so I resumed the trek to my stand.

The number of pigs on this place was impressive.

A smaller trail broke off to stand 7, where I found a small clearing with a feeder on the right (north). A tripod was set up in some eastern red cedars to the right of the feeder. Matt and Mike had recommended a ground blind to the east of the feeder. With the prevailing wind out of the west, I went with their recommendations.

Before I could enter the blind, however, a pig roared about one hundred to two hundred yards to the west. It sounded like a mature boar. The pigs were invisible in the thick brush west of the feeder, but they were close.

While we had been preparing for our hunt, Mike had told me, "Your heart will get to beating when you hear those pigs snorting and grunting on the way in." I couldn't agree more: the squeals and snorts coming from the woods had my pulse racing.

I tiptoed to the ground blind and pulled boards off the windows, placing my gear inside. I stepped back out with a bag of corn, scattering half of it from ten to fifteen yards in front of the blind. If pigs went to the feeder on the opposite end of the clearing, it would still be a reasonable shot. Mike had informed me, "Your feeder will be twenty-one yards from your stand."

The pigs kept up a steady racket in the woods to the west. Returning to the ground blind, I nocked an arrow and set my video camera in the window, adjusting it to make sure it was set to cover most of the feeder and the area in front before I turned it off to conserve the battery. Next, I adjusted the curtains to allow a shot to my front or left. Going to full draw, I found there was plenty of clearance and my position felt good. The best shot in the blind would be from a kneeling position.

Just as I set the bow down, a rustling to my left alerted me. Picking the bow up again, I heard the crunching of corn. A razorback sow was chowing down less than ten yards out. That was quick!

Before this hunt, I had told friends and family, "The first pig to walk into my sights gets shot!"

I reached over and turned on the video camera. The camcorder beeped twice, spooking the sow. The pig ran to the edge of the clearing, about thirty to forty yards away. The corn must have tasted pretty good, however, because the sow threw caution to the wind and charged back in.

At full draw, I put the ten-yard pin a little high behind the front shoulder, centering the lungs. Based upon my practice shots, the arrow would strike low. With the sow broadside facing right, I triggered the release.

The arrow flew through the sow, bounced off the ground, and landed in a mud puddle beneath the feeder. The sow wheeled and ran into the woods. It can be hard to judge a shot, but it looked like the arrow had struck too low. Picking up my remaining broadhead, I nocked the arrow.

As I exited the stand, the sow had a final message: *Uuurrrrrrrrr.* The closest thing to approximate this sound comes from distressed-looking actors on TV commercials emitting a sound of pain followed by, "Oh, my aching head" or "I can't believe I ate the whole thing." Mortally wounded pigs often make this sound just before they expire.

Picking up the camcorder, I walked toward the woods. Dry leaves rustled in the woods to my left. A red pig and a black pig were approaching. I figured they would see me and run away, but nothing doing. The pair stopped at the woods' edge about fifteen yards away. These two looked like they had come straight from a pig farm. The two pigs entered the plot behind me and started eating the corn. I turned around and filmed the pair vacuuming up the corn, thinking, "This is a little embarrassing."

Back to the task at hand, I had an excellent blood trail to follow, and it didn't take long to find the sow. The arrow had struck low, taking out the heart, which sits beneath the lungs. It was a relief to find the sow quickly, and I should have been ecstatic about reaching my ten-state goal, but I was already thinking about the other pigs in the woods surrounding the stand. How many more would come in? Should I shoot another?

The two domestic pigs backed off a little as I dragged the sow past the corn. Having quickly worked through their grief over the loss of their fellow porcine, they resumed eating.

I retrieved the arrow that had killed the sow. It was still straight and the fletching was intact. On the negative side, one of the three blades had broken off, and the arrow was coated with soupy mud from one end to the other, having landed in the mud puddle beneath the feeder.

Back in the stand, I checked the video camera. Unfortunately, though I had turned the camera on, I'd forgotten to hit the "Record" button. The video camera only had footage of me trailing and locating the sow.

The domestic pigs snuffled up the corn until the area was clean, then trotted north. But it sounded like there was a whole herd of pigs back in the brush. I scattered the remainder of the bag of corn in front of my stand. It was about 3:30 p.m.

There was time to sit back and contemplate the successful completion of my goal, but not for long. In just a few minutes, a herd of pigs filtered through the cedars and post oaks on the north edge of the plot. The pigs were about thirty-five yards out, waiting for the feeder to go off. I judged the herd to be at the extreme edge of my range, under good conditions. With only one good arrow and my bow hitting low, the pigs were about twice as far away as I wanted to shoot.

The pigs milled about on the edge of the woods. They were a mix of colors and sizes. A couple of pigs were a fair bit taller than the rest. The two tall pigs and a pretty spotted pig were all worthy targets. Given an opportunity, I would let fly at the first subject to provide a close-in, stationary shot from a good angle.

Before long, my decoy pigs went back to work. The black pig made a beeline for the corn scattered in front of the stand. The rest of the herd followed close behind. I hit the "Record" button on my video camera as they crossed the plot. Picking up my bow, I went to full draw as soon as the herd commenced eating. I drew a bead on one of the taller red pigs, but the shot was obscured by smaller pigs. The other tall pig circled to the edge of the herd on the left, clear of the smaller pigs.

The tall pig paused on the left, offering a broadside shot. Pivoting left, I put the twenty-yard pin on the center of the vitals behind the right front shoulder and triggered the release. The arrow thwacked into the pig, but did not pass through this hog, a taller, thicker boar. The boar wheeled, the arrow protruding from both sides as it ran into the woods, using the same exit path as the previously shot sow.

Within seconds, my friends the small black and red boars were back on the corn. As they crunched away, several of the feral hogs saw they were missing out, so they trotted back in to join the feast. Still in the stand, I watched the pigs mill around, cleaning up the corn. A couple of minutes after the shot, from the woods to the north I heard, *Uuurrrrrr.* A pause. Then again, *Uuurrrrrrrr.*

I nocked the arrow that had killed the sow. This was my only backup arrow on the boar. Picking up the video camera, I exited the stand. All of the feral hogs ran away, but not my two friends, now fully recovered from the dual tragedy of losing two acquaintances in less than one hour.

The feeder spun as I exited the clearing, throwing corn onto the surrounding soil and mud puddle beneath it. The boar brothers finished eating the corn near the shooting house and switched over to the feeder, where they went to work on the newly scattered corn.

A blood trail was not readily visible this time. Since the arrow had not passed clean through, it may have prevented blood from escaping the entrance and exit wounds. Pausing to examine my surroundings, I saw numerous pigs rooting in a nearby clearing. About a hundred yards out, I circled back to the left and entered some thick brush. The boar was lying on its side not more than twenty yards away. It was dead.

The arrow was still protruding from the pig's side, having struck a couple of inches higher than the spot I'd aimed for, but it was still a good lung shot. Two arrows had been traded for two dead pigs.

I dragged the boar back through the opening and laid the carcasses side by side, estimating the sow at 75 pounds and the boar at 140. It was only 4:15 p.m., and under normal conditions, it would have been pleasant to sit and film the pigs and/or exotics until dark. But it was the holidays, and time spent at Shiloh was time not spent with my family. I might be able to turn the rental car in early and return to Missouri sooner than expected.

I retraced my route from the cabins. The large black sow was back in the trail. It was the same pig I had stalked earlier on the way in to stand 7. Besides the sow, there were ghostly deer, pale to white, in the woods. These were fallow does. I circled past stand 5, where a nice black sow was eating corn beneath the feeder, about a hundred yards off the main trail.

Emerging into a clearing near the cabins, I saw a beautiful ram watching my approach. Not being familiar with the various species or types of goats and sheep, I was unsure of its breed. It was very pretty, and very tame—it walked in my direction before stopping about twelve yards out. With an extra broadhead and $450, the ram could have mine for the taking. Even if I had had both, I still would have passed. Shooting an animal this tame would be the same as buying a mounted head at an estate sale.

Back at the cabin, it was time to weigh costs and options. With just the sow, it would be possible to fit the meat in my cooler, packing my clothing around bagged cuts of meat. But with the boar added in, much of the meat would have to be left behind. Or I could fill the cooler to seventy pounds and pay for an extra bag to hold my clothing. This would require staying until my Sunday flight and paying at least $100 in extra bag and overweight luggage fees. But if I drove back to the farm in the morning, all of the meat and both heads could make the trip. As a bonus, I would get home a day and a half early.

I called the car company in Dallas and was put through to the manager. I started off, "My contract was for three days and returning the car to your office at Love Field. My hunt has ended early. I wanted to see if I could drop my car off at Kansas City International Airport."

The manager sounded annoyed. "Your contract was not for a one-way rental. There would be a fee."

That was obvious, but how bad were they going to stick me? "I figured there would be a fee. If it's not too much, I would like to drop my car off at the airport."

She replied, "Okay, you can do that and it will be between $150 and $200."

That was acceptable. "Are you sure it won't be something extreme, like $400?"

"No, I can't tell you the exact amount but somewhere between $150 and $200."

Something in my gut said, "This person is not trustworthy." But I decided to go with it.

The cabins had an intercom to Matt and Cheryl. I held the button down: "Matt and Cheryl, this is Mark."

Cheryl came on. "Go ahead, Mark."

"Hi, Cheryl. I was hunting at stand 7. I shot my first pig early so I decided to take another one. I've got a nice boar and a razorback sow."

"Congratulations, Mark. Did you drag them out to the road? And is there anyone else hunting that we would interfere with on the north side if we went to get the pigs?"

I told Cheryl, "I dragged both pigs out to the trail, but John is hunting on 5 or 6 and he is not out yet."

Cheryl said, "If John comes out, give me a call and we'll go get your pigs. Congratulations again."

Fifteen minutes later, John walked up. I asked him, "How did you do?"

He shook his head. "I got a little sow, but it took me three shots."

It wasn't that bad. "That's okay. At least you got it."

John told the story. "This black sow kept coming to the feeder but she was really spooky. I finally decided, 'It's now or never.' I jerked the trigger on my release and gut shot her. She ran off and I walked around until I saw her lying down. I was able to get in range and shoot again. The second time, the arrow hit the front shoulder and didn't penetrate. She got up and ran a short distance before she lay down again. The third time I said, 'I'm going to take my time on this shot,' and I hit her behind the shoulder. That one killed her."

Was his pig still in the woods? "Did you drag it out?"

"No, she's about a hundred yards back in the woods."

I suggested, "Let's call Matt and Cheryl, and let them know that we'll be at your stand dragging your pig out. Then we can go pick up my pigs."

John agreed, so I raised Cheryl on the radio. Cheryl said she would meet us at stand 5, where John had shot his sow.

John and I walked back to his stand. On the way, we heard a shot from the direction of stand 1A. It was 5:09 p.m. and darkness wasn't long away.

Back at stand 5, John led us straight to the sow. I assured him that his sow weighed over a hundred pounds. John was twenty to thirty years older than I, but in decent physical condition. We finished dragging the sow to the road just as Cheryl pulled up in an ATV. With the sow loaded up, Cheryl, John, and I hopped into the ATV. It was getting nippy but the windshield and roof made for a comfortable ride.

As we rode the ridge back to get my pigs, I quizzed Cheryl. "Where do you get your pigs from?"

She pointed across the fence. "Our neighbor traps them and sells them to us. He's had herds of pigs come in and tear up his Bermuda grass fields. Now that he can sell the pigs, he has turned an expensive problem into an extra source of income. Operations like ours have created such a demand that we've made feral hogs a commodity in these parts."

I was curious about the fences. "So these fences are sufficient to keep your fallow and sika deer in? Do the pigs burrow out?"

Cheryl answered, "Fallow and sika don't jump like whitetail deer." Looking at the height of her fence, I knew that a typical whitetail deer in Chariton County,

Missouri, or Covington County, Alabama, would jump a fence like this several times a day.

Cheryl continued, "We ride the fences everyday. We corn the roads to feed the pigs, and if we see any holes, we patch them up right away. We have a strong incentive to keep our pigs in, because we pay a minimum of $100 for a hog."

Since I had seen several pigs less than one hundred pounds, Shiloh was paying over $1 a pound for their smaller pigs, and that's more than most farmers get for domestic hogs.

Arriving at stand 7, Cheryl, John, and I got out and looked at the pigs. I asked Cheryl, "What do you think they'll weigh?" She guessed the sow at 90 pounds, 15 more than my guess. She guessed the boar at 140, the same number I had come up with.

John and I loaded my two pigs in the back, and we returned to camp. Driving past stand 5, we saw a pretty fallow buck standing by the feeder. I asked Cheryl, "What would that cost?"

"About $850."

It was a little less than I had expected. The fallow buck trotted away at our approach but stopped less than fifty yards away.

It was growing dark as we pulled up to the cleaning station. This operation had crossbars, gambles, and winches for hanging our kills. Cheryl demonstrated the skills of a professional guide, stretching out the two pigs and arranging them for a good photo. After our photo shoot, we cranked the pigs up on the scales. The sow weighed 80 pounds and the boar weighed 130. Cheryl and I had guessed fairly well.

Will from Georgia pulled up as I started gutting my pigs. He had killed a sow with his .30-06. A few minutes later, Mike returned with his camera.

Finally, Peter joined us, with the one sad story of the night. "I took a shot at a pig and I hit it a little low in the front quarter. It ran and fell down. It got back up and ran a short ways. Then it fell down again. It fell down a third time, before it got up and ran out of sight. It was too dark to follow a blood trail, so I came on out."

I skinned and quartered my sow as Mike, Cheryl, and John went with Peter to look for his pig. Matt pulled up just as I was finishing my sow. Will told Matt that the rest of them were out looking for Peter's pig. Matt was unhappy because Cheryl was sick with the flu. "The last time she did this it took her three weeks to get better."

Will decided to carry his pig to a local processor who worked up pigs for $60 a head. John just wanted his pig gutted. Matt gutted pigs for $10 a head. While Matt was gutting John's sow, Will complained, "There were a few good-sized pigs that came in early but they winded me and ran off. Then the 'petting zoo' came in—a bunch of goats and sheep and deer. They were eating up all the corn and standing in front of my stand. When the pigs came, they didn't want to come in because the 'petting zoo' was keeping them away. They could see me plain as day but they weren't scared at all."

Matt was clearly irritated. "They might not have been a challenge to experienced hunters like you and me, but we have physically disabled hunters come in here who have never had the chance to kill an animal."

Will had unwittingly pierced the illusion that was necessary for these operations to sell hunts. Hunters/shooters needed to believe these animals were "wild" and challenging targets.

Before leaving for the evening, Matt asked me, "Did you have fun?"

I answered honestly, "I did. I had a good time." The pigs were, in my opinion, the wariest animals on the property, excepting my friends the red and black boar brothers.

While I was still skinning my boar, the group returned from an unsuccessful search for Peter's wounded pig. Peter said, "We'll go back out first thing in the morning to look for my pig."

Feeling sorry for Peter, I said, "Do you want some of the meat off this boar?" Peter was all for it: "Sure!"

It turned out that Peter had a whole collection of knives, and he kept handing me new blades as I worked through the boar. Peter took two slabs of ribs and a hindquarter off the boar. The rest fit into my cooler on top of all the meat from the sow. Everyone else left for the warmth of the cabins or to deliver their pig carcasses to the processor.

With the pigs quartered, I washed up and drove seventeen miles into Ada, Oklahoma, to partake of an excellent Mexican supper. By the time I got back to

Shiloh, it was after 10:00 p.m., and Will and Peter were already sawing logs in the cabin. Lowering a ladder, I climbed into the loft and stretched out on a mattress. The day had started at 3:00 a.m. so it didn't take long for me to fall asleep.

I got up early the next morning, gratefully drinking the coffee Will offered. Per Matt's directions, I left the payment for my extra pig and started the drive home at 9:00. A few hours down the road, I called Mike in Missouri. "Hey, Mike!"

He was all ears. "How did it go?"

"I got my tenth state knocked out." Mike probably heard the relief in my voice.

"What did you get?"

I gave him a quick summary. "I took two pigs with my bow, including a razorback sow, within ten minutes of getting into my stand. I thought, 'What the heck, after spending all this time and money getting down here, why not pay a little extra and kill one more?'"

I asked Mike's opinion of hunts like this one. He was not as judgmental as I would have guessed. "It depends on your perception. For those guys hunting with you, that was probably a challenging hunt."

I agreed. "I don't want to run them down, because if you look at the hunting population as a whole, there aren't going to be that many guys who measure up to the knowledge, experience, or skill that you or Slim [Mike's brother] or John Dickson have."

Questioning Mike a bit further, I asked, "What would you call what I did [hunting a fenced and stocked area]?"

Mike answered, "You might have to trademark a name for that. I don't know if I would call it 'hunting,' but for some people it is probably as close as they will ever come."

When I arrived at the airport about 6:00 p.m., the rental car company representative looked up my contract on the computer. Clearly, the powers that be had decided they had me over a barrel. The company wanted a $999.99 drop fee. And although I was dropping off the car a day early, my other fees were increased—coming to a grand total of $1,300. Which was only $1,246 more than the original total of $54.

The poor girl behind the counter couldn't change the fees because there was no manager in Dallas to put a note in the computer about our agreement of $150 to $200. After nearly an hour of trying to straighten things out, the rental agent told me to come back the next morning. "We should be able to work things out when the manager in Dallas returns to the office at 9:00."

The countryside was still white from the snow that had fallen on the 28th. The temperature was in the low twenties the next morning as Mike and I drove to the airport. At the rental car office, the guy who looked up my record said, "Wow!" His computer showed that I now owed a $2,500 drop fee!

With the drop fee increasing by 250 percent daily, in only two weeks I would owe them $149,011,612. Since many of the major American banks were suffering a severe credit crunch tied to subprime mortgages, I would probably have to borrow the money from China or Dubai, just like the U.S. government.

There was no manager at the Kansas City office, but the manager in Dallas was in and she finally put the necessary note into the computer. The local agent, Hussein, was very agreeable, but he couldn't close out the account until his manager was on-site. Hussein promised me they would take care of it tomorrow.

Hussein was too nice for me to chew out, so I left with the resolve that if this weren't worked out, I would try my luck with the Alabama civil court system. If I weren't a satisfied customer by tomorrow, these buccaneers were going to become familiar with Alabama's infamous "jackpot" justice system. Having derided that aspect of Alabama's civil courts for years, I was starting to see it in a new light.

A few nights later, John Dickson gave me a call. He had big news from Bayou Cocodrie. "I've got to tell you about my recent hunt. I was duck hunting back in the 'Old Growth,' and I also carried my .22 Magnum because I figured there was a good chance of killing some pigs.

"I killed one duck and was checking the area out when I walked up on a sow with five piglets. I shot the sow with the .22 Magnum and it ran off. Walking through the palmetto, I found the sow. It had died and the piglets were nearby. I lined them up and rolled all three with one shot! I killed two and wounded the third."

The action didn't stop there. John told me he hit another sow that got away and he killed two more piglets, giving him his new personal record of six pigs in one hunt!

After John finished his story, I described my Oklahoma trip to him: the layout of the property (fence, blinds, feeders, etc.), the stocked pigs, and the clientele I had met. Then I asked him, "What would you call that?"

John was dismissive. "I don't think you can call it hunting. It doesn't meet the definition of 'fair chase.'" He continued, "I think with an operation like this you are buying the climax of the hunt. You're skipping the scouting, the buildup, the actual hunt."

His argument was convincing. "I hadn't thought about it quite that way. But that's an accurate assessment. If you compare our hunt in Louisiana to my Oklahoma hunt, the experiences couldn't be more different. Or the Florida experience, for that matter. It took twelve hunts in Florida to even *see* the first pig! In Oklahoma, I killed my first pig in less than twelve minutes on the stand!"

22 BAHIA GRASS

The author's name is familiar to the village folk as that of the man who has brought them relief from the great fear inspired by a cruel and malignant presence in their midst.

> —LORD LINLITHGOW, in the foreword to
> *Man-Eaters of Kumaon,* 1946

Bahia grass (*Paspulum notatum*): An introduced, perennial, sod-forming grass that is widely utilized for hay and/or grazing in the southeastern United States. Its thick foliage is anathema to the bobwhite quail. For that matter, replacing native ground cover with bahia grass probably reduces the carrying capacity for every important game species in North America.

Sometime during the first week of 2008, I finally got around to looking up the Chinese calendar on the Internet. I discovered that the first day of the Year of the Pig had been February 18, 2007. Coincidentally, February 18 had been the date of my first two kills at Fort Benning, Georgia.

The final day of the Chinese year would be February 7, 2008. My pig-hunting odyssey had just been extended! But this pig hunter wasn't up for more expensive, long-distance hunting trips. My goal of killing pigs in ten states had already been accomplished, as it turned out, in just under eleven months.

Unfortunately, my finances were on life support. After borrowing against my investment account and carrying over a significant balance on a credit card, it was going to take me at least a year, possibly two, to retire the debt incurred during the Year of the Pig. Consequently, I promised my wife, Katia, that any additional hunting in 2008 would take place close to home.

In January, I finally got around to scouting the long-neglected Dixon Center. The pigs had returned in force. A couple of weeks later, I received a long-awaited invitation to hunt pigs on property owned by my coworker Larry Stallings. This was the same guy who had killed and offered me a giant sow (which I kept) and a large young boar (which I passed on). On January 18, 2008, I drove to Larry's place for an afternoon pig hunt.

Just to the east of Larry's farm, a neighboring landowner owned a whole section (640 acres) that abutted the Conecuh National Forest. This landowner had leased his property to a group of Florida hunters. Coincidentally, the exploding pig population was closely correlated in time with the arrival of the Florida hunters on the lease. Now hogs were spilling out onto the landowner's neighbors' properties with increasing frequency, and tempers were flaring over the new agricultural scourge—feral pigs.

It was only a mile from the Dixon Center to Larry's farm and another quarter mile to his neighbor's section full of pigs. Quite possibly, this was the point of origin for many of the pigs straying onto the Dixon Center.

Pulling off the highway onto the southwest corner of the field, I engaged my four-wheel drive right away. The year 2008 had started with plenty of precipitation, and the field between the highway and a chufa patch was so soft that it felt like a sponge. Following the south edge of the field, I parked the truck and exited a couple of hundred yards south of the chufas.

Larry had shown me the chufa patch a few days earlier, on January 15. The amount of hog sign in the chufas was simply incredible. Virtually the entire patch had been rooted from one end to the other. Reading the tracks, I could tell there was an occasional large solitary pig, probably a boar. But most of the sign came from sows with piglets. It was impossible to judge just how many pigs were rooting here on a nightly basis, but it was more than a handful.

There were two hog traps set up in the southwest corner of the food plot. Earlier, I had asked Larry, "How many pigs did you trap here last year?"

Larry had been busy. "Thirty-nine pigs. I can catch the little ones. I need you to shoot the big ones that won't go into the trap."

Now the wind shifted from north to west and back again. Either direction was fine, but a west wind was a little better. A west wind would carry my scent to the open pasture to my rear.

It was cold. It was windy. And the ground was wet. Adding to the miserable weather, I was three days into my annual full-blown January sinus infection: coughing steadily from the drainage and running a low-grade fever.

I slung the 7 Mag over my right shoulder and the .17 HMR over my left. I still had a residual ambition of busting a sow with the 7 Mag and cleaning up the litter with the .17 HMR.

Just to the east of the chufa patch, a row of large round hay bales about four feet high stood in formation. Larry had suggested sitting behind the bales and waiting for the pigs to emerge.

The chufa patch, about 150 yards long and 20 to 50 yards deep, ran north and south alongside a dense, young loblolly stand. Behind or east of the bales, an open field offered good vantage. To the east of the field, Larry's house and his parents' house sat fifty yards off the county road. It was doubtful that the pigs would appear in the large open field and even if they did, I couldn't shoot with houses on the other side of the field.

I placed a blanket, several shirts, and a jacket into a waxed cardboard seedling box and carried it to the row of hay bales. Selecting a spot behind them and opposite the hog traps, I flattened the waxed cardboard box and laid it on the ground to form a waterproof barrier over the wet soil beneath. Next, I put on a couple of extra layers of clothing and loaded both rifles.

Within fifteen minutes of my arrival, a squeal arose from the timber to my left. Perhaps five minutes after that, there was another squeal from the timber to the right. I focused on my surroundings while leaning against a bale and watching the food plot. Grunts and squeals emanated from the woods with regular frequency.

A few minutes later, an alarm snort arose from the left, followed by more alarm snorts and huffs. Judging by the sounds, I assumed that the pigs had either entered the field just south of my truck or they had passed by close enough that they had seen my truck on the timber's edge. Either way, they had spooked and disappeared.

Parking so close to the chufa patch had been a bit lazy of me. If only I had parked on the road and walked the quarter mile to the chufa plot, my first pig could have been shot within thirty minutes of taking the stand.

The pigs to my left were now silent, but snorts and squeals continued from the right (north). Facing into the wind, I became chilled in just a few minutes, although the blanket draped over my shoulders provided some comfort as the wind continued to shift from north to west. When I had to cough, I just squatted down behind a bale and pulled the blanket over my head to mute the noise.

Since the sounds were coming steadily from the north, I shifted position about eighty yards, setting up behind the northernmost bale. Larry had cattle in a pasture to the north and he had given instructions to stay in this field because he didn't want me shooting around his cows across the fence.

After an hour passed with no pigs in sight, I returned to my original spot. There were still occasional squeals arising from the prohibited cow pasture. I wrapped up in the blanket, took a seat, and huddled out of the wind. It was getting progressively darker and colder as a front moved in. The temperature dropped to the low forties or high thirties. Several times I emerged from hibernation when the pigs sounded like they were on the edge of the timber, but they remained in the woods.

It had been two hours since my arrival and the same scenario had repeated itself over and over. Both daylight and my patience were diminishing. With all the pigs in the cattle pasture to the north, it sounded like a hog farm, and the slaughterhouse was waiting on the first delivery.

Still wrapped in the blanket, I walked north. A barbed wire fence separated the northern edge of the field from the cow pasture. At the fence, I hung the blanket on a post, lay flat, and scooted beneath the bottom wire.

The pigs were close. Grunts and squeals came from the edge of a small pond to the northwest. Step by step, I closed in. My heart rate was extremely elevated. My best guess is that when my ticker finally stops, it will be either during sex or when I'm stalking a sounder of pigs.

The hogs were strung out in some dense yaupon and privet that lined the banks above the water's edge. My distance from the pigs was only a few dozen yards and action was imminent. The wind was still in my favor, carrying my scent directly away from the line of hogs.

Shapes were moving in and out of the brush. It seemed like there were a few more pigs to the left so I eased in that direction, one step at a time. Several forms emerged from the brush to my left. A black sow with three or four piglets was crossing the bahia grass pasture. Having seen, smelled, or heard me, the pigs picked up speed as I tracked the sow with my scope.

I tightened the trigger and the 7 boomed, rocking me backward. The group of pigs disappeared into a solid wall of yaupon to the south. Two piglets broke from the brush and crossed the pasture not more than ten yards away. They passed unmolested. There were bigger fish to fry this afternoon.

Several more hogs broke from the brush to my right. I picked up another sow with piglets, tracking her for a couple of seconds before jerking the trigger. It was a horrible trigger pull and almost certainly a miss. This group also disappeared into the yaupon jungle.

There were still pigs down by the pond. It sounded as though a group had been foraging about fifty to eighty yards to my left, with another group at a similar distance to the right. Since no more pigs were breaking across the pasture, it appeared they were using the brushy fencerow for cover, escaping to the east or west.

Noisily picking my way through the brush and over a fence, I spooked another sow with piglets on the west edge of the pond. Pausing to load two more shells, I crossed back into the pasture.

It was silent and the light had faded. The pigs had dispersed for the night and it was time to look for blood trails, but it was too dark to see, so I illuminated the pasture with my light, walking back and forth perpendicular to the paths the sows had taken. The first shot had felt much better than my second shot, and my initial impression was validated by a river of red bahia grass where the first sow had crossed the pasture.

The blood trail ran straight to a solid wall of yaupon so thick that it appeared as though the sow had bounced off the brush before offsetting to the right and burrowing back in. Without a compass, I knew better than to crawl too deep into this nearly impenetrable mass. On the other hand, the exceptional blood trail I had to follow in could serve as my breadcrumb trail out.

For the umpteenth time in the Year of the Pig, I got down on my belly and crawled into thick brush with a long-barreled gun. It was long past time to acquire a sidearm.

The blood was heavy, so it was not difficult to follow the trail. Surely this pig hadn't run far. But was it dead? The blood trail led through thick yaupon and smilax, passing beneath a downed, dead red cedar. I belly crawled beneath the red cedar, stopping frequently to untangle myself from briars, grapevine, and yaupon stems. There was blood on my hands and clothes from crawling over the trail, further indication of a good shot placement.

The flashlight illuminated a large, prone object. It was the dead sow. It was much larger than I had first thought. At arm's length, this one looked like it could exceed two hundred pounds. Backing up about ten feet, I laid my rifle and light on the leaf litter before crawling back to the sow and attempting to pull her by the hind legs. Not able to budge the carcass from that direction, I tried the other end, grabbing the sow by the ears. Straining mightily, I finally dragged the head up and over, flipping the pig and pointing it toward the field edge.

My flashlight was growing dim. I turned around just as the batteries died completely. As I sat, contemplating my sorry situation, the first drops of rain started falling from the approaching storm front. Scratched from head to toe, buried in a yaupon thicket, covered with blood, sitting in the dark in a cold rain with a fever, a bad cough, and a two-hundred-pound hog carcass, the revelation hit me: "Maybe this is why more people go golfing than pig hunting."

23 PEANUTS

> *Nowhere in recent human history are our tribal, interdependent na-*
> *tures more realized than in farming communities; although these social*
> *units are not without dysfunction, ostracism, and strife, here the human*
> *spirit seems to thrive.*
>
> —JANISSE RAY, *Wildcard Quilt*, 2003

One week after killing the biggest sow of my hog-hunting career,
I followed Larry to another one of his fields during our lunch break. Larry had
forgiven me for shooting the sow out of his cow pasture, and I promised to pay
double market value for any incidental bovine takes. Having grown up hunting in fields full of pigs, cows, and horses, I was confident of my ability to dis-
tinguish between my quarry and Larry's livestock.

We pulled up to a field that was planted to peanuts in 2007. After the peanuts
had been harvested, Larry had planted a winter cover crop of oats and rye. The
pigs were coming into his field at night and rooting up the old rows looking for
peanuts missed in the 2007 harvest. There were hundreds of spots where pigs
had rooted the field, turning the soil and reducing forage production for the
cattle.

The east side of the field had an electric fence. The back (west) side had a
four-strand barbed wire fence separating the field from a pasture that abutted
the Conecuh National Forest.

Larry had given me written permission under his crop depredation permit.
Since I was now legal for night hunting, it was time to put the red light to use.
He showed me around the field, saying, "If you see a large light-colored boar,

shoot it first. That boar runs as soon as we shine the field. It may be light red, but it's a big one and you can pick it out of a group."

If this big pig was a frequent visitor to the field, I felt I had a good probability of shooting him. I assured Larry, "Consider that pig dead!"

It was pouring down rain when I returned to Larry's place at 7:00 that evening. I fell asleep while sitting in my truck, waiting for the rain to abate. Waking at 8:00, I noticed that the rain had stopped and the wind was out of the north. I walked toward a chufa patch with the red light mounted on my 7 Mag.

There were no pigs in the chufas or the area around the pond that had produced my big black sow. Walking the timber's edge south of the pond, I circled through more pasture and approached the southwest edge of the peanut field that the pigs had been tearing up. As I moved up a terraced slope into the field, a pig grunted above me, to the north and east. My position was safely downwind. Easing further upslope, I reached the top of the terrace, which allowed a good view of the surrounding field.

I stepped forward with the wind in my face, swinging the red light from right to left. Halfway through the arc, the light picked up a large, light-colored pig next to a smaller black pig. It was the one Larry had told me about!

The pair was about sixty to eighty yards out. I raised the rifle, placing the crosshairs on the light-colored pig as it walked up to the black pig and stopped. I pulled the trigger. The recoil rocked me back on my heels, kicking the red light off the scope.

With the red light dangling at my feet, I grabbed the light cord with my left hand while working the bolt with my right hand. The red pig was running to the left. It was headed for the west fence and, judging by its slow gait, it had been hit hard.

The black pig, on the other hand, was moving exceptionally fast and straight at me! It veered at the last second, passing about five feet to my left. I was already focusing on the big red pig as the black pig shot past. I just managed to get the crosshairs on the pig and pull the trigger as it ran under the fence and disappeared. The second shot rocked me back, knocking the light from my hands again. Damn the recoil!

Both pigs were gone. The black pig was probably in Florida by now, but the big hog couldn't have gone very far. Loading two more rounds in the 7 Mag, I walked up the hill to look for blood, spending a few minutes walking back and forth. There was no sign of a hit pig.

I crossed the fence, continuing my zigzag search pattern through the bahia grass. Perhaps the pig had cut back south and west? The search moved downhill. Fifty yards south of the fence, I saw a large, prone object in the field. It was the pig! It surprised me by standing up and starting to run straightaway. Dropping to one knee, I fired again as the rifle just touched my shoulder. The pig went down again. It was obviously gut shot and a long way from cover.

Dog fennel obstructed a clear shot. Taking a few steps to the right, I could see the whole pig. It was a big red hog with its head up and all four legs folded beneath. It was time to put this pig down for good. Dropping to a knee, I put the crosshairs just behind the right front shoulder and pulled the trigger. The pig squealed once and rolled over on its left side. It kicked twice and expired.

It was a very fat red pig. If this was the one Larry had been seeing, he was mistaken, not about the pig's size but about its sex. This was the fattest sow I'd ever killed. This sow looked like it was even heavier than the 205-pound sow I'd taken the week before. Was it as big as the sow Larry had taken a couple of months back? The sow weighed in at 215 pounds on the Dixon Center scales. It wasn't as big as Larry's sow, but it was a good one.

24 EATING THE PIG

I had to stop being a supermarket zombie.
—NICOLETTE HAHN NIMAN, *Righteous Porkchop*, 2009

Over the course of this quest, my health had been placed at significant risk. Two people I interacted with in 2007, Steven Ditchkoff from Auburn University and David Watson from Mims, Florida, both knew people who had contracted undulant fever (brucellosis) while handling meat from wild pigs. If there is real danger associated with pig hunting, it comes in the form of a bacterium named *Brucella suis*. For years I had field dressed and butchered pigs without latex gloves. No more. There is no cure for undulant fever, and it can be fatal to humans as well as pigs.

Don't let this information scare you away from feral pork, however. The risks of infection are associated mostly with the processing of raw meat. Any cut in the skin of the processor is a potential entry point for *Brucella suis*. So wear gloves and don't splatter fluids into your eyes, nose, or mouth. As soon as a pig is down, focus on taking care of the carcass so that it will produce the best-tasting and safest pork for consumption.

If I am hunting at the Solon Dixon Center, the carcass is usually a short drag from a fire lane, trail, or road. If the carcass can be hauled to our processing facilities within a couple of hours in cold weather, or within an hour at higher temperatures, then I don't bother with field dressing a pig. But if field dressing is required, I remove the innards and all reproductive parts (testicles and penis) from boars.

Be exceptionally careful while gutting pigs that have broadheads inside the body cavity. The blade from a broadhead on an arrow or bolt may seriously lacerate an incautious butcher. If you do screw up and cut something off, like the time I sliced off the top of one finger, get to the emergency room as quickly as possible. In my case, the flesh was hanging by a small piece of skin. First, the nurse thoroughly cleaned my blood- and gore-stained hand. Then the doctor glued the top of my finger back on and shot me full of antibiotics. After a rather protracted yucky-black phase, my finger was as good as new!

If the pig is hanging near a water source, wash the carcass well until the water runs clear. Most pigs will have recently rolled in mud, and it is easier to keep dust and/or mud off the meat if the carcass is washed prior to butchering.

Pigs range from a little to a lot harder to skin than deer. If the carcass is still warm, it is easier to pull and cut the hide off a pig. If it is a large pig that has been hanging in a walk-in cooler overnight, or up to a couple of weeks, then you'd better bring a whetstone because the hide will have to be cut loose from the carcass and it will probably take repeated sharpening of the skinning knife, especially if it is an old boar with a well-developed shield. In my opinion, heavy-duty pruning shears are vastly superior to meat saws for cutting through ribs, joints, and leg bones.

The pigs at the Dixon Center run large compared to many from other areas that I hunt. A typical Lower Alabama sow will weigh about 150 pounds. It takes me about two hours to process this average pig. For our family of three, this pig will yield:

Ribs: Two large slabs of ribs will provide four meals.

Bacon: Enough for four meals.

Roasts: When I cut up a hindquarter, it will usually yield two smaller roasts for one meal each and a larger roast/ham for two meals. Thus, two hindquarters at four meals each equals eight meals.

Loins: Two meals for each loin or four total.

Tenderloins: The two tenderloins will be eaten as one meal, generally the day after the pig is harvested.

Shoulders: A front quarter/shoulder may be smoked or baked in the oven, as is, for approximately two meals per quarter, yielding four meals altogether.

I save excess fat for future use in smoked sausage.

Because freezer space is often a limiting factor, we don't freeze the bones, but they are good when cooked with soup beans and eaten with hot cornbread.

If it is a particularly good-looking pig, we throw a shoulder or a back bone on the grill and cover it with barbeque sauce. Or, even better, rub the meat with fresh minced garlic, some lemon salt, and seasoned salt. For the truly sublime, use fresh minced garlic and a butt rub like Dixie Dirt! Fresh minced garlic goes very well with feral pork.

To sum it all up, one pig can produce ribs, bacon, roasts, loin, tenderloin, and various bones that will provide enough pork to feed a family of three around twenty-two meals! There are no known diseases that can be contracted from eating well-cooked pork, and wild pigs are delicious!

As I've said before, I grew up on a small farm in north central Missouri. After I left the farm for college, I kept wondering why supermarket pork, chicken, and eggs were so poor in taste in comparison to what we had produced on the farm. I came to realize that today's tasteless meats are all one can expect from modern factory-farming practices.

When I was a young farm boy, the term "free range" was not in vogue, but that is exactly how we raised our pigs, chickens, and cattle. All of our animals had access to expansive areas of grass, forbs, trees, shrubs, and streams. We didn't have to pump our animals full of antibiotics and hormones to keep them healthy and make them fat. Our animals were not crowded into cages and forced to live in their own wastes. Our herbivore livestock were not coerced into eating animal by-products. We used selective breeding, but none of our cows, pigs, horses, ducks, or chickens had their genes modified in a laboratory.

Most of the feral hogs I kill today taste similar to those free-range pigs we raised back on the farm in Missouri.

If you do not have access to feral pigs and you want to know what good pork tastes like, buy a pig from a local farmer who gives his pigs access to the out-of-doors. As Nicolette Hahn Niman puts it in *Righteous Porkchop*, "Finding foods from traditional farms and ranches involves being something of an explorer and a detective."

My knowledge of which pigs are best to eat has been greatly refined after trying boars, sows, and shoats from many different environments. The best feral pork comes from fat pigs. The more fat, the juicier, milder, and more tender the cut. Boars, especially lean older boars with broken tusks, should go directly into smoked sausage. Broken tusks are a good indication that the boar has been fighting other boars, and the meat will probably contain elevated male hormones. Cook a rack of ribs or a roast from a grizzled, dominant old boar and the smell may fall somewhere between a shark fillet that wasn't properly bled and the odor of stale urine. Old razorback sows, like the ones I shot in Texas or Oklahoma, can be a little on the tough side. The flavor is pretty good but these pigs are ideal for breakfast sausage. On the other hand, young boars, fat sows of any age, and all shoats are excellent table fare.

In Spain there is a pork version of "Kobe beef." These pigs spend most of their time foraging in the woods under the watchful eyes of swineherds. Their meat sells for twenty to forty times the price of American mass-produced, hormone- and antibiotic-saturated pork. Sophisticated consumers recognize a great product and will pay many times the standard price for the benefits of taste and health. As an effective pig hunter, I can secure meat with similar qualities by the ton.

Big agriculture derides anything that doesn't fit into its economies of scale, but I believe that big agriculture cares little about the health of its pigs, the quality of its product, or even the health of the consumer. Big agriculture has decimated small farms across America. It's time for all of us to stop being "supermarket zombies."

CONCLUSION

One of the penalties of an ecological education is that one lives in a world of wounds.

—ALDO LEOPOLD, *A Sand County Almanac,* 1949

What did I learn from the Year of the Pig?

Pig hunting is fun, challenging, and exciting. I had discovered this long before the Year of the Pig, of course, but my appreciation for and understanding of the sport were greatly reinforced.

Pig hunters can and should play a vital role in controlling pig populations. Pig hunters, especially hunters who use dogs, are particularly effective at catching large numbers of feral hogs in extremely challenging environmental conditions. If sport hunting is excluded from public lands, the government will end up hiring professional shooters and trappers to do what hunters do for free.

That said, it is also true that, like it or not, pig hunters are a big factor in the explosive spread of feral hogs across the United States. Blaming pig hunters for the spread of feral hogs wouldn't be all that controversial at the annual meeting of the Association of Southeastern Biologists. But how would a bunch of good ol' boys with four-wheel-drive trucks and dog boxes full of curs and pits take it if someone told them, "You all are to blame for the loss of gopher frog habitat because of the pigs you brought in ten miles down the river"? Standing on principle is a matter of perspective and geography.

I believe hunters must resist the temptation to move pigs to areas that are currently pig free. The ecological and economic repercussions of introducing pigs to virgin territory may be profound. This requires self-policing and message reinforcement by hunters of all stripes.

Over time, land managers will probably develop one of two attitudes toward feral pigs. I know several land managers from Georgia and South Carolina who have developed a visceral hatred for the feral pig. They spend tens or hundreds of thousands of dollars managing their properties for quail or ecological restoration—while feral hogs are working just as diligently to undo all their efforts and expenses.

On the other hand, I also interact with several longtime land managers and/or hunting guides who have come to respect, if not outright admire, the feral pig. David Watson, Deedy Loftus, Rodney Perreira, and Ken Gould all fall in this category. After decades of guiding hunters in pursuit of feral hogs, they rarely if ever kill pigs themselves. They derive their pleasure from working their dogs and/or guiding those with less experience to a successful conclusion of their hunt.

My attitude toward feral hogs falls squarely in this second category. In my humble opinion, the feral pig is the smartest large game animal in North America.

In the big picture, feral pigs are only one of many factors negatively affecting our environment.

On January 17, 2008, I left the Solon Dixon Center for a two-hour drive south to Fairhope, Alabama. Roger Reid (author of *Longleaf*) and I were scheduled to address the Alabama Coastal Foundation. The foundation had heard about the series of presentations we had delivered to middle schools across Alabama, and it was interested in sponsoring additional presentations to schools in south Alabama.

At our presentations, Roger would talk about writing *Longleaf,* a novel for young adults, the characters in the book, and his inspirations. I followed with a description of the longleaf forest, its dependence on fire, and why it is such a great place to walk in, to hunt, to own, to burn, and to manage.

Along the way to Fairhope, I looked forward to passing through the Flomaton Old-Growth Tract on U.S. 29. The Flomaton Tract was a sixty-acre stand of old-growth longleaf pine. I had visited this tract dozens of times and directed hundreds of people there so they could see the last known stand of old-growth longleaf in Lower Alabama. This tract was like an old friend.

There were once millions of acres of virgin longleaf in Alabama, but the longleaf forests have been cut, and cut, and cut some more, so that finally, this tract was the sole significant remaining stand of old-growth longleaf, at least in this portion of the state. Over the centuries, the Flomaton Tract has been owned by several companies. Most recently, this long-studied and admired tract was owned by Resource Management Services (RMS) of Birmingham, Alabama, which purchased it from International Paper as part of 2.6-million-acre acquisition. More than likely, the 60-acre stand was the only area of old-growth longleaf in the entire sale.

Approaching the Flomaton Tract that fateful day, I was uneasily aware that the landscape seemed wrong. I checked surrounding landmarks to make sure of my location. Tragically, this was indeed the site. I came to realize that the Flomaton Old-Growth Tract was gone.

I pulled to the side of the road and parked the vehicle. As I walked among the stumps and fresh logging slash, my spirit seemed to leave my body and seep away into the sandy loam beneath my feet. The entire portion of the Flomaton Tract on the north side of the road had been clear-cut. Less than five acres remained on the south side of the road. For all practical purposes, Alabama had no remaining old-growth longleaf pine.

The CEO, the forester, the logger, and probably even the developer will sleep well tonight. The only ones to suffer from this loss are the handful of naturalists, historians, ecologists, and foresters who knew, studied, and valued a sixty-acre tract of three-hundred-year-old longleaf pine.

Wild hogs may invade a Florida "steep-head" and wipe out an endemic salamander, but they can't clear-cut old-growth longleaf. Feral pigs can root up and damage pitcher plant bogs, but they can't exclude fire from vast forests of upland pine. Pigs can and should be controlled in our pristine ecological areas, but these areas comprise perhaps 1 percent of the landscape.

Real ecological damage is inflicted by human beings: forest conversion to dense loblolly, slash, and sand pine plantations; fire exclusion; urbanization; and the introduction of invasive plants, animals, and fungi. These are the real factors destroying our native forests.

It is our action, or inaction, that continues to remove diversity from God's creation. In comparison, the pig is a minor irritant, and a poor imitator.

EPILOGUE

So if you have loved some woman and some country you are very fortunate and, if you die afterwards it makes no difference.
—ERNEST HEMINGWAY, *The Green Hills of Africa*, 1935

Of the sports in which I participate, hog hunting is way low on the risk spectrum. No rational life insurance company would write me if they knew everything I've done, do, and, more than likely, will continue doing. So, in the event of my untimely demise, I'd like to get this on record, so my friends and family will know what to do.

On a recent drive to Virginia, I was listening to the Preservation Hall Jazz Band, and I got to thinking about dying. When my time comes, I would like a procession in the funeral. And while I am lying back, taking it easy in that casket, I want to hear some New Orleans brass. That would sure sound sweet.

And I got to thinking about something an old blues singer said or sang. Behind that New Orleans brass band, I'd want to hear a whole bunch of pretty women hollering and carrying on. But not all of them! Some should just weep quietly, in a dignified manner.

Then, I got to thinking about something my brother said.

Every year, as is tradition, I drive north to our farm in Missouri where the Powell and Pennington boys and I lay waste to the local squirrels, rabbits, quail, ducks, geese, and other assorted and unfortunate edible animals.

One year, as the holidays were wrapping up, I was packing to head south and my little brother, Curtis, said, "When you cross that state line, all the surviving animals are going to snort, whistle, chirp, and jump in the air to click their hooves and paws, because they'll know they made it through another hunting season with you gone back down south."

So I figured, after the band, and after all those pretty women in black, there needs to be a way for the animals to celebrate my passing. So, to those who own up to being my friend—please fall in line carrying a mounted deer head, or a stuffed hog, or a trophy fish, or whatever is handy, to fill out that procession.

Yes, Lord. Before you carry me home, I sure would enjoy being a witness to all that.

FURTHER READING

Associated Press. "Monster Pig Was Huge—Just Not Wild," MSNBC.com, June 1, 2007, http://www.msnbc.msn.com/id/18989526/.

Bass, Rick. "Activism's Paradox Mountain." *Orion,* November/December 2007.

Capps, Ronald Everett. *Off Magazine Street.* San Francisco: MacAdam/Cage, 2004.

Capstick, Peter Hathaway. *Death in the Long Grass.* New York: St. Martin's, 1977.

———. *Death in the Silent Places.* New York: St. Martin's, 1981.

Corbett, Jim. *Man-Eaters of Kumaon.* With a foreword by Lord Linlithgow. London: Readers Union, 1946.

Ditchkoff, Steven. "A Landowner's Guide to Wild Pigs, Part I." *Wildlife Trends,* May/June 2006.

Earley, Lawrence S. *Looking for Longleaf: The Fall and Rise of an American Forest.* Chapel Hill: University of North Carolina Press, 2004

Gooch, Bob. *Hunting Boar, Hogs and Javelina.* Tabor City, NC: Atlantic, 1989.

Hall, John C. *Headwaters: A Journey on Alabama Rivers.* Photographs by Beth Maynor Young. Tuscaloosa: University of Alabama Press, 2009.

Hemingway, Ernest. *Death in the Afternoon.* New York: Charles Scribner's Sons, 1932.

———. *The Green Hills of Africa.* New York: Charles Scribner's Sons, 1935.

Krakauer, Jon. *Into Thin Air.* New York: Doubleday, 1997.

Kramer, Gary. *The Complete Guide to Hunting Wild Boar in California.* Long Beach, CA: Safari, 2003.

Leavell, Chuck. *Forever Green: The History and Hope of the American Forest.* Dry Branch, GA: Evergreen Arts, 2001.

Leopold, Aldo. *A Sand County Almanac.* Oxford: Oxford University Press, 1949.

Mayer, John J., and I. Lehr Brisbin Jr. *Wild Pigs in the United States: Their History, Comparative Morphology, and Current Status.* Athens: University of Georgia Press, 1991.

Mitchell, Robert J. "Silly Shit I Say All the Time" Unpublished Manuscript.

Nation, Fred. *Where the Wild Illicium Grows: Historic Plants of South Alabama and the Central Gulf Coast.* Bay Minette, AL: Lavender, 2002.

Niman, Nicolette Hahn. *Righteous Porkchop.* New York: Collins Living, 2009.

Polancy, Toni. *So You Want to Live in Hawaii: The Guide to Settling and Succeeding in the Islands.* Hawaii: Barefoot, 1998.

Pollan, Michael. *The Omnivore's Dilemma.* New York: Penguin, 2006.

Ray, Janisse. *Ecology of a Cracker Childhood.* Minneapolis: Milkweed, 1999.

———. *Pinhook: Finding Wholeness in a Fragmented Land.* White River Junction, VT: Chelsea Green, 2005.

———. *Wildcard Quilt: Taking a Chance on Home.* Minneapolis: Milkweed, 2003.

Reid, Roger. *Longleaf.* Montgomery, AL: Junebug, 2006.

Robb, Bob. *Hunting Wild Boar in California.* Lakeland, FL: Larsen's Outdoor, 1996.

Robbins, Tom. *Still Life with Woodpecker.* New York: Bantam Books, 1980.

Sturkey, Dave, and Craig Marquette. *Wild Hog Hunting: Everything You Need to Know to Get Your Hog!* Sarasota, FL: Wildlife, 1998.

Swindle, Michael. *Slouching towards Birmingham.* Berkeley, CA: Frog, Ltd., 2005.

Triplett, Todd. *The Complete Book of Wild Boar Hunting: Tips and Tactics That Will Work Anywhere.* Guilford, CT: Lyons, 2004.

White, Bailey. *Quite a Year for Plums.* New York: Knopf, 1998.

Wilson, E. O. *Naturalist.* Washington, DC: Island Press, 1994.

I respectfully request that my readers consider joining and supporting organizations that work to protect, restore, and conserve our native forests. One organization working to restore longleaf to some semblance of its former glory is:

The Longleaf Alliance, Inc.
12130 Dixon Center Rd.
Andalusia, AL 36420
334-427-1029
www.longleafalliance.org